LYNCHING
IN COLORADO
1859–1919

LYNCHING
IN COLORADO
1859–1919

Stephen J. Leonard

University Press of Colorado

© 2002 by the University Press of Colorado

Published by the University Press of Colorado
5589 Arapahoe Avenue, Suite 206C
Boulder, Colorado 80303

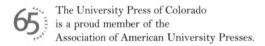 The University Press of Colorado
is a proud member of the
Association of American University Presses.

The University Press of Colorado is a cooperative publishing enterprise supported, in part, by Adams State College, Colorado State University, Fort Lewis College, Mesa State College, Metropolitan State College of Denver, University of Colorado, University of Northern Colorado, University of Southern Colorado, and Western State College of Colorado.

The paper used in this publication meets the minimum requirements of the American National Standard for Information Sciences—Permanence of Paper for Printed Library Materials. ANSI Z39.48-1992

Library of Congress Cataloging-in-Publication Data

Leonard, Stephen J.
  Lynching in Colorado, 1859-1919 / Stephen J. Leonard.
    p. cm.
Includes bibliographical references (p.) and index.
  ISBN 0-87081-680-2
  1. Lynching—Colorado—History—19th century. I. Title.

HV6465.C6 L46 2002
364.1'34—dc21

                                                    2002011499

Design by Laura Furney and Daniel Pratt

11   10   09   08   07   06   05   04   03   02   10   9   8   7   6   5   4   3   2   1

To Mary L. Nation (1940–2002)
and
Frank W. Nation

and all other Coloradans who have suffered injustice,
who have fought injustice, who have shown mercy,
particularly Look Young, Washington H. Wallace,
Jacob Weisskind, Sheriff William Cozens,
the Reverend Robert Servant,
and the Reverend James Sunderland, S.J.

CONTENTS

ILLUSTRATIONS

ACKNOWLEDGMENTS

T he story of the past does not write itself. Like gold, history must be mined, refined, and beaten into shape. Many people participate in that arduous process, only a few of whom enjoy the luxury of writing books and articles, arranging and burnishing the precious metal others have provided.

The coauthors of this book and most nonfiction books are the librarians and archivists who maintain and make available the treasures that keep civilization alive. Colorado is blessed in having several splendid institutions, staffed by equally splendid professionals, that for scores of years have collected and organized literally tons of printed and manuscript material. To thank them all would be nearly impossible, but some, with apologies to those inadvertently omitted, must be acknowledged.

For many years the late Eleanor Gehres fostered the national reputation of the Denver Public Library's Western History and Genealogy Department. Recently Jim Kroll, supported by City Librarian Rick Ashton, has kept that diamond of a department sparkling. Philip Panum and Barbara Walton have done much to develop the collections and to make them accessible. I owe much to their dedication, as I do to Kay Wisnia, Brent Wagner, Jennifer Thom, Janice Prater, Colleen Nunn, the late Augie Mastrogiuseppe, Brian Kenny, James Jeffery, John Irwin, Bruce Hanson, Don Dilley, Nancy Chase, Marilyn Chang, and Lisa Backman.

The Colorado Historical Society's collection is also rich in the newspapers and scrapbooks on which I heavily relied. Director of

Library Services Rebecca Lintz and her staff—Barbara Dey, Debra Neiswonger, Karyl Klein, and Margi Aguiar—were most helpful. Larry Lintz kindly gave me much of the lynching material from Jean and Don Griswold's *History of Leadville* before that massive work was published. At the Historical Society I was also assisted by Chief Historian David F. Halaas, Publications Director David Wetzel, and curators Stan Oliner, Keith Schrum, and Bridget Burke. Clark Secrest, for many years editor of *Colorado Heritage*, encouraged me in my insanely obsessive research and published somewhat different versions of this study's Introduction and Chapter 4 in summer 1999 and autumn 2000 issues of *Heritage*. Fortunately, additional research for this book has allowed me to correct several errors that appeared in those articles.

At the Auraria Library I used the excellent collection created by Head Bibliographer Terry Leopold and others supported by Library Dean David Gleim. I also thank Terry Ketelsen and the staff at the Colorado State Archives, Sylvia L. Rael of the Vehr Theological Library in Denver, Paul de Paoli at the Reddick Library in Ottawa, Illinois, and the Colorado State University Library. Joanne West Dodds of the Pueblo Library District proved more helpful than she or I knew at the time when she gave me a copy of her booklet on Custer County, which turned out to contain a good lynching story. Phimister Proctor Church of the A. Phimister Proctor Museum in Poulsbo, Washington, graciously allowed use of illustrations by his illustrious grandfather. I am, of course, in debt to many historians upon whose research I have relied and whose ideas I have sometimes borrowed.

One of those scholars, Thomas J. Noel, has listened at least as patiently to my stories about lynchings as I have to his descriptions of historic buildings. In the time it took me to write this book, he finished at least half a dozen volumes. James H. Madison at Indiana University and Norton H. Moses at Montana State University provided numerous suggestions for improving the manuscript. Michael L. Radelet at the University of Colorado shared his research on legal executions with me. At Metropolitan State College I am in debt to President Sheila Kaplan, Provost Cheryl Norton, and Dean Joan Foster. I thank my colleagues in the History Department, including Thomas Altherr, James Drake, Dolph Grundman, and Frank Nation—all of whom made helpful suggestions. I am continually beholden to History Department Administrative Assistants Gloria

Kennison and Nita Froelich and to student assistant Bill Magette for sparing me numerous burdens.

Metropolitan State College students also contributed to this study. Russell Lohse wrote an excellent paper on John Preston Porter Jr. David Lutter gave me copies of newspaper accounts on Bob Harris that helped me see the significance of Harris's not being lynched. Eric Skougstad took an interest in the McCurdy lynching, and Tanya McAvoy provided information on the 1919 Pueblo killings. Those cases I had previously discovered, but Ramona Percarek added a fresh tidbit to my larder by discovering the attempted lynching of Albert H. Flood.

Darrin Pratt, Laura Furney, Kerry P. Callahan, David Archer, and Daniel Pratt of the University Press of Colorado merit thanks on many counts, including their willingness to work with my archaic word processing program. Copyeditor Cheryl Carnahan did a splendid job and saved me from many mistakes. Christopher Altvater, a Metropolitan State College history student, deserves special thanks for undertaking the laborious task of converting the entire manuscript into a usable word processing format. He also added lynching locations to the map and restored several old newspaper drawings. Denise Hull, a student, did similar good work.

LYNCHING
IN COLORADO
1859–1919

INTRODUCTION

Unfortunately, grasshoppers are not the only source of
annoyance to the people here. The country is infested
with those superfluous incumbrances [*sic*] to the well
being of society, horse and cattle thieves. . . . The people
lose confidence in the efficiency of the law for their protection. Can not some change be effected so that the
people may not have occasion to resort to the court of
Judge Lynch for the better protection of their lives and
property?

—*Colorado Chieftain* [Pueblo],
July 20, 1871

Seated on a black coffin that he would soon occupy, William
Van Horn asked Sheriff William Cozens to hurry. Cozens
obliged. It took only a few minutes for the wagon carrying the
sheriff and his prisoner to reach the gallows three-quarters of a
mile east of Central City. There troops from the First Colorado
Cavalry and thousands of others watched silently as Van Horn was
hanged at 11:20 A.M., December 21, 1863.[1]

Two months earlier Van Horn had shot and killed Josiah
Copeland, his rival in love.[2] Convicted of that unremarkable crime,
he might easily have slipped into oblivion except that his death
vested him with a distinction. The troops lent authority, and the
crowd signaled community approval. More importantly, as Central
City's *Miner's Register* noted, the execution was "a vindication of

laws." For the first time in Colorado a felon had been legally hanged, a milestone that marked the advance of civilization just as schools, churches, and newspapers did. "Henceforth, mob law or lynch law has ended, and the people will rejoice in it."[3]

Ridding Central City of lynch law came at risk to Sheriff Cozens, who after Van Horn's arrest faced a mob armed with a hangman's rope. With the toe of his boot the sheriff traced a line across the dirt street, warning that he would shoot anyone who crossed it. The rabble pressed forward until Cozens fired in the air. They backed off, reluctantly accepting civilization at the point of a gun.[4]

Lynching might have ended at an early date in other parts of Colorado had every lawman boasted Cozens's backbone. Accused felons guarded by such upright men counted themselves lucky compared with those who faced angry mobs alone or fell into the hands of officers less brave or honorable than Cozens. The Durango posse that lynched Jack Roberts in March 1881 did not bother with a trial. In January 1884 Sheriff Charles Rawles told Ouray vigilantes to go to hell. Instead they seized his prisoners, Margaret and Michael Cuddigan, and hanged them.[5] After John Preston Porter Jr., an African American youth, was burned at the stake near Limon in November 1900, Sheriff John W. Freeman refused to arrest well-known mob members because, he said, "it would involve Lincoln County in a needless and fruitless litigation against its own citizens."[6]

Lynching arrived in the western reaches of Kansas and Nebraska Territories with the Pikes Peak Gold Rush of 1859. No one probably knew then, nor do scholars know today, when or where the practice originated. As early as the 1760s South Carolinians, known as regulators, operated outside of the law to rid their region of outlaws. Charles Lynch of Bedford County, Virginia, may have inadvertently lent his name to extralegal punishments when he and his friends informally tried and whipped pro-British sympathizers during the American Revolution. The term *lynching*, initially used to describe a variety of chastisements ranging from whippings to hangings, remained in the spoken language for decades, apparently first appearing in print as "Lynch's law" in 1817.[7]

Antislavery crusaders hijacked the word, using it to condemn killings such as those in 1835 near Vicksburg, Mississippi, where whites brutally crushed a rumored slave uprising. Southerners hated being called lynchers, so although they embraced the practice, their newspapers shunned the term. As lynching moved west the word shed much of its negative baggage. During the 1849–1850 California Gold Rush, westward-bound emigrants routinely accepted the occasional necessity of executing transgressors.[8] By the mid-1860s westerners, contending that they had a right to defend themselves against lawless ruffians, had made lynching—often personified as "Judge Lynch"—almost respectable. They even added a new word to the language—*vigilantes.*[9]

Given its deep roots and western popularity, it is not surprising that lynching flourished in Colorado. Between Colorado's first recorded lynching in 1859 and its last in 1919, approximately 175 people were killed without benefit of legal trial. Few Colorado towns of any size went without at least one lynching. Alamosa, Antonito, Boulder, Cañon City, Colorado City, Del Norte, Denver, Durango, Empire, Evans, Fairplay, Florence, Fort Collins, Fort Lupton, Georgetown, Golden, Greeley, Gunnison, La Junta, Lake City, Laporte, Las Animas, Leadville, Montrose, Ouray, Pueblo, Rico, Salida, Silverton, Trinidad—the list of lynching venues goes on and on.

The number of persons lynched will never be known. First there is the problem of determining who should be included. Vigilantes and mobs often used hanging to rid their communities of unwanted persons, finding in that standard means of execution a cloak legitimizing the killings as traditional, albeit somewhat irregular, applications of justice.[10] Because hanging was used so often, lynching is often equated with illegal hanging. Yet a person shot by a mob or beaten to death or burned at the stake was just as dead and just as lynched as one who was hanged.

If means of killing does not define a lynching, what does? W. Fitzhugh Brundage, in his model study *Lynching in the New South: Georgia and Virginia, 1880–1930,* provides a useful definition of lynching, one used by antilynching crusaders in the 1940s: "There must be legal evidence that a person has been killed, and that he met his death illegally at the hands of a group acting under the pretext of service to justice, race, or tradition."[11] Most Colorado lynchings— be they by hanging, shooting, beating, burning, drowning, and yes, even lethal injection—fall neatly within that formula. But a few do not.

The eleven Mexicans some say were hanged by Ute Indians at Jimmy's Camp on the plains about 25 miles northeast of Pikes Peak in 1833 probably do not meet the definition because even if the legend were true, the Utes of that period could hardly be expected

EXECUTION OF THE ROBBERS.

0.1 U.S. troops shot members of the Reynolds gang in September 1864 without bothering with the formalities of a trial. The drawing shows six gang members, but probably only five were killed. Courtesy, Denver Public Library, Western History Collection.

to conform to European American ways.[12] Do James Gordon, Marcus Gredler, John Stuffle, Moses Young, and Patrick Waters—all condemned to die by Denver's People's Court after formal and open trials in 1859 and 1860—rate inclusion among the lynched? The answer, as explained in Chapter 1, is technically "yes" because the People's Courts lacked legal jurisdiction.[13]

Should the two Espinosas shot in 1863 without being given a chance to surrender be counted?[14] What about the Reynolds gang, self-proclaimed Confederate guerrillas held prisoner by Union troops? Samuel E. Browne, U.S. attorney for Colorado, charged that in September 1864 "the whole five were butchered, and their bodies with shackles on their legs, were left unburied on the plains."[15] A few months later U.S. troops, "a group acting under pretext of service to justice, race, or tradition," massacred more than 160 Native Americans camped along Sand Creek in eastern Colorado. Were those deaths lynchings?

What of Pepino Tologrino, a truck farmer who lived in the South Platte River bottomlands near downtown Denver? In May 1891

Tologrino enraged his neighbors when he killed a sixteen-year-old boy. A mob, hangman's rope ready, chased him along the river until he plunged in and drowned while his pursuers, having undergone a change of heart, tried to save him.[16] Was Tologrino lynched? What of immigrants killed in the tradition of Old World vendettas? Should they be counted among the lynched?

Beyond the definition question lurks the record problem. Judge Lynch did not keep a diary. Vigilantes and mobs operating outside the law sometimes feared that the law would operate on them if their doings were known or feared retaliation from vengeful friends of the lynched. Communities, anxious to appear safe and stable, found impromptu hangings dangerous to their reputation and hence may sometimes have hidden their dark deeds. Gothic, a mining town north of Gunnison, reported that it had hanged a Chinese man in effigy. When the hoopla was misreported as an actual lynching, the town's newspaper scrambled to set the record straight.[17] Yet at other times towns took pride in their lynchings and trumpeted their toughness on crime to scare would-be miscreants away.

Even if lynchings were accurately chronicled, newspaper files were often lost. Much information that remains is scattered in tens of thousands of pages of unindexed and sometimes unreadable microfilm. Reluctant to wade through dismal swamps of material, some scholars have relied on the lynching lists published by the *Chicago Tribune* during the late nineteenth and early twentieth centuries.[18] Unfortunately, those compilations, although useful, are sometimes inaccurate. For example, the *Tribune* reported that on January 9, 1895, George Witherill, desperado, was lynched in Cañon City. In fact, George Witherill, desperado, had been lynched in Cañon City on December 4, 1888. Worse still is the *Tribune*'s list for 1882. It reckons Arnold Howard as lynched, although he was not, and it counts George Betts and James Browning twice. So its total of fourteen lynchings in Colorado for 1882 appears to be off by three. But by a stroke of accountant's luck the *Tribune* missed at least one and perhaps two other lynched persons, making the total for 1882 twelve or thirteen rather than fourteen. The devil is in the details, and many of the details are provided in the list of lynchings in this book's appendix.[19]

Despite the limitations, much can be known. The venerable general index of the Denver Public Library's Western History and Genealogy Department includes scores of references to lynching.

Splendid local histories such as Allen Nossaman's volumes on Silverton and Don and Jean Griswold's 2,374-page *History of Leadville and Lake County Colorado* provide reams of information, as do the manuscript, newspaper, and scrapbook collections at the Colorado Historical Society.

In eight years of mining this material I have unearthed more than 175 Colorado lynchings, starting in 1859 and ending in 1919, with all but two occurring before 1907. In those years lynching—used to punish alleged thieves, rapists, and, most frequently, murderers—far outpaced legal executions as a means of disposing of suspected criminals. Before Van Horn enjoyed the honor of a legal hanging, Judge Lynch had killed at least fifteen men in Colorado. In 1879 the state legally executed one person; it lynched at least nine. In 1900, a year without any legal executions, the state saw three lynchings.

The 175 count is conservative, leaving out most cases in which lawmen returned with their prey dead rather than alive. It omits the Sand Creek Massacre and other army encounters with Native Americans, and it skips most instances, such as the Espinosas, in which pursuers may have gotten trigger-happy. It includes those executed by People's Courts, the Reynolds gang, and Pepino Tologrino. It also includes a few cases, such as the Lake County killing of Judge Elias Dyer, in which groups murdered in defense of what they considered their traditions or interests; but it excludes private vendettas apparently born of foreign traditions. It undoubtedly fails to list every lynching. Were I to attempt that, I would spend the rest of my life reading newspapers and would still have only a partial list.

The fact that so many Coloradans lost their lives without due process of law only partly tells of Judge Lynch's influence. He did not always get his man, but he often played his deadly game. If he had consistently prevailed, scores, perhaps even hundreds, of other accused persons would have died without a fair hearing. In 1861 W. W. Clifton, an alleged thief sentenced to death by a miner's court near Hamilton in South Park, escaped. In 1867 he again faced lynching, and again he escaped. A few years later he accidentally shot and killed himself, thereby permanently cheating Judge Lynch.[20]

A felon named Jenks, if one can believe a bizarre story, was more fortunate. Tried in the northwestern Colorado town of Craig, he was sentenced to the penitentiary by Judge Tom Rucker. That evening Rucker cut himself a plug of chewing tobacco, carelessly dropped the knife on his bed, flopped down, and impaled himself. When he was found, bleeding and unconscious, people concluded that Jenks had stabbed him, and they prepared to lynch the man. Luckily, Rucker revived, and Jenks survived.[21]

Steeped in lynchings, attempted lynchings, lynching threats, and occasional legal hangings, Coloradans grew so used to the practice that they may not have been surprised to read of a game called "Lynching Missouri Jack," played by newsboys in Leadville in 1886. Nor perhaps were they shocked by the Leadville schoolboys who hanged their classmate Willie Maguire. Rescued by a passerby, Willie, his throat badly bruised, lived.[22] A mock hanging in Montezuma in 1879 turned out less happily. Several drunks, angry with one of their companions, Red Mike, tied him to a tree, noose around his neck. The joke turned sour when they sobered up in the morning and found Mike dead.[23]

James Cutler in *Lynch-Law*, a 1905 study, wrote: "It has been said that our country's national crime is lynching."[24] In committing that crime Colorado easily kept pace with the rest of the nation between 1882 and 1903. *Chicago Tribune* compilations, summarized for selected states in Table A.3 in the appendix, allow for rough comparisons. Between 1882 and 1903 Coloradans lynched 64 people, tying North Carolina as the fifteenth-most lynching-prone state in terms of the number lynched. That put Colorado well behind Mississippi, Texas, Louisiana, Georgia, and Alabama—each of which counted more than 240 lynchings—but well ahead of Ohio, Illinois, Michigan, Pennsylvania, and New York, none of which had more than 25 lynchings.

If one makes allowance for the difference in population between Colorado, which had fewer than 200,000 people in 1880, and North Carolina, which had more than 600,000 the same year, on a per capita basis Colorado had a far higher lynching rate than North Carolina and a rate higher than most other states. Indeed between 1882 and 1903, Montana, Wyoming, Colorado, New Mexico, and Arizona formed a kind of lynching belt that outdid most of the South in lynchings on a per capita basis.

Per capita rates, however, may be distorted by small population bases. Moreover, assumptions based on 1882 to 1903, the years summarized by James Cutler, are open to question. Colorado, for example, had an even higher lynching rate before 1882 than it did after 1882. After 1902 Colorado counted only three lynchings, while southern states far outstripped Colorado and the rest of the West in the number of lynchings. The annual *Chicago Tribune* list of lynchings for 1903 included thirteen in Arkansas, twelve in Georgia, eight in Florida, seven in Texas, but none in Colorado, Kansas, and Utah. Populous New York, Pennsylvania, and Ohio also reckoned no lynchings that year.[25] Never having gained a significant foothold in most eastern states, by 1900 Judge Lynch was no more than a wispy specter of the past in much of the East. In the South he continued to feast. In Colorado he prowled like a wolf until 1903, after which he rarely found a victim.

Judge and wolf: the images both clarify and cloud. Judge implies a degree of reason and deliberation that many lynchings lacked. But a few, especially executions ordered by People's Courts in 1859 and 1860, had most of the trappings of decorum and proper procedure that marked legal executions. Moreover Judge Lynch is a useful metaphor because the honorific title given a horrific practice accurately implies that many lynchings enjoyed community support.[26]

Wolf suggests the packlike nature of mobs and the barbarity of many lynchings: for example, John Preston Porter Jr., engulfed by flames, praying "Good Lord, have mercy!" as the Limon mob "shook with pure enjoyment of the situation."[27] Together the images, judge and wolf, illuminate the devolution of lynching from an orderly, open process in its early People's Court manifestations into an uncontrolled beast.

Historian Patricia Nelson Limerick has described a division of western historians into two groups: "Those who deal in ideas and those who deal in facts have set up their booths at opposite sides of the bazaar, and more often than not those booths face away from each other."[28] Both camps can benefit from studying lynchings— case by case, state by state, region by region—until they piece together a whole picture.

For starters, historians need more facts. They have dissected individual lynchings, but they have not adequately analyzed Judge Lynch's western career. The blindness results in part from historians' failure to adequately explore violence in the West. Lynching, like western violence in general, has long been considered the rightful domain of television and popular writers and hence as more or less beneath scholarly notice. Moreover, the subject of lynching is distressing to those who love the West. Without complaint, perhaps with a sigh of relief, they have let the lynching discussion in recent decades focus more on the South than on the West.[29]

There are good and bad reasons for that attention. In the twentieth century lynching was far more common in the South than in the West. Southern lynching reveals much about racial relations, a topic of great importance. And southern barbarisms give westerners a way to sidestep their own misdeeds. In Owen Wister's *The Virginian*, a novel set in late-nineteenth-century Wyoming and published in 1902, Judge Henry takes the West off the moral hook by explaining that western lynching "done by the swiftest means, and in the quietest way" differs from "semi-barbarous" southern lynchings marked by torture and public display.[30]

Judge Henry was conveniently unaware of many of Colorado's lynchings. Did George Witherill's spirit give thanks that he had lived in the West when, after he was lynched in Cañon City, citizens abandoned their plan to pickle his body and instead preserved his lip and mustache—which as late as 1969 remained on display at Denver's Frontier Hotel?[31] Were the ghosts of the Espinosas pleased to know that one of their skulls served as a drinking cup for some of Colorado's most illustrious citizens?[32] Was Joseph Dixon, an African American, thankful that the Ouray jail prevented lynchers from reaching him, prompting them to torch the building and burn him to death?[33]

In excusing western lynching Wister was in good company. The historian Frederick Jackson Turner wrote admiringly of the no-nonsense approach of the frontier backwoodsman: "intolerant of men who split hairs, or scrupled over the method of reaching the right."[34] Turner blazed the trail, followed by several generations of western historians. LeRoy Hafen, long Colorado's state historian, and Carl Rister in *Western America* (1950) found two types on the western frontier: "the honest home-builder and the outlaw." Siding with the home builder, Hafen and Rister admitted "there were times when popular tribunals temporarily got out of hand," but they concluded that "the Westerner's sense of justice was an excellent stabilizer."[35] Similarly, Ray Allen Billington in *Westward Expansion: A History of the American Frontier* (1974), a widely used textbook, wrote of vigilance committees' efforts to control "roaring reprobates . . . shifty-eyed saloon keepers . . . and Mexican outlaws."[36] Few historians before the 1980s explored the territory charted by Richard Maxwell Brown in *Strain of Violence* (1975), which delved into lynching in both the South and the West. One of the most insightful scholars, Richard Slotkin, found large national issues and attitudes expressed in vigilantism.[37]

That many western historians were either blind to the evil of lynching or unwilling to embarrass the West perhaps explains their failure to thoroughly treat the subject. The notion, once widely held by western writers, that vigilantes were simply speeding up the process of justice protected westerners from accusations of injustice. Basing their work on biased sources, usually newspaper reports or antiquarian histories financed by local boosters, many writers accepted the common view that due process of law was unimportant and that the lynched got what they deserved. Wanting to believe that lynching bespoke civilization rather than barbarity, those writers concentrated on the lynchings that appeared to be reasonable responses by the "best men" to threats against their communities. San Francisco's vigilance committees of the 1850s, Denver's People's Courts in 1859 and 1860, the vigilantes of Montana in the 1860s, and the supposedly noble cattlemen of Johnson County, Wyoming, until recently were lauded by historians.[38]

Western historians paid less attention to scores of other lynchings, including the hanging of a "Mexican" in Golden in 1867, which prompted other Hispanos to leave the area; the Denver killing in 1880 of Look Young, a Chinese man who had committed no crime; and the knifing, hanging, shooting, and rehanging of Daniel Arata, an Italian, in Denver in 1893. Those inconvenient, embarrassing cases and many others matched southern lynchings in their barbarity. Yet the Colorado lynchings have largely been ignored, except by scholars anxious to recount the sufferings of a particular group. That approach, although useful, has sometimes led to other errors. For example, Andrew Rolle, in *The Immigrant Upraised: Italian Adventurers and Colonists in an Expanding America*, reported a Gunnison lynching of an Italian in 1890, a Denver lynching in 1893, the slaying of six Italians in southern Colorado in 1895, and the killing of another four in Walsenburg in 1900. An Italian was lynched in Gunnison in the early 1880s and one in Denver in 1893; but in 1895 the number of Italians lynched was three, not six, and the record does not confirm the deaths of four Italians in Walsenburg in 1900.[39]

Once the fact-mongers have supplied their tents with accurate information, idea merchants, who in recent years have been willing to write about western warts, can borrow some facts to use as ballast for their booths. Fact and idea historians can learn from lynching as they try to make sense of the bazaar of western history. In doing that they will meet a checkered cast of characters: the stupid and the wise, the rabble and the responsible, some good, some bad, some merely men of their times, Sheriff Cozens, and Sheriff Freeman. They will also find that the drama has an ending worthy of a western movie. The good people triumph, and lynching dies.

That took time. The reports of Judge Lynch's death in Colorado were greatly exaggerated in 1863. He flourished through much of the late nineteenth century. Although doddering by the dawn of the twentieth century, he outlived Sheriff Cozens, who died in 1904, by more than a decade. Coloradans were driving automobiles, watching movies, and attending air shows when the old avenger finally exited the state after killing his last victims, José Gonzales and Salvadore Ortez, in Pueblo on September 13, 1919.[40] As late as April 1934 it seemed lynching might return, like some long-dormant Dracula, when men in Colorado Springs, blaming African Americans for an attempted rape, mobbed the jail and hanged and burned an effigy of a black man in the city's African American enclave.[41]

Historians warn students that the past is a foreign land, growing increasingly foreign as it fades into the misty decades of grandparents and great-grandparents. But just as grandparents and great-grandparents shape their descendants, the 60 years of lynching in Colorado and the more than 200 years of lynching in the United States have influenced who we are. That Texas, which had one of the highest lynching rates in the nation, today has the highest number of prisoners on death row in the nation is perhaps no accident.[42] Attitudes created by more than a century of lynching, like a persistent toxic waste, still pollute.

In 1782, as the United States was being born, J. Hector St. John de Crèvecoeur, a French observer, asked, "What then is the American, this new man?"[43] After two centuries of nation building, of wars and migrations, canals and railroads, pencils and Pentium chips, Jefferson, Red Cloud, Susan B. Anthony, Martin Luther King Jr., George Wallace, and César Chávez, the country still asks what it is and who we are. The answer, historian David Hollinger noted, is crucial because in defining ourselves we find the basis for understanding our past and the foundation for the direction of our future.[44] Among the many rivers that flowed into the huge reservoir that comprises us, lynching was, if not a Mississippi, at least a South Platte.

The nation is no longer, as Samuel Clemens once tagged it, the "United States of Lyncherdom."[45] But Judge Lynch's embers still sometimes flicker, as in the 1998 killing of gay college student Matthew Shepard near Laramie, Wyoming, or the 1998 dragging death of James Byrd Jr., an African American, near Jasper, Texas. In each case the killers acted with the pretext of service to race or tradition, but in neither instance was the pretext sanctioned by the wider community. For such aberrations we have coined a new term, *hate crime*, which can claim lynching among its ancestors.

Today few people would argue that Judge Lynch's putrefied corpse should be resurrected. Yet some hanker after what they imagine to be frontier justice. Vexed with slow and complex legal processes, some citizens, unmoved by the standards of much of the rest of the Western world, quietly ignore the inequities and savagery that still plague justice in the United States—including class and race biases, the election of "hanging" judges, assaults on the tradition of juries' responsibility for fixing punishments, and capital punishment itself.

Before anyone embraces twenty-first-century incarnations of Judge Lynch, they might be wise to meet the creature their eighteenth- and nineteenth-century ancestors made and their twentieth-century ancestors unmade.[46] How he came to Colorado; how he initially got a good name; when, where, and why he flourished; how he operated; whom and why he killed; and how he himself was finally killed are the questions raised in this book. They are answered only partially because lynching was a complex social and psychological phenomenon that still badly needs the continuing attention and insights of first-rate historians and sociologists such as E. M. Beck, Richard Maxwell Brown, W. Fitzhugh Brundage, Roberta Senechal de La Roche, James H. Madison, Stewart E. Tolnay, Christopher Waldrep, and Joel Williamson, to name only a few of the scholars who have investigated lynching.[47]

Perhaps they and other academicians will find grist for their intellectual mills in this narrative history of lynching in Colorado. General readers will, I hope, find an interesting, albeit disturbing, story. Chapter 1 covers the advent of lynching in the Pikes Peak country. Chapter 2 centers on lynchings before 1890 in larger towns: Denver, Pueblo, and Leadville. Chapter 3 looks at lynchings in smaller places. Chapter 4 details the lynchings of Margaret and

Michael Cuddigan and touches on the killings of others. Chapter 5 focuses on the tug-of-war between lynching's friends and foes. Chapter 6 examines race, ethnicity, and lynching. Chapter 7 tries to find the forest in the trees. In the appendix scholars may find helpful information, and genealogists may discover the names of their ancestors.

Quotations have been given as they originally appeared. In some instances newspapers made spelling and other errors. Those are noted by the word *sic* in brackets after the error, except in the many instances in which the word *hung* was used in place of *hang*. On occasion reporters tried to write in dialect or broken English. Those attempts are apparent, so *sic* has not been used. Nineteenth-century Americans often used derogatory racial epithets. I have generally quoted them exactly as they were given in the press. The thinking that prompted such slurs fed the mentality that fostered lynching, so it is important to be attuned to the language to understand lynching. To remove that language would be to soften the condemnation its users should bear.

1

PEOPLE'S COURTS AND VIGILANCE COMMITTEES, 1859-1861

We never hanged on circumstantial evidence. I have known a great many such executions, but I don't believe one of them was ever unjust.

—WILLIAM N. BYERS[1]

During the autumn of 1858 William Larimer, a versatile town developer, traveled more than 600 miles from Leavenworth, in eastern Kansas Territory, to Auraria, in western Kansas at the base of the Rocky Mountains, where gold discoveries promised potential riches to prospectors and speculators. On his arrival in mid-November he saw that Auraria's settlers had built cabins on the southwest side of Cherry Creek near its juncture with the South Platte River. On the creek's northwest bank Charles Nichols, representing the St. Charles Town Association, had partly completed a rude cabin. It was not fair, Larimer and his friends evidently rationalized, for such a poorly secured tract to interfere with their pursuit of property. So they ordered Nichols to quit his claim, or "a rope and noose would be used on him."[2] Nichols took the hint; Larimer took the site. Denver was born.[3]

A rope and a noose, intertwined though they were with Denver's founding, were not icons the town cared to engrave on its seal or emblazon on its flag. Such symbols did not sell real estate. William McKimens, an early booster who knew what prospective settlers wanted to read, wrote from Auraria to the Leavenworth *Daily Times* in January 1859: "Our population on the Platte and tributaries, exceed 1000 men. I believe five white women is all we can boast of at present, but I think in the space of one short year we can count them by the tens of thousands. We have preaching here semi-monthly, and the morality of our town is improving rapidly. It has never been my good fortune to be in a better disposed community."[4]

McKimens had cause for optimism. From midsummer 1858, when prospectors led by William Green Russell discovered gold in the South Platte, until early April 1859, the gold seekers avoided killing one another. A shooting in September 1858 led to the banishment of the perpetrator.[5] Russell and others stole land from the Cheyenne and Arapaho Indians. Larimer and his associates stole St. Charles. But as far as the spotty record shows, the few hundred pioneers of 1858 handled occasional friction without resort to murder.

Their demi-Eden was doomed. During 1859 and 1860 tens of thousands of young men—largely without the restraint of women, family, and elders—crashed like tidal waves against the base of the Rockies, eroding hastily constructed community foundations. William Parsons, another pioneer of 1858, saw in the advancing flood of gold seekers "the gambler, horse-thief, and the more accomplished metropolitan desperado." He warned, "The vice and hideous deformities incident to new countries grown suddenly populous, will be seen in this the newest one of all."[6]

William Larimer's diary proved Parsons's point. In it Larimer, who established Mount Prospect, Denver's first cemetery, tallied early burials. First was Abraham Kay, who died of lung disease; next came fifteen-year-old B. Marynall, who fell from a horse; third was Arthur Binegraff, who was murdered; fourth was John Stuffle, hanged for killing Binegraff; and fifth was Peleg T. Bassett, killed by John Scudder, who kept his name out of Larimer's book by leaving town. Those five deaths—three of them violent—were registered in less than a month, from mid-March to mid-April 1859. The Gold Rush was just beginning.[7]

The lust for gold triggered the area's first murder. On April 7, 1859, John Stuffle, prospecting on Clear Creek northwest of Denver, stole ten dollars' worth of gold dust from his brother-in-law Arthur Binegraff, murdered him, and hid his body behind a log. A telltale bloodstain on Stuffle's sleeve gave him away, and his confession sealed his fate. "The citizens," wrote historian Jerome Smiley, "decided to give the man the form, at least, of a trial."[8]

The trial, which took place outdoors, was conducted by a People's Court—a temporary assembly—presided over by Seymour W. Wagoner, recently elected a probate judge of Arapahoe County, Kansas Territory. Wagoner clung precariously to his judicial perch because, among other defects in his authority, his election had not been sanctioned by Kansas officials. Technicalities apparently did not concern the Fifty-Niners. Still, they tried to make their procedures proper by giving Stuffle a defense attorney and a jury trial. James Pierce, one of Auraria's founders, remembered: "The evidence was all heard in profound silence by the mass. I never witnessed a more orderly trial in any court in my life than this was. Of course we found him guilty of murder in the first degree." Some reports indicate that Stuffle was then bound over for appearance before a U.S. district judge, which, considering the lack of authority of Wagoner and the People's Court, was the proper thing to do.[9]

The proper thing never happened. Lacking a jail in which to keep Stuffle and facing a weeks-long trek to deliver him for trial in eastern Kansas, the people quickly decided to hang him. On April 9, two days after the murder and a day after the trial, he was taken by wagon to a cottonwood tree on Cherry Creek. "Noisy Tom," an experienced hangman, fixed the rope around Stuffle's neck. Tom and a preacher knelt to pray. Stuffle obstinately remained standing. Tom poked him in the ribs and asked "if he didn't know better than to act like a heathen."[10] Stuffle continued blaspheming until the angry crowd pulled the wagon from underneath him, leaving him to die miserably: "The contorted features and figure were so terrible in aspect that many turned away."[11]

Denver's first hanging, although messy and lacking legal sanction, was a public, daylight execution done by orderly people after an open trial. No mob battered down a jail door. No masked avengers crept through moonlit alleys at midnight. No doubt apparently existed as to Stuffle's guilt. It was nevertheless technically a lynching because Stuffle had "met his death illegally at the hands of a group acting under the pretext of service to justice, race, or tradition."[12]

That first lynching in Colorado served as a model for a handful of executions by the People's Court in Denver. The extralegal People's Court in turn established a precedent that could be used to help justify clandestine lynchings. What started as an open, orderly process became a secret, often disorderly monster. There was a world of difference between the careful process that ended in the condemnation of John Stuffle in Denver in 1859 and the riotous attack on the Arapahoe County jail in Denver in 1893, which ended in the slashing, hanging, and rehanging of Daniel Arata. To fathom how Coloradans devolved from Stuffle to Arata, one must first examine the People's Courts.

The *Rocky Mountain News*, the area's first newspaper, published its first edition two weeks after Stuffle's death. In its brief account of his hanging the *News* avoided the term *lynching*. The People's Court may not have been fully legal, but it was the best the isolated community could muster and was better than mob law. Judge Seymour did not enjoy the blessing of U.S. or Kansas officials, but he had the people's sanction: "we the people who are the power here."[13] Larimer summed up community sentiment in his register of Mount Prospect burials: "John Stuffle, German" was "hung after a fair trial."[14]

The governmental void that plagued the Rocky Mountain towns between 1859 and 1861 gave the People's Court a degree of legitimacy. What would become Colorado Territory in 1861 was in 1858 largely Indian domain within New Mexico, Utah, Kansas, and Nebraska Territories. Most gold discoveries took place in western Kansas, but Kansas didn't organize effective courts in the Pikes Peak region. Even had that been done, such tribunals would have rested on shaky ground because Kansas's power did not extend to Indian lands. The U.S. Congress could have unloosed the legal knots, but tied up in pre–Civil War bickering over whether new territories should be slave or free, it did nothing.

Desperate for government, in 1859 some Pikes Peakers formed a do-it-yourself territory they called Jefferson. Lacking federal sanction and local support, it languished. George M. Willing, one of Jefferson's would-be delegates to Congress, complained to U.S. Secretary of State Lewis Cass in December 1859: "It cannot be expected that we can protect ourselves against lawless persons and the incursions of savages with a provisional Government [*sic*]."[15] The People's Courts partially filled the jurisdictional vacuum. With

A STATE OF SUSPENSE.

1.1 Commenting on Denver's People's Court, Albert D. Richardson wrote: "The Denver people are a law unto themselves." In his account of his western travels, Beyond the Mississippi (1867), Richardson included a sketch of a pioneer lynched by other pioneers. Courtesy, Thomas J. Noel Collection.

nearly a dozen major cases between April 1859 and December 1860, Denver provides the fullest record of these temporary assemblies.

Shortly after Stuffle was buried, Denver reckoned its second homicide. On April 16, 1859, John Scudder tussled with Peleg T. Bassett, killing him.[16] Scudder, fearing hasty injustice, fled to Salt Lake. He returned a year later to be acquitted by the People's Court. W. J. Paine, an African American blacksmith who claimed self-defense to justify his October 1859 slaying of Oliver Davis, another African American, was also acquitted by the People's Court.[17]

Justice stayed on its moderate course during the first nine months of 1860. According to historian Smiley, in early 1860 Auraria's citizens banished five turkey-thieving "bummers" from the Cherry Creek settlements. Some returned later, but "as they behaved conservatively they were not hanged."[18]

Moses Young was not so fortunate. He peppered William West with buckshot on March 13, 1860, killing him. The next day the people gave Young an elaborate and open trial featuring three judges and a twelve-man jury. They found him guilty and two days later hanged him from a scaffold on the west bank of Cherry Creek between Larimer and Market Streets. They selected the location because it was "exactly over the pool of blood that yet marked the spot where West was shot down and died."[19]

At the next trial, March 30, 1860, of John Rooker for killing Jack O'Neil, Rooker was acquitted. O'Neil was buried in Mount Prospect Cemetery, which in popular parlance became "Jack O'Neil's ranch." In April "Pocahontas," an Indian woman who killed a saloon keeper named Labine, fled from Denver before she could be arrested.[20]

Marcus Gredler, who axed Jacob Roeder to death on June 12, likely wished he had followed Pocahontas's example. Tried by the People's Court, he was convicted. On June 15 nearly 4,000 people, practically the entire population of Denver, watched him hanged from a scaffold on the east bank of Cherry Creek near the Curtis Street intersection. To one spectator, George T. Clark, it was an interesting but not overly bothersome event: "There was a great crowd and a good many ladies present. He was very cool to the last moment. Had a prayer and his confession read. Did not make a struggle after he dropped. Everything about the hanging went off quiet. Took a walk after tea."[21]

William Hadley, who killed J. B. Card with a butcher knife on June 20, also enjoyed an open trial. Convicted and ordered to be hanged, he was given two days to tidy up his affairs. He used the time to escape. The *Western Mountaineer* noted, "In consequence of the absence of Hadley the hanging did not take place on Monday."[22]

Nor was there a hanging in July after Charles Harrison, a prominent gambler, slew "Professor" Stark, an ex-slave. "Murder is murder," said the *Rocky Mountain News,* "whether committed upon the body of an unknown and unrespected human being, or on the highest citizen of the land."[23] Some evidence, however, supported Harrison's claim that Stark had started the fight. So weighty was Harrison's influence, so lightly did the community value an ex-slave's life, that the gambler was not brought to trial.[24] Later in 1860, Harrison was again summoned before the People's Court for killing a white man named James Hill. Harrison pleaded self-defense and was released, perhaps because the jury was slipped a basket "filled with grub, cigars and flasks of whiskey which the jury-men took out of the basket and put into themselves."[25] They got drunk, fought among themselves, and failed to reach a verdict.

That fiasco underlined what some settlers realized by midsummer 1860. Openness and citizen participation allowed the People's Court to drape itself in the mantle of civilization. But virtues could be vices. Openness and citizen involvement subjected the People's Court to the vagaries of opinion and the manipulation of juries.

Those shortcomings saved Carl Wood. Reacting to a spate of violence including the Stark murder, the *Rocky Mountain News* on July 25, 1860, attacked "the rowdies, ruffians, shoulder hitters, and bullies generally that infest our city," warning them that "the very next outrage will call down the vengeance of an outraged people."[26] Such talk irked Wood and two of his friends. They seized William N. Byers, editor of the *News,* took him from his office, and marched him to the Criterion saloon—Harrison's bailiwick. Byers recalled that as they walked, "Wood would thrust his revolver up against my ear and say God d—n you, I have a mind to kill you right here." At the Criterion the thugs urged that Byers be killed, but Harrison spirited him out a back door.[27]

Byers and his coworkers barricaded themselves in their office. Wood and his companion George Steele lurked nearby, intending to shoot Byers. Growing impatient, Steele fired on the *News.* He in turn was shot, fled, was shot again, and later died. Wood was captured. Taken before the People's Court, he was charged with attempted murder. "It was a forgone conclusion," said the *News*, that the prisoner would be brought in "Guilty."[28]

That did not happen. Wood was ably defended by, among others, attorney A. C. Ford. Curiously, the prosecutor, George W. Purkins, helped the defense by making remarks that "served to excite sympathy" for Wood. One juror insisted on acquittal reportedly because he considered the death penalty too harsh a punishment. The crowd decided to banish Wood rather than hang him. His drinking buddies gave him "an ovation" as he rode out of town.[29] "Our people's court," lamented the *News*, "has become little better than a farce."[30]

Wood's release, coupled with a rash of horse thefts, led the *News* to demand harsher punishments even at the expense of abandoning the People's Court: "Much as we deprecate mob violence, or the working of Lynch law . . . we can at this juncture see no other alternative."[31] In seeking that alternative the advocates of lynching willingly abandoned democratic processes.

The capture of "Black Hawk," a white man despite his name, on Saturday, September 1, 1860, led to his confession before a secret group. He admitted "that he was a member of a great organization of horse-thieves that operated through the country all the way across from southern Wisconsin."[32] The next day, in a radical departure from the orderly operation of the People's Court, Black Hawk was secretly hanged from a cottonwood outside of town. Before he died he revealed the names of the theft ring's leaders—attorney A. C. Ford and John Shear.

Shear, "a big, fat and rather dissipated man," was a member of Denver's City Council and a founder of the town's library.[33] Neither bookish merits nor political standing could shield him from angry frontiersmen. The *News* on September 4 reported that his body had been discovered a mile south of town, hanging from a poplar tree near the South Platte. A note explained: "This man was hung. It was proven that he is a horse thief." Interviewed by the *News*, some people held that "every man should receive a fair trial." Others argued, "A fair trial in this community means . . . a farce."[34]

Ford, perhaps aware of Shear's death, boarded a stagecoach on Monday, September 4. About 8 miles southeast of town he was kidnapped, taken into the prairie grass, and shot by a few members of Denver's newly organized vigilance committee. His unburied, buckshot-riddled body was discovered on September 8 without his valuables, which had evidently been stolen. Months later a member of the vigilance committee found the thief in El Paso, Texas, recovered Ford's gold watch, and returned it to his widow. Clearly, Ford's executioners were willing to go to great lengths and distances to keep from being blamed for the watch theft, a venal act unworthy of pure-hearted community watchdogs.[35]

Who were those watchdogs? The fact that *News* editor Byers supported them suggests that they were men of his type, the emerging power elite. Perhaps he was one of them. Less than a decade after the hangings of 1859–1860 the *News* indicated that Alexander C. Hunt, later Colorado's territorial governor, headed the vigilance committee. Henry L. Pitzer, whose memoirs were published in 1938, recalled two vigilance groups—one embracing 100 men, the other an inner circle of 10. John M. Chivington—the local leader of the Methodist church—William N. Byers, and William Larimer were, Pitzer speculated, among the 100. Sheriff William Middaugh, blacksmith Tom Pollock, and sawmill operator D. C. Oakes may have been among the inner circle. A report in the *Rocky Mountain Herald* for September 3, 1860, indicated that a group of "mounted men" was "to overhaul and to bring to punishment the thieves, be they Indians or Whites." Among those organizing that group were Larimer, Pollock, and attorney Hiram P. Bennet.[36]

Jerome Smiley listed three victims of the committee: Black Hawk, John Shear, and A. C. Ford. All others, he reported, were executed openly by the People's Court. He dismissed as "pure fiction" the stories of numerous hangings: "It was a tribute to the forbearance of the people of those times that the trees did not more frequently bear in the morning fruit that was not on their branches the night before."[37]

Smiley, booster historian to the core, was apparently either wearing rose-colored glasses or naively relying on the memories of old pioneers. Black Hawk, Shear, and Ford were probably not the only men lynched near Denver in September 1860. On September 5 the *News* dismissed speculation that seven men had been found hanged near the city. On September 12 the paper reported that "rendezvous" of the thieves had been uncovered, that a party was going after them, and that "we shall not be surprised to hear of a reduction in the number of gentry now in the horse business."[38] Seventy years later George Willison, in *Here They Dug the Gold*, indicated that indeed at least half a dozen other hangings occurred in September, including that of Jim Latty, a stable keeper. Stanley

Zamonski and Terry Keller, in *The Fifty-Niners: A Denver Diary*, also reckoned nine September lynchings including those of Black Hawk, Ford, Shear, Latty, and five unidentified men. Three men or nine, the fact remains that if the democratic People's Court would not punish criminals, the self-styled patricians among the Pikes Peakers were willing to help Judge Lynch kill in secret. They were willing, as social historian Richard Hogan has observed, to adopt "private solutions to the problem of public order."[39]

But "mysterious and terrible" retribution was not what the best people regularly wanted. The *News*, although it defended the September lynchings, called for the organization of government to secure orderly legal processes.[40] The *News* also fretted about the "mysterious committee, secret inquisition," praying "to God that we may never again be called upon to record a hanging by Lynch law."[41] With the horse thieves subdued, a revived commitment to stern justice, and the recognition that secret executions were a last resort, Denver revived the People's Court in late September 1860. For the fresh opportunity to demonstrate the righteousness of their ways, the people owed thanks to a drunken bully of unrighteous ways.

Twenty-three-year-old James Gordon, a popular Denver saloon owner—decent when sober, wild when drunk—brutally killed John Gantz on July 20, 1860. The unarmed Gantz, also a well-liked young man, did nothing to provoke Gordon who in a drunken fury seized Gantz by the hair, held him down, and put a gun to his head. Four times the gun misfired. The fifth shot killed Gantz.

Gordon fled. Besieged at a ranch outside of town, he boldly escaped by riding through his pursuers. Tracked by Denver's sheriff, William H. Middaugh, Gordon eluded capture for five weeks before being apprehended in eastern Kansas. Middaugh wanted to return Gordon to Denver for trial, but Kansas authorities insisted that he be taken to Leavenworth. That angered people in Denver who had to ante up the money to send Middaugh and seven witnesses 600 miles to testify.

Their arduous stagecoach trip counted for nothing. John Pettit, chief justice of the Supreme Court for Kansas Territory, refused to delve into the murder. Gordon, he ruled, had done the deed not in Arapahoe County, which was within Pettit's jurisdiction, but in Montana County, a half-baked concoction of the Kansas legislature that, said the judge, was not under the authority of any court. Gordon could not legally be tried anywhere because he had the good fortune to have murdered Gantz in a jurisdictional void.

While Pettit split legal hairs, some onlookers grew boisterous, prompting the judge to threaten to "turn them out among the swine if they persist in making a noise."[42] That put them in a more churlish mood, and when Pettit ordered that Gordon be set free, the incensed assemblage bolted toward the door—an ominous sign that caused Gordon to blanch. Taken to jail to shield him from the maddened crowd, Gordon was attacked that evening by a mob that beat him, tore off his clothes, and put a rope around his neck in an attempt to hang him. Responsible men, including Sheriff Middaugh who was injured in the fray, rescued Gordon from the rioters.[43] Middaugh brought him back to Denver to face the People's Court.

Gordon's crime, flight, capture, rescue, and ensuing trial attracted national notice. "The eyes of tens of thousands in the States are turned to Denver," said the *News*.[44] Under scrutiny, the town put on a good show by giving Gordon an open trial presided over by three judges, including William Larimer. They allowed the prisoner a six-man defense team. The People's Court agreed to proceed "according to matters of fact, and the circumstances of the case, and not to forms of law."[45] Gordon denied the court's authority and asked to be tried by a U.S. court because he was, after all, in the United States. The jury took only twenty minutes to convict him. He was hanged on October 6, 1860, from a scaffold near Fourteenth and Arapahoe Streets.[46]

The *Western Mountaineer* praised the dignified doings: "They cannot be charged with rashness and barbarity, for though all the proceedings were extra-judicial, there was no indecent or indecorous haste, and all mercy and clemency was shown that public safety would permit." An orderly crowd quietly watched as "the black cap was adjusted, the drop fell, and the prisoner swung between heaven and earth, as though unfit for either place."[47]

Patrick Kelley was more fortunate. Accused of killing his partner, Richard Doyle, Kelley was tried in December 1860 by the Denver City Court, not the People's Court. Although it was clear that Kelley had killed Doyle, the jury set him free. Critical of the decision, the *News* predicted that the "citizens of Denver will again return to the plan of disposing of desperate cases in the People's Court."[48] Throughout the autumn of 1860, Denver's law and order element vehemently objected to court judgments with which it disagreed: decisions of the People's Court in Wood's case, the Kansas Territorial Court in Gordon's case, Denver's City Court in Kelley's case.

Having seen Kelley slip away, solid citizens were in no mood to let that happen to Patrick Waters, accused of killing Thomas Freeman. Waters was tried before the People's Court, judged guilty, and hanged on December 21, 1860, on the west side of the South Platte near the Fifteenth Street bridge. He turned out to be the last man hanged by a People's Court in Denver, although the city's taste for summary executions long lingered.[49]

Pikes Peakers outside Denver organized mining districts and local governments that attended to property rights and, as circumstances demanded, dealt with criminals. The Gregory District, 35 miles west of Denver in the Central City area, demonstrated its legal sophistication by allowing defendants to request a change of venue if they feared a prejudiced local jury. Union District, which embraced the town of Empire 40 miles west of Denver, did not like lawyers but wanted women. It threatened attorneys with twenty to fifty lashes if they appeared in court and offered women equal political rights with men. Another district banned lawyers and pettifoggers.[50] Nevadaville, a mountain mining camp near Central City, reduced attorneys' work by making its laws simple. Thieves and perjurers were to be whipped; "any person convicted of the willful premeditated murder, shall be hung by the neck until dead."[51]

Canada Charley, a thief, so angered people in Golden in November 1860 that they considered hanging him, but after a People's Court trial they decided instead to give him twenty-one lashes and banish him.[52] The next year a man named Davis shot but did not seriously wound another man in Lake Gulch a few miles southeast of Central City. Some wanted to hang Davis, but the People's Court ordered that one side of his head be shaved. Then, as witness H. J. Hawley reported: "He was taken to the spot where he had done the deed, tied to a tree and five men gave him his regular fifty lashes on the bare back that made him get up and stir about—there were eight hundred or a thousand men present all shouting to put it on harder. . . . This is rough business for Sunday but such things must be attended to."[53]

Whipped and banished, Canada Charley and Davis escaped with their lives. Between September 1859 and April 1861 Edgar Vanover, W. W. Aitkins, Solomon Kennedy, and at least one unidentified man were condemned and hanged, usually with more dispatch but less decorum than was typical of the People's Court in Denver. Vanover had not killed anyone. He shot at a barkeeper in Golden and threatened others in early September 1859. Captured, he faced citizens who, if one believes the story in the *Rocky Mountain News*, "after cool deliberations" decided "for the safety of the inhabitants he should be executed. . . . A committee was appointed to carry out the will of the people and the sad duty was performed."[54] Libeus Barney, a gold seeker, saw Vanover's end differently: "His career [was] suddenly brought to a close by an infuriated mob who seized, bound, tied and hung the desperado all within the short period of 20 minutes." Barney's version rings true in light of a letter to the *News* in which leading businessmen of Golden condemned the "mob" that hanged Vanover.[55]

Judge Lynch similarly cast off the cloak of civilization in early 1860 when he rudely hanged Aitkins, a man better known by his nickname Pennsyltuck. Tuck took an ineffective shot at Arapahoe County sheriff Jack Kehler, who in turn wounded him. Tuck then threatened to kill Kehler and four others. In the dead of night on February 29, 1860, a mob of at least 100 men broke into the house of a doctor in Missouri City, a village near Central City, where Tuck was recuperating. They grabbed him, gagged him, and hanged him from a tree. Responsible residents, regretting the hasty action, later apologized to the doctor.[56]

Kennedy received fairer process but similar punishment. In a drunken rage he killed John Mailey, a shopkeeper in Lake Gulch, on April 11, 1861. A correspondent for the *Rocky Mountain News* reported that he received a fair trial. More than 1,000 people jammed the gulch on April 13 to witness the execution. Kennedy confessed his crime, blaming it on drink. A sympathetic liquor dealer tried to save Kennedy by arguing, "He was the last man to vote for hanging for such a crime, committed under the influence of liquor, for he sold it himself." That plea did not hold water with the crowd. Kennedy was hanged.[57]

An unidentified man may have been hanged for murder on the headwaters of the Cache la Poudre River in 1859, and another described only as a "Mexican" may have suffered a similar fate for horse theft in El Paso County in the summer of 1860.[58] He received a hearing attended by 200, who sentenced him to die by voting with their feet. Those judging him guilty gathered on one side of the street; those favoring acquittal congregated on the other.[59] And if a story published decades after the event is true, a man named Bill Flemming was hanged by a People's Court for killing his partner near the headwaters of Cherry Creek southeast of Denver.[60]

Congress finally made Colorado a U.S. territory in late February 1861, removing whatever claims the People's Court had to legitimacy based on necessity. That did not stop people in Cañon City, 115 miles southwest of Denver, from trying Charles Brown for horse theft in July 1861. After a "committee" was appointed "with discretionary powers to extract from him all that he knows," Brown confessed and was ordered hanged. He managed to escape.[61]

Citizens of Apex, a mountain hamlet northwest of Central City, recognized their People's Court was no longer supreme in July 1861 when they judged John Bishop guilty of horse theft. They properly decided to send him to the U.S. marshal in Denver. Bishop never made it. Abducted "by parties unknown," he was hanged. Such "justice" distressed Benjamin Hall, newly appointed chief justice of Colorado's Territorial Supreme Court, who condemned "self-commissioned executions" as "unnecessary . . . unlawful, barbarous and murderous."[62] But Hall's preaching did not save Joseph W. Briggs, an accused horse thief lynched north of Denver near the St. Vrain River in early September 1861.[63] People's Courts largely faded away. Lynching lived.

For more than half a century Judge Lynch prowled in Colorado, in part because he could claim that from 1859 to 1861 he was an angel of civilization, often operating through the People's Courts, bringing order from chaos. The fact that James Gordon enjoyed three judges, six defense attorneys, a jury, and an orderly execution bespeaks a community thirsty for civilization or at least striving to seem civilized. Judge Lynch could also often argue that he worked for and through pillars of the community, men such as William N. Byers, John M. Chivington, Alexander C. Hunt, and William H. Middaugh. Draped in the mantle of popular sovereignty—the American belief in self-government—and lauded by local patricians, the judge could easily style himself a servant of the people.

Coloradans long portrayed Judge Lynch if not as a mythological hero, at least as a helpful handyman. They sang his accomplishments, praised his manners, and excused his dark deeds. They largely ignored the hard cases such as the hangings of Edgar Vanover and W. W. Aitkins in which lynchers were more wolflike than judgelike.

They glossed over citizens' unwillingness to accept the decisions of courts if they disagreed with those decisions. The selective memories of pioneers became the truth for the next generation. "We never hanged on circumstantial evidence," Byers told Jerome Smiley. "I have known a great many such executions, but I don't believe one of them was ever unjust."[64]

Early chroniclers such as Smiley rarely raised questions of class, religion, or race when assessing the People's Courts. Did the unidentified "Mexican" lynched in Colorado City die in part because he was Mexican? Did Patrick Waters's Roman Catholic faith, his Irish ancestry, and the fact that he killed a Mason put him at odds with those who judged him guilty—most of whom were not Roman Catholics? Why were William Larimer's friends free to threaten Charles Nichols with hanging so they could grab the St. Charles site? Why could an influential gambler such as Charles Harrison kill Professor Stark, a black man, and James Hill, a white man, and yet go untried for one offense and unpunished for the other? It seems obvious that class and race played their roles in the drama. Still, at least in the Gold Rush period, class was not always a determining factor. A. C. Ford and John Shear were men of standing in the community prior to being lynched in September 1860.

Over the course of the 1860s and into the 1870s, lynching, having gotten firmly rooted during the Gold Rush, remained popular. Outlaws plagued Colorado during its territorial days (1861–1876) and for a few years after. Citizens might have controlled them without recourse to lynching had communities been willing to spend money for jails and police, brook delays, and run the risk of escapes and acquittals. "Why bother?" many asked. After all, Judge Lynch worked quickly and cheaply.

2

MAJOR TOWNS, 1860s–1880s

The community would seem to have no way of protecting itself but to run well-known ruffians down, as it
would wolves, and kill them.
—*ROCKY MOUNTAIN NEWS*, NOVEMBER 23, 1868

Musgrove and Duggan, Coe and Tex, Phebus and McGrew,
Stewart and Frodsham, among many others, fed Coloradans' appetite for lynching from the 1860s into the 1880s.
Those thieves and "brigandish boys" so angered law-abiding citizens
that many judged it as proper to kill them as it was to massacre
Indians or shoot wolves.[1] They were, like the Native Americans, seen
as a threat to the civilization that justified European Americans in
their drive to fulfill what they proclaimed to be their manifest des-
tiny, their God-given right to sweep across the continent, summarily
removing everything—Arapaho or Cheyenne, bison or brigand—
that stood in their way.[2] In killing desperadoes Coloradans fostered
a culture of lynching that also brought death to lesser criminals,
hapless little fish netted with the large.

Yet although dozens of suspected outlaws were summarily killed in the 1860s, 1870s, and early 1880s, respectable people in larger communities such as Denver, Pueblo, and Leadville turned against lynching. Vying with one another to attract labor and capital, up-and-coming cities did not want to do anything to hurt business. They rapidly reproduced the societies they had left behind in Chicago, St. Louis, and Cincinnati—complete with churches, schools, jails, and courts. Once they put on the trappings of civilization, they no longer needed or wanted vigilantes.[3]

Lynching lasted as long as it did in Colorado less because it persisted in large places than because of its constant rebirth in new towns.[4] In those communities lynching of outlaws and common crooks usually marked a locale's early history. As in Denver and Pueblo, later lynchings in smaller places tended to be punishment for what those communities considered serious crimes or to be the work of mobs drunk on ethnic and racial hatred.

For a few years after the Gold Rush lynching went a-begging in Denver. With the frenetic activity of 1859–1860 tapering off during the Civil War years, the town temporarily settled down. One of its early marshals, David J. Cook, compared it to a New England village, "a paradise of quiet and repose."[5]

How reposeful that paradise really was or was not is suggested by crime statistics. In 1859, Denver tallied four murders, in 1860 thirteen. The population fluctuated, so it is difficult to determine the homicide rate. If the 1860 census number of 4,749 holds for 1859, there were approximately 84 homicides per hundred thousand population in 1859 and 274 per hundred thousand in 1860. In 1860, Denver suffered a murder rate roughly 34 times greater than its 1999 rate of less than 8 per hundred thousand.[6] After 1860 the rate dropped, with probably no more than 13 homicides in the city from 1861 to 1865. Although the per capita rates—based on a low population base—are suspect, they strongly suggest that frontier Denver was a violent place during 1859 and 1860, after which it became less so. Even in its calm years it was far removed, geographically and spiritually, from peaceful New England villages.[7]

Outside Denver the crime picture has been less studied and hence is less clear. William Van Horn's Central City execution in December 1863 was the territory's only legal hanging in the Civil War years. Scattered hamlets sometimes lacked newspapers, or if they had them, many have not survived. Accounts produced later—

some the foggy memories of aging pioneers, others the work of copy-hungry newspapermen—lack the reliability of contemporary reports.

Irving Howbert, an observant pioneer, recalled that a "Mexican" accused of stealing a horse was hanged in Colorado City in the summer of 1860 after trial by the people.[8] Perhaps that was the same "Mexican" the *Western Mountaineer* on August 2, 1860, said was lynched in Colorado City. Was another "Mexican" thief hanged in May 1860, also in El Paso County, as chronicled by A. Z. Sheldon?[9] Or has one man been multiplied into two by the passage of time or two men into three? On May 9, 1863, Central City's *Tri-Weekly Miner's Register* noted that a man named Baxter was summarily executed near Fairplay 80 miles southwest of Denver, and perhaps another also suffered lynching in the Fairplay area.[10]

The Reynolds gang, claiming to be Confederate guerrilla fighters, shattered the peace of central Colorado in 1864 by robbing stagecoaches. Five gang members were captured and sent to Denver, from whence Colonel John M. Chivington dispatched them as prisoners to Fort Lyon on the Arkansas River in early September 1864.[11] "I told the guards when they left that if they did not kill those fellows, I would play thunder with them," Chivington reportedly bragged later. Shortly after they left Denver, shackled and under heavy guard, the guerrillas supposedly tried to escape and were all shot to death. If indeed they tried to flee, they cannot be numbered among the lynched. But if, as U.S. Attorney Samuel Browne contended and Captain Theodore G. Cree, who commanded the guards, confirmed, "the whole five were butchered with shackles on their legs," their deaths can be laid at Judge Lynch's feet.[12]

A few months later, on November 29, 1864, Chivington reminded his troops that Indians had "murdered women and children on the Platte" shortly before the troops attacked Cheyenne and Arapaho camped at Sand Creek in southeastern Colorado.[13] To include the more than 160 Native Americans who died that day among the lynched might stretch the definition of lynching, but the soldiers' disregard for life sprang in part from the mind-set that also countenanced lynching. At least one native woman died by hanging. Chivington reported her death as a suicide; later generations could easily see it as emblematic of many murders at Sand Creek.[14]

Among his own people Chivington apparently valued proper legal procedures. He may have been a member of the vigilance committee of 1859, but his attitude toward extralegal hangings changed after Colorado became a territory. In December 1863 he quieted a mob bent on lynching a pimp who had killed a drunken soldier at Aunt Betsy's, a brothel in Highlands across the South Platte from Denver. Aunt Betsy, "a wretched woman, ripe for the bottomless pit," got little sympathy from the press. Yet Chivington calmed the crowd: "Two wrongs never can make one right. We live in a land of Law— where every man has meted out to him equal and exact justice. . . . If you should hang him without a trial you would be just as guilty of a cowardly murder as he is." The mob relented, taking vengeance by torching Aunt Betsy's house.[15]

The Civil War, coupled with a mining slump, slowed the region's growth in the early 1860s. Renewed migration after the war turned Cook's "tranquil repose" to violent waking. Garroters, evidently choking their victims until they coughed up their money, stalked citizens in October 1865, prompting the *Rocky Mountain News* to propose the creation of a vigilance committee. Blaming the crimes on outlaws from Montana, the *News* complained, "It's getting mighty rough, boys. How long shall we stand it?"[16] Patience evaporated in early 1866 as the city tallied nearly a dozen lynchings within 25 miles of town. The most notorious victim, Frank Williams, was suspected of having driven his stagecoach en route from Helena, Montana, to Salt Lake City into a trap where Williams's secret confreres killed several passengers and escaped with $60,000 in gold. Williams left Montana and began spending money freely.[17] Montana vigilantes sniffed him out at the Planter's House, a Denver hotel. Learning of their arrival, he hastily boarded an eastbound stage. The avengers pursued him and brought him back for examination before local vigilantes; one can only imagine their methods. After three days of questioning, "Williams broke down, confessed his guilt, and gave the names" of others. He was taken outside of town and hanged from a cottonwood in late January 1866. On his breast someone pinned a drawing of a "mysterious coffin and a red cross."[18]

Community watchdogs tacked coffin-shaped, cross-emblazoned slips of paper on Denver doors and scattered the grim warnings about town. On January 30 three unidentified corpses—"on the breast of each was a coffin painted in black and in the center of each a red cross"—were found hanging from a cottonwood near the South Platte a couple of miles from Fort Lupton, 30 miles north of

Denver. A few days after the triple lynching, two more coffin-placarded bodies were discovered dangling from a telegraph pole east of Denver.[19]

Five dead men in less than a week was, said Jerome Smiley in his *History of Denver*, the extent of Denver-area vigilante vengeance in 1866.[20] But there were more. On January 20 the *Rocky Mountain News* reported: "It is generally supposed that a Vigilante Committee has been perfected in this city and vicinity and that at least four of the professors of the garote [*sic*], have undergone surgical operations under their hands within a few days, who now lie quietly not a thousand miles from the race track."[21] In late February J. S. Bartholomew, a Denver jail escapee and alleged robber, was hanged from an "umbrageous" cottonwood near Fort Lupton. A note pinned to his body explained: "This man is a Thief. Let thieves and those that harbor or countenance them beware. Vigilance Committee."[22]

Take Frank Williams, add the four most likely lynched in mid-January, add the five of late January and early February, and put in Bartholomew to make a six-week total of eleven lynchings. In comparison, the rest of 1866 seemed tame, with three more cases of speedy injustice: an unidentified man suspected of theft north of Black Hawk, an unidentified Mexican man accused of assaulting two women in Golden, and a suspected horse thief—"one poor cuss of the Irish persuasion"—in the Pueblo area.[23]

Those hangings, most only briefly reported in the press, were apparently quickly forgotten. Junius E. Wharton, who wrote the first history of Denver in late 1866, did not mention them. David J. Cook, in his memoir *Hands Up*, asserted that no one had been lynched in Denver between 1861 and 1868, a true statement only because the hangings in 1866 took place outside the city's legal boundaries. Jerome Smiley also winked at the killings in 1866, understating the numbers and stressing the role of the Montana vigilantes.[24]

The city wanted to forget that blizzard of death. Denver, described by John Evans, the territory's second governor, as "really the only tolerable place" in the region, liked to think of itself as the nascent cultural, moral, political, economic, and social center of Colorado.[25] Town fathers, their money tied up in local ventures, grieved when the Union Pacific Railroad bypassed Colorado to build its main line through southern Wyoming. Anxious to attract investors and settlers, would-be empire builders dreaded having their city seen as a violence-prone, lynching-addicted place.

Boosters fumed in 1867 when William Hepworth Dixon, an English traveler who had visited in 1866, published *New America*. He proclaimed Denver a "city of demons" where "justice is blind and lame, while violence is alert and strong." A secret vigilance committee, he said, hanged men from the "cotton-tree." He explained that in Denver the phrase "gone up" means a man has "gone up a tree," the local expression for having "been hung." Storekeepers, Dixon asserted, sometimes found "a corpse dangling from a branch" when they opened their doors in the morning, or more commonly, the malefactor's remains disappeared before dawn, thrown "into a hole like that of a dead dog."[26]

Dixon exaggerated and mangled some facts. There were no cotton trees. But there were cottonwood trees and in 1866 nearly a dozen lynchings outside of town, two legal hangings and one murder disguised as a lynching in the city, and three other unexplained killings.[27] Obviously, Dixon caught the spirit of the place. Unwilling to admit the truth, the *Rocky Mountain News* attacked Dixon for seeking "in an under-handed manner to intimate that we are a race of barbarians, thirsting for human blood."[28] To the boosters' dismay, Dixon's book was read in the United States and Europe. Thanks to him a new phrase entered the English language: "gone up," which E. Cobham Brewer's *Dictionary of Phrase and Fable* (1898) defined as meaning "put out of the way, hanged, or otherwise got rid of. In Denver (America) unruly citizens are summarily hung on a cotton tree, and when any question is asked about them the answer is briefly given, 'Gone up'—i.e., gone up the cotton tree, or suspended from one of its branches."[29]

Shortly after Dixon published *New America* the *News* condemned him for his "libels" and "outright falsehoods." In May 1868 the *News* published a sanitized history of local crime, minimizing the lynchings of 1859–1861 and totally ignoring those of 1866. Admitting to three mysterious deaths in 1866, the paper blamed those killings on stock thieves who quarreled among themselves.[30] Nor did the *News* mention five lynchings south of town in February 1868.

General James Rusling, another visitor in 1866, painted a picture that, although not rosy, was less damaging. He saw a mob threaten to lynch territorial governor Alexander Cummings, whose opposition to statehood for Colorado offended many. "Let the vigilance committee be recognized at once," said the *News*. "Something worse than horse thieves, guerrillas, and road agents demands its immediate attention."[31] Cummings prudently slept away from home and moved his offices to Golden. Fortunately, Rusling noted, nothing came of the threats: "No doubt she [Denver] liked Judge Lynch still, but she liked English capital and English immigration better, and would do nothing to offend either."[32]

In late 1868, Denver proved Rusling wrong. After the deaths of L. H. Musgrove, Sanford Duggan, and Ed Franklin, Denverites found it hard to live down their town's devilish reputation.[33] Musgrove, Duggan, and Franklin, according to David J. Cook, were representative of the wolves that scavenged in the temporary towns created by the Union Pacific Railroad as it pushed west in the late 1860s. Musgrove, his enemies said, left a bloody trail behind him in California, Nevada, and Utah before organizing a band of thieves headquartered on Clear Creek a few miles northwest of Denver. Arrested in the autumn of 1868 on suspicion of stealing horses, he was jailed in Denver where he waited for his fellow brigands to free him.

Two of them—Ed Franklin, a friend of Musgrove's, and Sam Duggan, a friend of Franklin's—spent some of their spare moments robbing people. They held up Justice of the Peace Orson Brooks late in the evening of November 20 and took $135 from him. Duggan threatened to "plant the damned old snoozer." Fortunately for Brooks, they let him go home to snooze another night.[34]

For Duggan and Franklin there was little rest. The City Council posted a reward for their capture, and two days later Cook and others traced them to Golden west of Denver. Cook cornered Duggan in a dark saloon, fired, and slew the saloon keeper's brother by mistake. Duggan fled. Later that evening Cook and another officer found Franklin sleeping in a hotel room. They woke him and then killed him as he resisted. "He had," said Cook, "sowed the wild oats of a reckless and useless life and he had reaped the full harvest." After paying the hotel proprietor fifty dollars for damages to the bed in which Franklin lay, Cook returned to Denver.[35]

Cook arrived on Monday, November 23, in time to see more oats harvested. Musgrove had been bragging that his friends would rescue him. In the midafternoon fifty men, a "body of our best citizens," went to the jail and seized Musgrove without opposition from law officers.[36] "I suppose you are going to hang me because I've been an Indian chief," Musgrove said. Although other transgressions could be laid at his feet, the charge of being an Indian chief seemed better than most. As the *Rocky Mountain News* put it, consorting with Indians, more than his other alleged crimes, "exasperated the people."[37]

Taken by wagon to the Larimer Street bridge over Cherry Creek, he was given a few minutes to write letters. "I am to be hung to-day on false charges by a mob," he told his brother, "take care of my pore [*sic*] little children."[38] Then the wagon was driven under the bridge, and a noose hanging from a beam was tightened around Musgrove's neck. Edwin Scudder, a grocer, objected to the lynching. He was quickly silenced. Musgrove calmly smoked a cigarette, throwing it away a moment before the wagon drove off. By jumping in the air, thereby bringing his full weight onto the rope, he assured himself of a broken neck and a quick death. An onlooker tried to slip a diamond ring from Musgrove's finger, but someone in the crowd bludgeoned the would-be thief, who crumpled under Musgrove's suspended body.[39]

Duggan, captured a few days later, was returned to Denver on December 1, 1868. He was quickly seized by a mob of nearly 100. Told he was to be hanged, he admitted robbing Judge Brooks but denied crimes meriting death. He asked for a Catholic priest. Unwilling to wait, the impatient crowd quickly hanged him from a cottonwood near Twelfth and Market Streets, about a hundred yards from where Musgrove had died a week earlier. His body remained there through the night, "swinging in the bright moonlight." The next morning photographers vied for exclusive shots until police broke up their bickering. People living near the hanging tree cut it down because they did not want it used for another lynching.[40]

Neither the denizens of Market Street nor the solid citizens of Denver relished the thought that theirs was indeed a "city of demons." So besides condemning the cottonwood, they scrambled to justify the lynchings. By the late 1860s the jurisdictional loopholes of the 1858–1861 period had been closed, and local courts were operating. Yet lynching had not died. Vigilantes had killed Musgrove and Duggan without even the trappings of due process that marked the People's Court nearly a decade earlier. Why?

On November 24, 1868, a day after Musgrove's demise, the *Rocky Mountain News* tried to justify his death. He was, said the paper, an outlaw, a bandit, a murderer, a "land pirate," the head of a group of horse thieves, and he had been the "leader of one of the bands of Indians that ravaged our settlements last fall." In making

Lynching of Musgrove.

*2.1 L. H. Musgrove smoked a cigarette before he was hanged from Denver's
Larimer Street bridge over Cherry Creek in late November 1868. His alleged
crimes included being an Indian chief. Courtesy, Denver Public Library, Western History Collection and Phimister Proctor Church, A. Phimister Proctor
Museum.*

2.2 Sam Duggan's corpse dangled in bright moonlight near Twelfth and Market Streets in Denver until the morning of December 2, 1868. Courtesy, Colorado Historical Society (F6426).

those charges the *News* advanced little proof except Musgrove's admission that he had been "an Indian chief."[41] In a society that saw itself mandated by God to clear away Indians and that felt equally justified in suppression of crime by any handy means, being a criminal and an Indian chief was a deadly combination.

Satisfied that Musgrove's past justified his death, the *News* then considered the propriety of the "proceedings of yesterday," never once referring to the hanging as a lynching. The courts, said the *News*, rarely convicted murderers—only three men had been legally executed in seven years of Colorado history. Because of the size of the region and its sparse settlement, criminals could easily escape. Moreover, Musgrove had allies: "Such was the thief's prestige in the popular mind, that it was feared he might bring a band of Indians or Quantrell raiders upon the town, resulting in its conflagration, in bloodshed, in everything terrible." Unable to hold him securely and fearful of the terror he might bring upon them, "the people took him out of jail and hanged him decently until he was dead."[42]

The press also damned Duggan. Before he died he confessed to robbing Judge Brooks and admitted that he had killed a man in self-defense. He argued that he had done nothing to merit hanging, but neither his logic nor his cries for mercy did him any good. Central City's *Register* summed up popular attitudes: "When scoundrels endanger life and property and keep them in constant danger, vengeance is seldom long delayed, and it is to this fact that we owe our safety."[43] The self-protection rationalizations held kernels of truth. Shortly before Duggan's and Musgrove's lynchings Denverites had read of widespread lawlessness in Bear River City, a temporary town on the Union Pacific Railroad in extreme western Wyoming.[44] Indians on the eastern plains had been hostile since the Sand Creek Massacre in 1864. Local fears, not totally unjustified, were nevertheless overblown. Denver, a town of around 4,000 people, had never been attacked by Indians and was far more stable than temporary Union Pacific construction camps. Nor did the excuse that criminals could easily get away because the territory was large and sparsely settled bear close examination. Cook's detective agency quickly tracked Duggan and Franklin to Golden, and when Duggan escaped to Wyoming he was apprehended.

To the charge that its courts sometimes stank, particularly between 1861 and 1866, Colorado had to plead guilty. The territory's federally appointed jurists, who collectively served as a three-member supreme court and individually as district court judges, secured their posts through connections in Washington, D.C., where politics often counted more than ability and integrity. The Pikes Peak country, a region as rude as it was remote, initially attracted some second-rate judicial oddities in search of a bench.

Benjamin Hall, the first chief justice, did credible work, but he only served from 1861 to 1863. S. Newton Pettis, one of the two original associate supreme court justices, arrived in Denver in June 1861. He reported that the people "have for a long time been suffering the effects of mob law and violence." Pettis concluded, "This court is clearly of the opinion that it will never marry the Territory of Colorado."[45] Charles Lee Armour, the third member of the first supreme court, once fined a court bailiff and sentenced him to an hour in jail for repeating "Hear ye, hear ye, the honorable court is now in session" four times instead of the customary three.[46] Alleged to be "a weak man at best, an inveterate opium eater, and considerably shattered in his upper story," Armour was also considered a "cuss" and a "cranky, inscrutable, many-sided tyrant."[47] To restrict him the Territorial Legislature limited his district court jurisdiction to two southern counties, which he refused to visit. Corralled but not vanquished, he stayed home where he "sipped his toddies, of which he was fond, drew his salary of which he was fonder, and held out his term as a gentleman of elegant leisure."[48]

Several succeeding territorial justices were no better. Allen A. Bradford, who replaced Pettis, flabbergasted the fastidious: "He would go around with his shoes unlaced, his pants flap unbuttoned, his Prince Albert coat unbuttoned, his shirt and clothes all covered with drippings from his food."[49] Perhaps to cover what was underneath, Bradford sometimes draped himself in a Mexican serape or a tobacco-stained linen duster.[50]

Stephen Harding, who followed Hall as chief justice, was accused of adultery and considered so unfit to hear cases that lawyers refused to appear before him. He resigned.[51] Associate Justice Charles F. Holly, who beat an adultery charge on a technicality, also failed to ennoble the court. A correspondent of the *Rocky Mountain News* castigated the wayward jurist: "Conscious of his guilt, he evaded investigation. A craven vagabond, his name is a disgrace to the title of Judge. Himself, a moving insult to the profession of the law, and his immoral conduct an outrage upon society."[52]

But even ill-suited, ill-tempered, and morally ill judges could dispense efficient justice. Bradford was accounted an able man who was especially hard on mule thieves.[53] When William Van Horn was tried for murder in 1863, the court acted swiftly to condemn him to death. In early January 1866 Franklin Foster and Henry Stone, two former Union soldiers, were charged with a double murder. Their cases were quickly heard, and they were legally hanged in Denver on May 24, 1866, an event that pleased the *News* because "the law [was] upheld by a people who are evidently looked upon by the 'all-civilized' people of the east as little better than barbarians."[54]

Had the vigilantes of early 1866 wished to avoid being branded barbarians, they could have used the courts. The lynchers of 1868 had even less of an excuse because by then the judicial jetsam of the earlier period had been washed away. With judges of the high caliber of Moses Hallett serving at both the district and supreme court levels, there was no reason Musgrove and Duggan could not have received honest legal trials.

Despite its rationalizing, the *News* admitted, "Although every citizen of Denver is glad that Musgrove is out of the way, there are many who are sad and humiliated at the way it was done."[55] The *News* knew a "city of demons" frightened investors and immigrants. To contend that lynching was justified was to admit that the "brigandish boys" were so powerful and society so disorganized that investors and settlers would be wise to stay away. After 1868, Denver did not care to make that self-deprecating argument. During the next forty years the city would witness three more killings that met the definition of lynching, but never again would the community as a whole claim that Judge Lynch was a more appropriate enforcer of the laws than the regular courts or that the best men sanctioned lynchings.

Pueblo, 112 miles to the south of Denver, and Leadville, 103 miles to the southwest, also hoped to become important places. Their solid citizens, as did Denver's, came to see that illegal executions damaged their towns' reputations. Consequently, they changed their minds about lynching desperadoes.

Pueblo was little more than a dusty hamlet in early 1868 when it witnessed the hanging of William Cyrus Coe, the adroit leader of a large band of thieves. Operating from a stone fortress in what later became the panhandle of Oklahoma, Coe's gang reputedly had stolen thousands of sheep and cattle. Seized by U.S. soldiers, Coe escaped from Fort Lyon, was recaptured, escaped again, was again recaptured, and was jailed in Pueblo. Fifty vigilantes decided he would not escape a third time, and late in the evening of April 11, 1868, they hanged him near the banks of the Fountain River—not far from the home of the untidy jurist Allen A. Bradford.[56]

In the 1860s the deaths of such thieves were more a cause for rejoicing than for reproach. Pueblo had no newspaper in April 1868 to record the reaction to Coe's death, but in 1871 the *Colorado Chieftain* recalled that after the hanging from a "noble old cottonwood," the vigilantes "returned to town with flying colors."[57] Denver's *News* dismissed those who might think of Coe's end as a tragedy as people with "weak nerves."[58]

Two horse thieves, one unidentified and the other named Tex, once Coe's lieutenant, were hanged in Pueblo during the night of August 1–2, 1870. Their bodies, suspended from a telegraph pole, "the tongues protruded with the hideous leer of convulsive death," were left to greet the morning stagecoach as it pulled into town. All and all, said Pueblo's *Chieftain*, the sight was "a trifle ghastly and startling." The *Chieftain* wished the two outlaws had been killed elsewhere, "rather than our town should have to bear the odium of their wretched taking off." Offering no apology for planting the felons in the "hangman's garden," the paper editorialized: "Until we have jails, and a penitentiary, and a less tardy mode of meeting [*sic*] out justice to these horse thieves by the courts, this summary mode of punishment seems justifiable, and the only one likely to prevail."[59]

Nor did Pueblo regret the lynching of Bill White, a sneak thief, on October 31, 1872.[60] The town's next lynching—that of Nickel Smith, accused of rape—in September 1880 met with a mixed reaction from a Pueblo correspondent of Denver's *Rocky Mountain News*, who noted that "we had all hoped that our town had advanced so far beyond the condition of western towns as to render Judge Lynch's court a matter of tradition only."[61]

Both Denver and Pueblo shed many of their homespun western ways during the 1870s. Denver connected to the national railroad network in the summer of 1870, setting off a boom that made it the largest city in Colorado in 1880, with a population of 35,629. In June 1872 the Denver and Rio Grande Railway reached Pueblo, making it a town of high hopes and 3,217 people by 1880.

To forge dreams into realities, Pueblo needed capital and labor. That is largely why it bewailed the lynchings of William T. Phebus and Jay W. McGrew on March 31, 1882. Accused of stealing cattle in Pueblo County, they were arrested in early March, acquitted at one trial in Denver, then jailed again in Pueblo. Unable to post bond, they were awaiting another trial when fifteen to twenty men overpowered the jailers and seized the prisoners in the middle of the night of March 30–31. The masked vigilantes, rumored to be members of the county cattle growers' association, quietly hanged the suspects from a cottonwood near the corner of Tenth Street and Santa Fe Avenue not far from the jail. Giving lie to the notion that western lynchings were clean, sanitary affairs, the *Chieftain* reported that "one of Phebus' eyes had been forced from the socket and protruded upon the cheek of the victim" and that McGrew also presented a grim picture of strangulation, with his tongue hanging out and blood trickling from his mouth.[62]

"No doubt," said the *Chieftain*, Phebus and McGrew were bad men, "integral parts of an element of bummer cussedness that prefers to steal rather than make a living by honest toil."[63] Yet that did not justify the way they were killed. Lynching might have been acceptable in frontier times, but now Pueblo was a modern city, having exchanged "the woolen shirt and bull trains of the pioneer for the streetcar, the telephone and other appliances, of civilization." The outlaws, even if guilty, were not charged with murder. A cruel death by lynching was not an appropriate punishment for cattle thieves. Moreover, Phebus left behind a good wife—"a determined and brave little woman"—and a widowed mother who depended on him for support.[64]

Neither Phebus's dislodged eyeball nor his grieving wife fully explains the *Chieftain's* fusillade against the "lynching outrage." The paper also worried that immigrants would shun the city "when it is learned that masked mobs of men have a cheerful habit in Pueblo of breaking into jails and hanging criminals on the charge of cattle stealing." Moreover, "the responsible men of the community, the solid real estate owners, those who build business blocks and pay taxes are unanimous in their expressions of disapproval, and declare that a foul blotch has been fastened upon us which will require years to efface."[65]

Denver gloated: "We thought Pueblo was more civilized than that." David J. Cook, who well remembered his town's hangings of Musgrove and Duggan in 1868, noted, "It is a hard thing for Pueblo and is going to hurt the place with eastern people."[66]

The *Chieftain* retorted that in 1880 a Denver mob had killed a Chinese man simply because he was Chinese and that a few weeks before Pueblo hanged Phebus and McGrew, Denver hoodlums attacked a Chinese burial party and desecrated a corpse. Such a place, the *Chieftain* admonished, should not throw stones, especially since its courts had failed to properly punish Phebus and McGrew when they were tried in Denver.[67]

E. RINEHART,   DENVER. COLO.

2.3 *Lawman David J. Cook criticized Pueblo for lynching William Phebus and Jay McGrew in March 1882. Less than two years earlier Cook had helped quell Denver's anti-Chinese riot. Courtesy, Denver Public Library, Western History Collection.*

Distancing its town from the lynchings, the *Chieftain* blamed the deaths on "cow punchers not citizens of Pueblo."[68] Soon after the Phebus-McGrew lynching another vigilante group, reportedly largely made up of the same angry cattlemen who conducted the in-town lynchings, hanged S. P. Berry, a man named Chastine, and another surnamed Ormsby—all supposedly in league with Phebus and McGrew—10 miles south of Pueblo.[69]

Pueblo regretted the lynchings, particularly those that took place in town, more because of the bad publicity than because of the crime itself. "The mob outrage . . . will injure Pueblo city and county to the extent of many thousands of dollars," said the *Chieftain*.[70] Eight weeks earlier the paper had railed against robbers by suggesting that "the hanging of one or two of those thieves would be a good thing and the first one caught should be treated to a short rope and a long shift."[71] The April lynchings gave the paper what it had asked for in January. The *Chieftain* of April 1, 1882, which condemned the lynchings, seemed to wink at its own moral indignation by running a short squib asking that the town spare an old cottonwood because "the cottonwood is the only tree in this country that bears gallows fruit."[72] Pueblo's ambivalence toward the killings reflected competing economic interests. Stockmen outside of town were happy to be rid of Phebus and McGrew. Businessmen in town worried that their enterprises would suffer if the area got a bad reputation. The *Chieftain*, more attuned to its in-town supporters and advertisers, was willing to slap the stockmen on the wrist.

The wrist slapping did not translate into action against Phebus and McGrew's killers. Nor did the 1868 lynchings of Musgrove and Duggan, despite the *Rocky Mountain News*'s mild expressions of regret, bring punishment to their lynchers. A dozen years after the event, William Vickers, in his *History of the City of Denver*, facilely excused Denverites for killing Duggan: "The citizens hanged him, which was perhaps the best use they could have made of him for the benefit of society."[73] Historian Jerome Smiley noted that Musgrove and Duggan's lynchers were well-known, but "no such thought of prosecuting any of them for their acts occurred to anyone."[74]

Like Denver and Pueblo, Leadville lynched brigands, regretted it, but did little to chastise the lynchers. On November 20, 1879, shortly after the lynching of Edward Frodsham, a reporter for Leadville's *Evening Chronicle* visited Frodsham's widow and small daughter, who was asking questions. "Mama, papa hung. He was hung by neck. Papa dead. Won't papa tum [*sic*] home pretty quick? Mama, who killed papa?"[75] A sad child, a grieving widow, a lynched land pirate, a dead footpad, and an unlikely hero barber delimited the one-night stand of Judge Lynch in Leadville.

In November 1879, Leadville was little more than a year old, having been incorporated and named in 1878. Focal point for a great silver bonanza, the village turned into a city almost overnight. As the world rushed in, men profited from the opportunities and chaos. Money could be made more or less honestly: Horace Tabor, Simon Guggenheim, and Charles Boettcher—destined to be among the state's wealthiest men—owed much of their success to Leadville. Or it could be made without any pretense of honesty. Sneak thieves, called footpads because they robbed on foot, terrorized the town. Robert G. Dill, a newspaper editor, recounted those lawless days: "Footpads were to be found lurking in every corner lying in wait for belated business men or wealthy debauchers, on their way home. The ominous command, 'Hold up your hands,' accompanied by the click of a pistol was heard almost nightly."[76]

Other crooks jumped mining claims and snatched town lots from their rightful owners, sometimes bouncing them out of their cabins at night. John Lord, a freighter, recalled that once when he and his crew were delivering timber to the Buckeye Belle Mine, a fight broke out between the mine owners and claim jumpers led by Edward Frodsham. Lord arranged a brief truce so he could move his wagons. Then the battle raged until Frodsham was driven away.

Leadville's skimpy police force was either unable or unwilling to protect citizens. City Marshal George O'Connor was murdered on April 25, 1879, by one of his four deputies, James Bloodworth—a man rumored to be entwined with the town's weedy lowlife. After shooting O'Connor, Bloodworth rode away, "never to be seen again."[77] Later in the year one of O'Connor's successors, Marshal Patrick A. Kelley—sometimes an associate of Frodsham's—was accused of protecting criminals and charged with "malfeasance, misfeasance, and nonfeasance in office." Bereft of feasance, he was forced to resign.[78]

Such was the chaotic state of affairs on November 15, 1879, when Carl Bockhaus, a barber, made his way home at night. Fearful of footpads, he whistled to calm his nerves and held a pistol in his trembling hand. Patrick Stewart and Harry Clifford, robbers, not seeing that Bockhaus was armed, ordered him to put up his hands. Instead he shot them both. Clifford staggered away and died on a

2.4 *Leadville's small police department was inadequate to protect citizens against footpads and other outlaws. Courtesy, Denver Public Library, Western History Collection.*

nearby porch. The wounded Stewart was captured a few minutes later.

Barber Bockhaus, the footpad foiler, became an instant hero. The next day a crowd gathered near his shop, hoisted him onto a chair, and accompanied by musicians, paraded through the streets. Winding up at the city jail, the revelers devolved into a mob intent on lynching Stewart, who had threatened to take vengeance on Bockhaus. Lawmen dispersed the crowd and transferred Stewart to the more secure county jail. As a wounded and unsuccessful thief he might have safely stayed there except that on November 19 he had the misfortune to be joined by Frodsham, arrested for disturbing the peace after a claim-jumping incident. Frodsham had offended his fellow citizens even more than Stewart, for if one accepts stories published after his death, he was roundly hated as one of the town's worst lot snatchers.

Early in the morning of November 20, fifteen to twenty men— all masked and some wearing long black robes—forced their way into the jail, took Stewart and Frodsham to a nearby cookhouse, and hanged them both. To Frodsham's request that he be given time to write a letter to his wife, the dark avengers responded, "we will let you write it in hell."[79] The vigilantes pinned a note to Frodsham's back. Headed "Notice to All" and signed "Seven Hundred Strong," it warned: "Lot Thieves, Bunko Steerers, Thieves, Foot Pads, Highwaymen, together with their Pals and Sympathizers and all other Classes of Criminals. This is only the Commencement and this shall be Your Fate. We Mean Business. This is Our Last Warning. Cooney, Adams, Connor, Ed Champ, Hogan, P. A. Kelley, Ed Burns and Many Others are Already Marked by this Organization."[80]

During the next few days those who favored the hangings tussled with those who did not. In the end the anti-Frodsham group won. Most of the men mentioned in the note left town, although ex-marshal Kelley remained and later again became marshal. The history books, belonging to the victors, reviled Frodsham. Still Leadville, like Denver and Pueblo, eventually came to regret the lynchings, not because of a guilty community conscience but because of bad publicity.

In 1882, playwright Oscar Wilde puffed his way up to 10,000-foot-high Leadville to lecture miners on the "Ethics of Art." After he poked fun at them in *Impressions of America*, many of the Cloud City's best men wished he had stayed in London. Wilde told of a sign he saw in a saloon: "Please do not Shoot the PIANIST, He is doing His Best." Even worse, he said he had been told that the stage on which he lectured had shortly before hosted the informal trial and hanging of two murderers.[81]

With good reason Leadville could quibble with Wilde's facts. It had only lynched Frodsham and Stewart. They died near the county jail, not on stage, and the lynchings had occurred three years before Wilde visited. It had legally executed two murderers, Merrick Rosencrantz and Frank Gilbert, in July 1881 on a gallows near the high school. That execution, witnessed by several thousand, might have given Wilde grain for his literary mill had the hanging machine's 350-pound weight pulled the men's heads off as some feared it would. As it was, Rosencrantz and Gilbert—dead after being jerked 7 feet into the air—graciously retained their heads, thereby sparing Leadville embarrassment.[82] Most Leadvillians would probably have disagreed with Wilde's opinion: "One is absolutely sickened, not by the crimes that the wicked have committed, but by the punishments that the good have inflicted."[83] But Leadville's boosters knew lynching was bad for their community's reputation. It did them no good to be portrayed in Edward L. Wheeler's *Deadwood Dick in Leadville* as a place where in a single episode of that dime novel, two people were lynched, including the noble road agent Deadwood Dick himself.[84]

In 1884, when Cyrus Minich was charged with murder, the *Evening Chronicle* insisted he be given a trial: "Leadville cannot afford to have a lynching . . . the stigma will rest upon the community for all time." Minich was properly tried and legally executed after addressing the thousands who came to watch him die: "I know I am a sinner. All men have sinned. Some of you here today will meet me again, and some of you will not because you will not be able to go to where I go to. I am an innocent man. Good-bye to all. Good-bye." To which the crowd replied in unison, "Good-bye, Cy. Good-bye Cy."[85] Leadville also bid a quick good-bye to lynching. In the Cloud City Judge Lynch died on November 20, 1879, the night of his first and only appearance, the night he killed Frodsham and Stewart.

"Denver is not the greatest city in the world, but it is great, as beautiful and highly improved, relative to Colorado as Paris is to France."[86] That braggadocio was, in effect, true. By 1890, Denver, with 106,000 people, was home to more than a quarter of the state's population and was the center of its government, commerce, and culture. Pueblo, with 24,558, dominated southern Colorado, and although it continued to host Judge Lynch, it appears he was not welcomed by the city's best men. Colorado Springs, the third largest city with 11,140 people, boasted a college and society refined enough to earn it the nickname Newport in the Rockies. Even Leadville, its 10,384 people making it fourth among Colorado towns, still entertained delusions of grandeur matching the mountains that surrounded it. Lynching did not suit the best men, "the solid real estate owners, those who build business blocks and pay taxes," of would-be Parises.[87] In fact, Colorado Springs, if it did not count the hangings in and near Colorado City in the 1860s, could claim a history free from illegal executions.[88]

Many people in smaller places—less worried about their reputations, less willing to spend tax money on jailing and trying outlaws, perhaps more threatened by outlaws and bullies than were larger cities—continued to welcome Judge Lynch. Yet even in the hinterland, lynching, acceptable in the 1860s and 1870s, became far less so by the mid-1880s.

3

THE HINTERLAND

If in his old age Judge Lynch doted on his golden youth, he must have fondly remembered the years 1859 to 1870 when, often in broad daylight, he killed more than sixty men—sometimes for such relatively minor offenses as making threats. In the 1870s and 1880s he increasingly punished serious crimes. After 1884 he killed no more horse and cattle thieves. Eight dead in 1874, nine in both 1880 and 1881, and at least a dozen in 1882—his record remained impressive. But measured on a per capita basis his deadly grip was weakening. In 1870, one in 4,000 Coloradans was lynched; in 1880, one in 22,000; in 1888, one in 41,000. After that the rate plummeted. An unlucky dozen or so were lynched in the 1890s. After 1902 only four persons died at Judge Lynch's hands.

Banished from Leadville and usually shunned in Denver, for decades the judge was still welcome in smaller places and able to prowl in Pueblo. From 1870 through 1919, 3 people were lynched in Denver, 2 in Leadville, and perhaps as many as 14 in Pueblo. In rural areas and small towns vigilantes and mobs killed more than 100. In Cañon City, 39 miles west of Pueblo, lynchers disposed of 5 men; in Trinidad, 86 miles south of Pueblo, they killed at least 4. Near Walsenburg, between Trinidad and Pueblo, they also took at least 4, as they did in Ouray. Alamosa, Golden, Rosita, and Silverton each tallied at least 3 lynchings.

Approximately 125 people were lynched in Colorado between 1870 and 1919, roughly one-fourth of them suspected thieves. Many were accused of stealing horses and cattle, several of robbing stage-coaches, one of pilfering from hotel rooms. After 1884 practically all the lynched were accused of murder, rape, child molestation, or both murder and sex crimes. Some, both before and after 1880, were not taxed with any transgression. Of those, a few were murdered and their deaths made to look like lynchings. One, Judge Elias Dyer, ran afoul of powerful men in Lake County in 1875. They charged him with "being pompous."[1]

At least two were lynched solely because of their race or religion. Between 1866 and 1884, lynchings outside the major towns sometimes merited extensive newspaper coverage, but often, especially in the 1860s and early 1870s, the press wasted little ink on them. Brief to a fault, the *Rocky Mountain News* overlooked the crime that brought John Donahoe to his death in May 1869: "They hung a man named John Donahoe to a telegraph pole at Bryan last Thursday evening, and left him out all night. The next day they had a funeral. He deserved it."[2] Sometimes, without newspapers to report them, the names of the quickly dead faded fast. The parade of the ghostly unidentified stretches from the western mountains to the eastern plains, with the unnamed reigning mainly on the plains. "Report prevails that the murderer was overtaken at Iron Springs and shot to pieces," summarized Pueblo's *Colorado Chieftain* in its account of a probable lynching in July 1869.[3] A year later two un-named "Mexican" prisoners were shot also at Iron Springs, a stage stop northeast of Trinidad.[4]

A mob in Kit Carson in eastern Colorado broke into the town jail in 1870, seized an accused murderer, and "mildly hung" him, evidently without learning his name.[5] From Granada in southeastern Colorado came an 1874 story of the death of an unidentified "Negro" who, after being taken from a deputy sheriff, was found "hanging to a tree, shot through the body."[6] The next year Granada dispatched another accused horse thief "to that bourne from which no horse thief ever returns and it didn't cost the country a cent."[7]

Nor did taxpayers part with a penny to get rid of a man found hanging on Cottonwood Pass west of Buena Vista in July 1880. His killers pinned a note on his back:

Cottonwood Gulch

June 18, 1880

Hung for stealing a horse

and killing a man in Leadville

———

Stole the horse to-night[8]

The unidentified dead seemingly had little in common except that almost all were accused of murder or horse theft, they were lynched in small places mainly in eastern Colorado, and many were ethnically Hispanic. They were, as more fully explored in Chapter 6, a people apart, almost universally called "Mexicans" by Anglo Americans blind to the fact that the Spanish speakers of southern Colorado were just as much U.S. citizens as the English speakers of northern Colorado. Bound by deeply rooted prejudices, newspaper correspondents put a low priority on identifying the "Mexicans" lynched at Golden in 1866, at Iron Springs in a double killing in 1870, at Jimmy's Camp east of Colorado Springs in 1871, at Trinidad in a double lynching in 1873, at Rosita in 1883, and perhaps three at once hanged with baling wire in Pueblo in 1888.[9]

The execution of horse thieves brands the West in the popular imagination. The harsh punishment, so the assumption goes, was justified because stealing a man's horse might cause him to lose his livelihood, perhaps even his life. "We do not know of anything," said Lake City's *Silver World* in 1875, "that would afford our citizens more pleasure than the hanging of a horse thief."[10]

The record shows that Coloradans often enjoyed the pleasure of hanging a horse thief, but it also demonstrates that not every good citizen considered stealing horses a terrible crime. Territorial laws permitted executing horse thieves, but what the law allowed it apparently never did. In 1866 Floyd Bailey, convicted of stealing two horses, was sentenced to thirty days in jail, a wrist slap that prompted

Central City's *Tri-Weekly Miner's Register* to pine for the good old days "when men were hung for such offenses."[11]

All hangings of horse thieves before 1866 were illegal, and it appears all those after 1866 were also illegal. What the law could do but would not, Judge Lynch did. Many Coloradans, particularly in the 1860s and 1870s, approved of his work. William Toll realized that fact in the small hours of June 24, 1867. A few days earlier he had stolen two horses from his employer and hidden out with a party of Arapaho Indians. Jailed in Boulder, he was seized by five men, taken to a cottonwood near Boulder Creek and Pearl Street, and hanged in what turned out to be that town's sole lynching.[12]

Donaciano Sanchez died for a similar sin. Accused of stealing two horses, he was seized at gunpoint from Sheriff Fullerton of Saguache during the night of January 7–8, 1871, and hanged from a cottonwood 200 yards from the sheriff's house. As with Toll and as was the verdict after many lynchings, a coroner's jury determined that Sanchez's killers "to the jury were unknown."[13]

Big-time thieves also feared Judge Lynch. "Nothing," said the *Rocky Mountain News*, "is so calculated to discourage stock raising as the knowledge that it will be stolen."[14] The *News* in June 1868 made short work of two thieves, as did their lynchers in southern Colorado: "Two deserters, named Charles Watson and Frank Hudson, stole four horses, were followed by the settlers a hundred miles, caught, confessed, and hanged."[15] Pueblo's *Colorado Chieftain*, reporting Watson's and Hudson's deaths in its premier issue, joked that a "high court of impeachment" was set up to try them, and "without loss of time or expensive preparations they were hanged to the limb of a 'noble old cottonwood.'"[16]

A twenty-four-hour trial in December 1870, conducted by vigilantes at Frankstown southeast of Denver, wrested confessions from Tom Madison, Frank Cleveland, and Jack Mason that they had stolen forty to sixty horses.[17] The county sheriff, who tried to protect them, was forced "to adjourn homewards," and the three men were hanged.[18] Sheriff Alex Barron of Elbert County was similarly unsuccessful in his attempt to prevent a lynching. Fifty masked men overpowered him and took Tip Marion, his brother Joshua, Dick Thompson, and Jerry Wilson to a grove near Middle Kiowa and hanged them in late August 1874. As often happened, the thieves were killed within days of their capture. Arrested Saturday, hanged Tuesday, the Marion brothers exited so quickly that their mother's attempt to sell her furniture to raise $1,000 bail was in vain.[19]

Juan Graviel, an alleged cattle thief, missed his opportunity to do penitentiary time because he had the misfortune to be in the Alamosa jail at an inopportune time. A large mob gathered in Alamosa on Tuesday night, January 6, 1880, hoping to punish Utes for the 1879 massacre of whites in northwestern Colorado. The *Colorado Chieftain* reported, "Finding them [the Utes] guarded by about fifty soldiers they concluded it might be somewhat dangerous to tackle the wards of the Government," so the mob "proceeded to the jail where a Mexican horse thief [Graviel] was confined and took him out and hung him."[20] Charles Adams, an Indian agent who accompanied the Utes, reported that Graviel was "hanged to a tree in full sight of the Utes. The crowd was bound to hang somebody that day, and they did it."[21]

Less is known about the hangings of an unidentified horse thief on Cottonwood Pass in July 1880 and of T. W. Waters on the banks of the Frying Pan River west of Leadville in September 1881. In each instance the corpses bore short notes. Waters's killers explained his offense, "stealing horses," on a strip of bark from the tree on which his body dangled just out of reach of scavenging mountain lions.[22]

Intermittently dealing death between 1882 and 1884, Judge Lynch completed his harvest of horse and cattle thieves. In one day, March 31, 1882, he disposed of Phebus, McGrew, Berry, Chastine, and Ormsby in or near Pueblo, as noted in Chapter 2. Earlier the same month more than 100 cowboys stormed the Del Norte jail, intent on killing accused cattle thief Arnold Howard. Howard and his jail mate, Frank Young, stood close to the door, and when the mob battered it down they ran into the crowd and separated. Young was shot. Howard jumped over a fence, hid in a ditch, and later fled Del Norte.[23]

Years later Frank Case, a Del Norte pioneer, reminisced about that wild night. Cattle stealing, Case said, was common in the San Luis Valley in the early 1880s. A rancher "would not knowingly take anything from another stockman [he] could not reasonably be expected to get away with. . . . But quite often the thing was over done. Unintentionally of course." Case counted Howard among the many who overdid things and among the few who had the bad luck to be caught. Young, one of Howard's hired hands, was jailed as a witness against Howard. Wounded as he fled from the mob, Young was taken to a nearby building where he was given a dose of morphine by a fake doctor who proclaimed: "There I have given that fellow Morphine [*sic*] enough to kill a mule." "But," said Case of that unusual lynching by lethal injection, "he killed an innocent young man instead."[24]

A lucky researcher may someday unearth a rival to Black Pete for the unenviable distinction of being the last horse thief lynched in Colorado. Until then he can rest his claim on a brief entry in Denver's *Rocky Mountain News* for August 5, 1884: "The body of a noted horse-thief and all-around rustler, known as Black Pete, was last week found in the lava beds below Cebello [*sic*] with a bullet hole through his head. The coroner's jury returned a verdict of 'killed by a thunderbolt from heaven.'"[25]

Judge Lynch hurled his thunderbolts less frequently at those who stole money than at those who ran off with horses and cattle. Duggan in Denver, White in Pueblo, Frodsham and Stewart in Leadville—all covered in Chapter 2—were lynched because they either stole or tried to. And William Dodge, who stole $250 in Laporte, 75 miles north of Denver, in late February 1869, died for that theft.[26]

If the value of property taken could justify lynching, then Major Graham's death in Rosita in October 1875 came closer than most to being justified. Working for two swindlers, known as Colonel Boyd and Walter Stuart, Graham and twenty henchmen held the Pocahontas Mine, which Boyd and Stuart had stolen from its rightful owner. Although versions differ, some reports indicate that Graham, after terrorizing the town, was killed by a mob that shot him more than 125 times.[27] Colonel Boyd was more fortunate. He was jailed to protect him from lynching and was later exiled from Rosita.[28]

The Rosita War could inspire makers of western movies. So too might the short lives and quick deaths of Arthur and Silas Pond, brothers known by their aliases, Billy LeRoy and Sam Potter.[29] Arthur Pond began robbing Colorado stages in the autumn of 1880. Captured and sentenced to ten years in the federal penitentiary at Detroit, Michigan, he escaped by jumping from a moving Kansas Pacific train. Recruiting his brother Silas to assist him, Arthur returned to Colorado where on May 18, 1881, they robbed passengers and mail on a coach in the San Juan Mountains, wounding a man in the process. Apprehended, they were taken to Wagon Wheel Gap where a reporter interviewed them. Arthur denied ever killing anyone, admitting only thefts including pies in Leadville and a gun in Lake City. Told he might be killed, Silas reflected, "Any man who would follow stage coach robbing is none too good to be hung." "Their ideas of eternity," said the *San Juan Prospector*, "were as naught, having never read up much on the hereafter."[30]

The Pond brothers had little time to bone up on the hereafter. They were jailed at Del Norte for only a few hours when forty masked men overpowered the sheriff and took Arthur and Silas to a tree near the town's pesthouse and hanged them. The next day their bodies, "stiff as crow-bars . . . were balanced against the jail and photographed by I. I. Cornish," who put the photos up for sale. Sans sympathy to brigands, the *Prospector* bid them a terse goodbye: "Adios Pond Bros.—road agents."[31]

George O'Connor, justice of the peace in Antonito near the Colorado–New Mexico border, was also accused of being both a thief and a bully. In his capacity as the town's judge he protected robbers with whom he was in league and fined upright citizens arrested on trumped-up charges. Sick of injustice, vigilantes hanged him in a slaughterhouse the night of July 21, 1881, attaching a note to his body ordering that it not be cut down until after 9:00 A.M.[32] "The action of the vigilants' committee," reported the *Rocky Mountain News*, "meets with the approval of every citizen."[33]

Hot Sulphur Springs citizens also reveled in the death of local bully Charles Wilson, known as Texas Charley, who made men hop by shooting at their legs. On December 9, 1884, Charley fell dead, riddled with bullets from the guns of fifteen men who had concealed themselves along the town's main street. Afterward, no one testified against the "public benefactors" who killed that "beastly enemy to man."[34]

Denied a cemetery burial, Texas Charley still enjoyed a minor honor, for he and James McLees, hanged in Montrose in 1886, were apparently the last persons lynched in Colorado for making threats.[35] After the mid-1880s practically all of Judge Lynch's victims were accused of murder or sex crimes or both. Even before that time, murder ranked with horse theft as the transgression most likely to prompt a lynching. Between 1859 and 1884 at least fifty men were lynched for murder—some between 1859 and 1861 by People's Courts and many more by less formal groups after 1861. In most

3.1 *"Buzzard Meat"* *ran the headline in Del Norte's* San Juan Prospector *heralding the May 1881 deaths of Arthur and Silas Pond, accused robbers. Courtesy, Colorado Historical Society (F5978).*

instances the lynched had stepped well beyond the bounds of spilling blood on the barroom floor. Indeed, although Judge Lynch often punished murderers, the regular courts just as often seemed to wink at their crimes.

Dr. William Bell, a Scottish traveler who visited Colorado in 1867, reflected on frontier justice: "The proper amount of punishment necessary for murder depends upon circumstances and the social status of the murderer." Anecdotal evidence supports Bell's observation. Killing an opponent in a fight was rarely considered a misstep demanding execution or even a long prison sentence. Accused murderers able to afford sharp lawyers such as Thomas M. Patterson, who reportedly secured acquittals in fifty-seven of his sixty-two murder cases, often escaped serious punishment.[36]

Examples of lenient treatment of murderers abound. In Hinsdale County, R. O. Lacy, a doctor, killed his friend Henry Vittle. Lacy was jailed for a year, sometimes being released to tend his patients.[37] Richard Mackay, given eighteen months in jail for manslaughter, got along so well with his Georgetown jailers that he was allowed to go out for his dinners without a guard.[38] When John Foster killed Alex Peterson, a bully, in the Paradox Valley, the deputy sheriff said, "well somebody had to." After a jury freed Foster, grateful citizens collected money to buy him new clothes.[39] In Denver in 1884, O. H. Haller, slayer of his adulterous wife and her paramour, was acquitted because of "emotional insanity."[40] In March 1891 the *Denver Republican* noted that during the previous four years sixty-five homicides had occurred in the city, with four garnering first-degree murder convictions and only one resulting in an execution.[41] Of the eight murder trials held in Denver in 1895, six resulted in acquittals.[42] The eighteen homicides reported in Denver in 1905 brought no executions and no lynchings. Defending the city's bloody citizens, the *Denver Post* editorialized: "When provoked the instinct born in every man and woman was uppermost—to take a gun in hand and shoot down the antagonist."[43]

The murderer and cannibal Alfred G. Packer was convicted of five homicides and sentenced to die on May 19, 1883. Hinsdale County sheriff Clair Smith issued invitations to the execution, but before citizens could savor the spectacle Packer's attorneys appealed to the Colorado Supreme Court, which had earlier ruled that the state's statute against first-degree murder had been inadvertently repealed by the legislature. May 19 came and went; the invitations fluttered into wastebaskets; Packer stayed alive. Sentenced to forty years on five counts of manslaughter, he lived long enough to be conditionally pardoned by Colorado governor Charles S. Thomas in 1901.[44]

County sheriffs conducted legal executions before 1890, after which they took place at the penitentiary in Cañon City. Between 1863, when William Van Horn was executed near Central City, and 1889, when José Abram Ortiz was hanged in Antonito, it appears that fewer than twenty-five men were legally executed. In the 1890s the state executed a dozen murderers at Cañon City but none between 1892 and 1895, largely because Populist governor Davis Waite opposed capital punishment. Seven hangings followed in 1895 and 1896. In 1897 the legislature abolished capital punishment but restored it in 1901 after a spate of lynchings convinced legislators that the people wanted blood.[45]

The law's failure to execute many murderers gave lynchers an excuse for their executions, as did the short penitentiary sentences many murderers served. Charles Bennett, doomed to life in prison in October 1871, was pardoned in 1879; David Manzaners, also given life in 1871, was freed in 1874. James Wilson got a year for murder in 1871. Norman Patterson, Frederick Lottes, and Moses Fox—sentenced in 1872—were pardoned in 1874. Rare was the murderer such as George Witherill who served sixteen years of a life sentence before he was released. Of around 100 men sent to Cañon City for murder or manslaughter between 1871 and 1884, few stayed in prison more than five years.[46]

Paradoxically, in the decades during which lynching flourished, the law was not particularly harsh on those who managed to evade vigilantes and mobs. That may have been in part because lynchers killed the ugly big fish, leaving those more worthy of leniency to the courts. The paradox was not total, though. Lynching advocates defended impromptu hangings because they spared communities the expense of imprisoning felons and holding trials. Releasing prisoners from the state penitentiary also saved money. Mercy and lynching served the same frugal ends.

The unlynching of Lytleton F. Symmes and the lynching of James N. McLees demonstrate that taxpayers did not always care how they cut costs. On September 25, 1886, Del Norte's *San Juan Prospector* chronicled a death: "Symmes the Montrose murderer was lynched on Monday night last." Six days later Ouray's *Solid Muldoon* resurrected him, reporting that he was in the Ouray jail. Vigilantes had abducted him from the Montrose jail and run him out of town, but he had not gotten far. The *Muldoon* advised its neighbors: "To get a man out of this country, buy him a railroad ticket, put him on a train and tip the conductor. It's all in knowing how." The *Muldoon* could also have advised Montrose to hire Judge Lynch. It did so three weeks later when its vigilantes hanged James N. McLees, who had threatened the town marshal. "Montrose," said the *Prospector*, "is tired of paying for the prosecution of murderers and criminals."[47]

In snickering at Montrose, the *Solid Muldoon* risked being accused of hypocrisy because Ouray also put money ahead of justice. Reporting on the district court in October 1886, the *Muldoon* complained of the leniency shown one thief and the release of a man charged with assault "on the promise that he would leave the county." Chiding citizens for coddling "to mock mercy in order to save their pocket-books," the paper suggested sentencing wrongdoers to long penitentiary terms because that cost less than jailing them locally.[48]

Saving money was only one of many justifications for lynching. The courts' mercy, inefficiency, and legal hairsplitting sometimes provided another excuse. "When the law fails to deal out justice," said Leadville's *Evening Chronicle*, "there is but one resort left."[49] Well supplied with people whose ethnic backgrounds, low social status, and alleged crimes suited them for lynching, Colorado had no problem providing candidates for that last resort.

One such accused felon, William Magee, arrested in Trinidad for murder in 1867, also confessed to having axed to death Cheap John, "a simple unoffending" resident of Denver who sold second-hand goods. The tall, red-haired Magee—an illiterate eighteen-year-old, probably of Irish lineage—was initially examined by a Trinidad People's Court, which ordered him held for district court trial. Lacking a jail, the people placed him under guard, and "the citizens took him from the guard and hanged him."[50] Dr. William Bell, who slept soundly while "the corpse of this miserable man swung to and fro from a tree in a coralle [*sic*] within a few yards of my window," admitted that although Europeans might consider such "rough justice barbarous and uncivilized," it might be better than "the systematic evasion of justice which is commonly practiced throughout the Western country."[51]

Both class and color apparently worked against Edward Bainbridge. Described as an ex-Mormon and a "half crazy coon," he shot James

Martin supposedly without provocation after a card game in Georgetown in April 1867.[52] Arrested and put under guard, Bainbridge
was sleeping in a second-story room when three men scaled a ladder and entered through a window. Two of them pitched him out
the window while the third thumped the guard on the head with a
pistol. The mob took Bainbridge to a tree and hanged him with a
clothesline. Martin, although badly wounded, unexpectedly survived.
Bainbridge's skeleton, rumor had it, wound up in the Central City
offices of Dr. Aduddel who had tended Martin—macabre payment,
in its way, for the doctor's service.[53] The fact that Bainbridge's guard
was injured may be true, or the story may have been concocted to
protect the guard from retaliation. The press often reported that
lawmen bravely opposed mobs; rarely was an officer so brave as to
get hurt.

Lynchers easily had their way with Charles Coats and John
Murrays, accused of murdering John Hull near Castle Rock, south
of Denver, in mid-February 1868. After being captured by a New-
foundland dog that held him down until ranchers could nab him,
Coats was warned by a local justice of the peace: "I have bound you
over to the court and intend to take you to Frankstown and put you
in jail, if I can. But here is [sic] one hundred and fifty armed men
that say I will never get there with you. I don't know whether I will
or not."[54] Horsemen overawed the lone guard protecting Coats. They
gave him a few minutes to pray and to write his mother in England
before they hanged him from a pine tree. His partner, John Murrays,
apprehended south of Castle Rock, was also lynched. Coats was
buried in a shallow grave, and his skeleton was later unearthed.
According to one account it was sent to Denver to be reassembled,
then returned to Castle Rock where it was used in the school to
teach anatomy and, one suspects, good conduct.[55]

A gathering with the trappings of the People's Courts of the
Gold Rush era assembled in Evans, 52 miles north of Denver, in
November 1869 to try Joel Carr, who half an hour earlier had mortally wounded Daniel Steele, a popular hotel keeper.[56] Richard B.
Townshend, an Englishman who observed the excitement, later remembered that Pat Egan, a local functionary, objected to the illegal
proceedings: "By rights this hyar man's my prisoner, and I can't
consent to no proceedings of this sort. . . . I can't give up the man
without some excuse, ye know I can't." Within minutes a big man in
the crowd aimed a "formidable weapon" at Egan and asked, "Mr.

Egan will that do ye for an excuse?" Egan replied, "Certainly, certainly, quite sufficient; that will do."[57]

After a speedy trial Carr was judged guilty and by vote of the assemblage was sentenced to die. He was given time to write to his wife and to pray, a favor he rudely declined. "H—l," he said, "my prayers would not go seven feet high."[58] He was hanged from a cottonwood along the South Platte River. The vigilante leader told the crowd: "Let this be a sign that in this town the people don't mean to tolerate any such goings on. We know there were men who encouraged this miserable wretch to do this thing that brought him to this—yes and lent him the pistol to do it with. . . . They'd better get." As a reminder to those who had "better get," Carr's body was left hanging until the next morning.[59]

Common threads run through many of the lynchings. Vigilantes used their deadly rituals, most of which involved public hanging, to dramatically signal that they would not tolerate crime. By pinning notes on their victims, leaving their bodies dangling, and sometimes denying them a decent burial, community watchdogs made certain other would-be miscreants got the message. The memory of Willie Dubois, an alleged robber lynched by a posse near old Burlington, likely lingered long because after he was killed his corpse was returned to Burlington, "picked up by his hair and carelessly thrown upon the porch of the drug store with his long black hair matted with blood from a bullet hole in the head, making a striking object lesson for all the boys who might have thought they had ambitions to become bad men."[60]

Still, the avengers maintained some balance. Hanging, which usually involved slow death by strangulation, was hardly a pleasant way to die; and prisoners were sometimes beaten before they were hanged, especially when they tried to resist. But normally, the men lynched between the mid-1860s and the early 1880s were not sadistically tortured. Occasionally, a little humaneness crept into the ghastly process: time for prayer, time to write a mother or a wife, time for a cigarette. Bainbridge, thrown from a second-story window, was treated especially harshly, suggesting that a man of color was at greater risk of rough treatment than a white man.

In the 1860s, resistance to Judge Lynch was usually slight. Officials normally objected to having their prisoners taken. Just as commonly, lynchers obligingly overpowered lawmen, thereby getting them off a legal hook for failing to protect their prisoners. Often

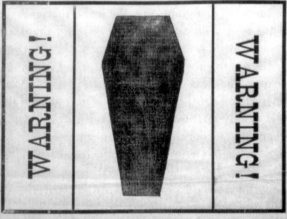

WARNING!

WARNING! **WARNING!**

FOOT-PADS, THIEVES AND DANCE-HOUSE LOUNGERS MUST GET OUT OF LAKE CITY AND STAY---OTHERWISE HANG.

The Foot-pads who are known to be in this city are hereby warned to leave immediately and

SAVE THEIR NECKS!

The proprietors of the Dance Houses are notified to close them immediately, and saloon keepers are notified that they will be held accountable for any injuries that may occur to persons or property. Miners are requested to go to their respective places of work and remain there. Parents are enjoined to keep their children off the streets at night.

By order of THE VIGILANTES.

3.2 Vigilantes often used the threat of lynching to rid their towns of riffraff. Courtesy, Colorado Historical Society (F38008).

the vigilantes of the 1860s did not seem to care if they were recognized. The men who hanged Musgrove in Denver in 1868 did their daylight work without disguises. The *Rocky Mountain News* in its report on Carr's death in 1869 revealed that Richard Sopris, a respected pioneer and later mayor of Denver, presided over the open-air court. Dr. William Bell's account of the hanging of Magee in Trinidad in 1867 does not suggest that the vigilantes hid their faces. Nor does it appear that the men who killed Toll in Boulder in 1867 or Coats and Murrays in Douglas County in 1868 masked their identities. Public opinion in the late 1860s so favored Judge Lynch that his votaries usually saw little reason to hide. During the 1870s and into the early 1880s, vigilantes continued killing murderers, albeit at a lower per capita rate than in the 1860s. Taking more trouble to disguise themselves than they had previously, the avengers of the 1870s demonstrated their realization that lynching was becoming less acceptable.

Men usually organized, conducted, and witnessed lynchings; it was rarely women's work. Reacting to the Rosita hangings of John Gray and Frank Williams in January 1884, Sarah Warner wrote, "[To] Pa and Ma and Cora: We did not know they were hung so close so when I got up early this morning and peaked [*sic*] out the front room door they both hung facing tord [*sic*] me, and it was offal [*sic*]. Their parents and all their folks live here, their mothers did not come to see them but their fathers did, both old men. I felt so sorry for them."[61]

Prostitutes in Trinidad provided a rare exception to male dominance in lynching. In early 1874 a man named Spinner beat Moll Howard, a lady of the night, to death with a rock. "On hearing this confession," the *Rocky Mountain News* reported, "the mob seized him and took him down to the bottom near the town, where he was hanged by a party of prostitutes, friends of the murdered."[62]

Lynchings in the late 1870s, although often enjoying community approval, were often more secretive than those in the early 1870s. Night hangings became the standard after the mid-1870s. Felipe Salas and Joe Talmadge, accused of killing their employer in 1876, were seized by a Cañon City mob of 100 and hanged at night. "Everybody," said the *Rocky Mountain News*, "approves the act."[63] A night hanging conducted by 75 vigilantes disposed of Marcus Gonzales, accused of two murders near La Veta in 1877. A few months later Andreas Barela, charged with the attempted murder of Issac O. Perkins near Costilla in the San Luis Valley, was grabbed from his guards at night and hanged from a cottonwood.[64]

In southern Colorado, many of its counties heavily Hispanic, Anglo vigilantes wisely disguised themselves when lynching Hispanics. But fear of retaliation alone does not explain the shift toward clandestine lynchings. There were no racial overtones to the lynchings of accused murderers Charles G. Walrath and James H. Craft in Alamosa in early July 1879. But the men who seized them at night were disguised, and they took their victims out of town to kill them.[65]

The avengers who hanged accused murderers Joseph Seminole and Samuel Woodruff in Golden in December 1879 had little to fear from Seminole's Sioux relations. There were few, if any, Sioux in Golden. The taxpayers, saved at least $5,000, were reportedly gladdened by the accused miscreants' hasty exit. Thirteen residents, interviewed by a reporter, agreed: "It was the best thing possible, and we are all glad of it."[66] Nevertheless, the vigilantes worked at night, blackened their faces or wore masks, cut the telephone wires to the jail, and put guards around the sheriff's house so he could not get word that his prisoners were about to die.[67]

Henry Cleary, accused of killing James Brown, a popular saloon keeper in Silverton, stayed in jail only four days. In the predawn hours of August 31, 1879, he was hanged from an ox-shoeing frame. "The work of the vigilants stands approved," noted the *Rocky Mountain News*. Yet true to the pattern common after the mid-1870s, those "vigilants" also operated under cover of darkness and wore masks.[68]

As they buried their bosses in late April 1882, the "habitues, male and female," of the San Juan Central, a Lake City dance hall run by George Betts and James Browning, may have wept.[69] If so, their lamentations did not reflect community sentiment. Perhaps as many as 500 people participated in hanging Betts and Browning from a bridge near the Ocean Wave smelter. The mob was incensed over the killing of Hinsdale County sheriff E. N. Campbell, who along with Lake City marshal Clair Smith had surprised two burglars as they rifled a house. One of the thieves shot and killed Campbell. Smith said he recognized the murderer, George Betts, by the light of a match. On the strength of that flickering evidence Betts and Browning were seized and, after scarcely a day in jail, were hanged.

So many residents of Lake City joined in the predawn lynching that practically everyone must have known who did it. But the Lake

3.3 In the early 1880s, A. Phimister Proctor, who had not yet fully developed the artistic talents that would one day make him a well-known sculptor, depicted the Golden hangings of Joseph F. Seminole and Samuel Woodruff on December 28, 1879. Courtesy, Denver Public Library, Western History Collection, and Phimister Proctor Church, A. Phimister Proctor Museum.

City *Silver World* mentioned none of the lynchers' names. With studied grandiloquence the paper editorialized: "When in the course of human events it becomes apparent to an order-loving people that statutory law is weak or inadequate to suppress or punish crime, or is inefficiently administered, then it becomes necessary to invoke the highest law of the land—the law of dire necessity, the edict of the people."[70]

The grand words masked a grim reality. The law was never given a chance to punish Betts or Browning. Protesting overly much, the *Silver World* explained that the lynching was done "by the best and most solid men of the country, not by an uncontrollable mob fired by excitement, revenge or liquor." Why, if those lynchings were so justifiable, did the *Silver World* find it necessary to explain them to the outside world, which the newspaper complained judged "merely on surface facts"?[71]

"Surface facts," two men killed on the basis of an identification made by the light of a match, were important. In 1860, Denver had justified executions ordered by People's Courts on the same grounds of necessity Lake City used in 1882. Even as late as 1868, with far less justification, Denver used the necessity argument to countenance the hangings of Musgrove and Duggan. The rationalization was not strong then, but at least Coloradans could claim to be living in a sparsely populated territory without the right to select its own judges. After Colorado became a state in 1876, citizens took charge of their own judicial affairs. If judges and juries failed, Coloradans largely had themselves to blame. Moreover, with a population of at least 200,000 by 1882, the state could no longer easily claim to be so sparsely populated that it could not control criminals or afford jails and trials.

By the late 1870s and early 1880s, "surface facts" mattered even in small towns. Condemning the attempted lynching of a man named Johnson at Garland in the San Luis Valley in 1878, a correspondent wrote to the *Rocky Mountain News*: "With the railroad and the telegraph at our door, in a state well settled and protected by law, Garland has no need of a vigilance committee."[72] Trying to save accused murderer Marcus Gonzales, imprisoned at La Veta in southern Colorado, jail guard F. D. McHolland asked a member of the mob on whose authority they acted. "By the authority of the voice of the people," the vigilantes' spokesman declared. "I told him," said McHolland, "that wouldn't do—they could not have him."[73]

70

The lynchers took Gonzales anyway and hanged him. Their authority, however, was far from absolute by the late 1870s. No longer was the voice of the people, clamoring for lynching, paramount. That was apparent in early 1884 when the hangings of Margaret and Michael Cuddigan triggered a statewide debate on lynching and provided a milestone along the long road of Judge Lynch's slow death.

4

THE CUDDIGAN
AND OTHER LYNCHINGS,
1884–1906

As a rule, there is too much sentimentality about lynching. Some of our exchanges blame the people of Ouray
for hanging the Cuddigans. In our opinion, they did right
and deserve praise rather than condemnation.
        —*SAN JUAN PROSPECTOR* [DEL NORTE],
                                JANUARY 26, 1884

In the cold, dead, predawn hours of Saturday, January 19, 1884,
vigilantes in Ouray lynched Michael Cuddigan and his pregnant wife, Margaret, both accused of murdering their ten-year-
old ward, Mary Rose Mathews. As he eyed the ridgepole of Tommy
Andrews's cabin, Michael observed, "Fellows, that ain't high enough
to hang a man on." They strung him up there anyway, briefly allowing him to survive by standing on his tiptoes until four men grabbed
his legs and pulled, strangling him to death.[1]

By 1884 Coloradans were abandoning lynching as a means of
disposing of horse thieves and ordinary murderers. But the hanging of Michael Cuddigan, brutal as it was, did not overly trouble the
state's collective conscience because his alleged crime was so heinous it
seemed to demand stern and swift retribution. Michael's death

pointed toward a new order of lynching in which summary executions were usually reserved either for those accused of weighty crimes or for those whose race made them special targets. Alleged killer of a child, Michael fit neatly into the loathsome crime pigeonhole.

Margaret Cuddigan—also strangled, hanged from a tree across from Andrews's cabin—was a thornier and more embarrassing nettle. She was taxed with the same despicable crime as Michael, but she was female. The lynching of a woman was so rare that some Colorado newspapers reported she was probably the first of her gender to be lynched in the United States.

They were wrong. Miners in Downieville, California, lynched Juanita, a Hispanic woman, in 1851. Of the more than 3,000 people lynched in the United States between 1882 and 1902, about 60 were women, 20 of them white. A Hispanic woman may have been lynched in Trinidad in 1873, perhaps robbing Margaret Cuddigan of the distinction of being Colorado's only female victim of Judge Lynch. But the rumored and poorly reported Trinidad killing is by no means certain.[2] Margaret was clearly lynched, and because she was a woman her hanging triggered considerable debate over the merits of lynching. "The case," predicted the *Gunnison Review-Press*, "will go down in history as a remarkable one and to the dishonour of Ouray."[3]

Ouray, today a recreational center in the San Juan Mountains, 300 miles southwest of Denver, was incorporated in 1876, the year Colorado became a state. Named for the Ute chief Ouray, it occupied land that until 1873 had belonged to the Utes, who had long enjoyed the locale's hunting and hot springs. Smitten more by mineral riches than by mineral baths, European Americans made the San Juans one of Colorado's top gold and silver producers. Near Ouray, Thomas Walsh's Camp Bird Mine helped launch his daughter, Evalyn Walsh McLean, into Washington, D.C., society, where she glittered as the owner of the Hope diamond.

Set like a gem in a ring of mountains, Ouray also sparkled. "Words are inadequate to describe the appearance of these wild scenes," wrote George Crofutt in his 1885 *Grip-sack Guide of Colorado* as he portrayed the "wreck of matter . . . exploded world piled up" that surrounded the town.[4] Ernest Ingersoll, another visitor, also viewed that wild scene but made clear that Ouray itself was not wild: "There are few western villages that can boast so much civilization."[5]

4.1 In addition to its beauty, Ouray was noted for its lynchings. William Henry Jackson photograph. Courtesy, Denver Public Library, Western History Collection.

More than that, Ouray could boast of almost instant civilization. David F. Day, editor of the *Solid Muldoon*, greeted 1884 with a tribute to his eight-year-old town's swift progress: "Sampling mills and manufacturing establishments rise as if by magic from what a few short years ago was but a wooded grotto inhabited by the untutored savage and wild beasts of the forest."[6] By early 1884, Ouray counted three hotels; three churches—Episcopal, Methodist, and Roman Catholic; and two newspapers—the *Muldoon*, a popular, cocky Democratic sheet featuring a rooster as its mascot, and the *Ouray Times*, a more sedate Republican journal.

Besides scenery, mines, and civilization, Ouray had another advantage. A few miles to its north the mountains gave way to a magnificent valley watered by the Uncompahgre and other smaller rivers such as Dallas Creek. There farmers and ranchers kept stock and raised grain to feed San Juan miners.[7] Around 3,000 people—many adult males in the mining areas, more families in town and the farming districts—lived in Ouray and its environs in the summer, with the population falling during the winter. In those frigid, often dull months they soaked in the hot springs and spent long evenings in saloons and secret fraternal societies, "so numerous and varied," wrote Crofutt, "that very few of the citizens think of keeping a secret."[8]

Churched, schooled, organized, wined, dined, and bathed, the town's citizens seemed safe and content. Yet if they were so secure, why did David F. Day, Ouray's brilliant booster, boast so brashly? Was Ouray, where schools, churches, and lodges were only a few years old, uncertain of itself? Did that magic place fear it would disappear as quickly as it had appeared, starved to death as mines played out?[9]

Not if Day could help it. Winner of the Congressional Medal of Honor for bravery at Vicksburg, he retained his fighting mettle after the Civil War. Learning that Silverton, one of Ouray's nearby competitors, worried about its honor, Day mused, "In a village where the hotel and bar spittoons are nailed to the wall, stove pokers chained to the ceiling and barbed wire fences around the coal and marble yards 'honor and integrity' must be abundant." Grand Junction, 90 miles to Ouray's northwest but still a rival in sparsely settled western Colorado, became in one of Day's headlines "The Queen Fraud of the Sunset Slope An Empire Founded on Greed, Gall, and Prevarication."[10]

Day's jabs bespoke jealousy. Grand Junction and Silverton enjoyed railroad connections, giving them the economic lifelines without which braggart would-be cities often faded into ghost towns. "If the miners of Ouray pray at all," Crofutt observed, "it [is] for the coming of the 'Iron Horse.'"[11]

If Ouray's boosters prayed, perhaps they also prayed that Margaret Cuddigan and her unborn child, buried with Michael in an unconsecrated grave, would not rise to haunt them, to tell their secrets, to drift about whispering that Ouray—hungry as it was for capital, labor, and settlers—was far removed "from the delights of civilization."[12] Nor did Margaret hold the only spectral warrant. Mary Rose Mathews's spirit also had ample right to pace the town and revisit the farms on Dallas Creek. When she lived, those civilized people had done little for her. After she died, instead of letting her rest in peace they dug her body up, shipped it to Denver, and put it on display—hoping to show they had acted justly in killing the people they thought had killed her.

When had Mary Rose had a happy moment? Did she enjoy days in Denver after her mother died when her father, Charles Mathews, took her for walks? Or did she live in hell with Mathews, a man of "unenviable notoriety," a thief, and a companion of a prostitute named Julia Mullins? After Mary Rose's death some Denverites recalled that before she went to the Cuddigans her "body was almost covered with scars" and that "her own parents had mistreated her."[13]

Unable or unwilling to support his daughter, Mathews placed her in Denver's St. Vincent's Home, a Catholic orphanage. He did not visit her because, as one paper said, it would make her sad and would "unnerve him."[14] She remained with the nuns around three months until midsummer 1883. Then Father Robert Servant took her to the Cuddigans.

Servant, a French-born priest who had been ordained in Denver in late 1881, was newly assigned to a vast six-county parish in southwestern Colorado. It is unlikely he knew the Cuddigans well before he placed Mary Rose with them. He may not have realized that Margaret and Michael were first cousins, that their marriage had probably been forced, that insanity had touched Margaret's family.

Both Cuddigans were from La Salle County, Illinois, 75 miles southwest of Chicago. In the summer of 1882 Michael had abruptly broken his engagement to one woman and married his cousin, Margaret Carroll. Their son Percival, usually called Percie, was born in November 1882, six months or so after the marriage. Michael's change of plans, the rarity of Roman Catholic marriages between first cousins, and Percie's birth date all suggest that the Carroll-Cuddigan union was dictated by necessity rather than by plan.[15]

Margaret was nineteen when she married and twenty-one when she died. Her childhood, like Mary Rose's, was blighted by tragedy, for when she was ten her father went insane and later drowned himself.[16] Michael was probably a decade or more older than Margaret, but his age did not win him his wife's respect.[17] After the lynching the *Denver Tribune* reported that Michael "stated that his wife had been the means of making his home a hell, and that whatever he had done he was urged to it by her." Michael often went to Ouray with one of his brothers, where "they would go on a drunk, flourishing revolvers, and dare any man to face the 'bad men from the park.'" It took an especially bad woman to control such a bad

4.2 *The Cuddigans lived near the small town of Dallas north of Ouray. Some of the townsfolk pictured in this 1888 photograph may have been among Margaret and Michael's lynchers. Courtesy, Denver Public Library, Western History Collection.*

man. Margaret "made [Michael] sleep in a haystack for displeasing her."[18]

All that was apparently unknown to Father Servant. In late July 1883, when he took Mary Rose to them, Michael and Margaret were farming 160 acres on Dallas Creek, about a mile from its juncture with the Uncompahgre River 13 miles north of Ouray.[19] Percie was around eight months old, and Margaret was pregnant. Mary Rose would no doubt be of help. The match appeared a good one: Mary Rose's natural mother, Mary, had been Irish; so were the Cuddigans. "Before consenting to place the child with the Cuddigan family," Servant recalled, "the Right Reverend Bishop Machebeuf and myself made many and strict inquiries about its character, and such were the accounts received that we were satisfied the child would have a pleasant home and kind protection."[20]

By mid-December 1883, rumors reached Servant that the Cuddigans were not kind protectors. He visited them on December 16 and found Mary Rose "most lively and cheerful." He stopped again on Christmas Day, and when Margaret and Michael were temporarily absent he asked the child if they abused or whipped her. She said they did not. Servant inquired about cuts on the back of her head. She explained that she had fallen down a flight of stairs. Servant told her that if they hurt her, he would take her away from them.[21]

A stagecoach driver saw Mary Rose from a distance on Saturday, January 12, 1884. Later that day Margaret told her brother, James Carroll, that Mary Rose had died. Carroll went to Ouray to purchase a coffin. On Sunday George C. Morrison, a schoolteacher, stopped at the Cuddigans where he saw Mary Rose's body and noticed a bruise on her forehead. On Sunday afternoon he reported in Ouray that "Mary Rose Mathews had died and been buried that morning in a very mysterious manner, and charged that death resulted from barbarous and inhuman cruelty."[22]

On Monday Coroner Alex Hazard had Mary Rose's body disinterred and took it to Ouray, where on Tuesday and Wednesday a coroner's jury met. Dr. W. W. Rowan testified that both Mary Rose's feet, and probably her legs and thighs, had been frozen. He found a cut on one of her knees, wounds on her thigh, wounds and bruises on her arms, fingers and thumbs frozen on her right hand. "On the forehead, a little to the left of center . . . she had received a severe blow from some blunt instrument; also on the rear portion of head [I] found a very large wound, about the size of a silver dollar, caused by some blunt instrument." After the examination "the doors were thrown open to allow the public an opportunity to view the damnable extent of the torture."[23]

Rowan concluded that ill treatment and the head injury caused Mary Rose's death. The coroner's jury, based on the limited information presented, determined that she "came to her death from cruelty, maltreatment and inattention at the hands of Michael Cuddigan, Margaret Cuddigan, and James Carroll."[24]

On Monday, January 14, before the coroner's jury met, Sheriff Charles Rawles arrested the Cuddigans and James Carroll. He brought them and Percie to Ouray, lodging them in the Delmonico Hotel—judging, no doubt, that the rickety wooden jail was ill suited for both their confinement and protection. Rawles, two deputies, and two of Michael Cuddigan's brothers were also there, the brothers to protect Margaret and Michael. When they arrived a large crowd gathered, so Rawles pulled down the curtains because, as Carroll recalled, "the crowd was peeking in on all sides."[25]

The Cuddigans passed fretful days. Margaret, seven months pregnant, "raved and wanted flowers to surround her and desired to partake freely of pure water." That, the *Denver Tribune* claimed, was "the insanity dodge." Dr. M. A. Wheelock tended her, for which he later billed Michael's estate $40.26. Francis Fitch, a local attorney, agreed to defend the Cuddigans.[26]

The weekly *Solid Muldoon* appeared late on Friday, January 18, fanning the anti-Cuddigan furor: "brutes—worse than brutes that have heretofore passed as humans." As for James Carroll, he was "one of the monsters . . . who should be strung up with Cuddigan and his murderous wife." If, said the *Muldoon*, "the boiling indignation of the community were to mete out to the villains the punishment they so justly merit, red tape justice might be pardoned the exclamation! 'Well done, Judge Lynch!'"[27]

Having helped set the stage, editor Day won a part in the ensuing drama. Around 12:30 A.M., Saturday, January 19, he was approached by several dozen masked men who ordered him to warn Rawles and all others, except the two Cuddigans and James Carroll, to leave the hotel. Day delivered the message. Sheriff Rawles responded, "You can go back and tell your mob to go to hell." Rawles and Thomas Knowles, the Delmonico's proprietor, stood on the porch as the mob approached. Both men were soon overpowered, as were the Cuddigans' other guards, including two deputy sheriffs, two of Michael's brothers, and a brother-in-law, likely Martin Birtsh.[28]

Discretion defeated valor. Michael's brothers, following Rawles's example, did not lay down their lives to save their kin. Father Robert Servant also had some explaining to do. Learning of the Cuddigans' arrest, he had arrived in Ouray on Friday, January 18. "Had the slightest suspicion of the lynching entered my mind I would have seen the Cuddigans on that night," he later explained. "When next morning I learned what had been done during the night I was overcome with a sickening sense of shame and horror." The *Muldoon* snidely wondered how Servant, when "he slept, or pretended to sleep" in a hotel across the street from the Delmonico, could have failed to hear the shots fired that night.[29]

The vigilantes seized Carroll and the Cuddigans. Four men dragged Margaret screaming from her bed. They marched her shoeless over frozen ground, taking her and Michael slightly beyond the town's northern limits. Michael reportedly confessed to his tormentors that Margaret had forced Mary Rose out of the house. Two men held Margaret down in the snow. James Carroll remembered, "I heard the branches of the tree opposite the cabin squeak and I knew by her cries, and calling for her mother, and the sounds that followed, that they had hung my sister."[30]

A handful of men also hanged Carroll, releasing him before he choked to death, crediting his account that he had been away for more than two weeks before Mary Rose died. They ordered him to get out. He told the *Grand Junction News,* "I started and ran as long as I could."[31]

News of the lynching spread more rapidly than Carroll ran. Silverton reported it the day it happened. It took only a day to make the front page of the Sunday, January 20, *New York Times,* which, picking up errors from early accounts, misstated the Cuddigans' name as Cuddihee.

The novelty of lynching a woman ensured that the incident would attract more than the usual notice in Colorado, where impromptu hangings were so common they often received little attention. Fairplay, a mining town in central Colorado, witnessed the lynching of John Hoover, a convicted murderer, in 1880. Its paper praised Ouray for a "piece of exact justice." A Del Norte mob hanged the Pond brothers in 1881. Its paper defended Ouray: "The murderers were bad people . . . in said matters, it is safe to rely upon the judgment of the executioners." In Rico, a San Juan town to Ouray's southwest, the *Dolores News* agreed: "The vigilantes of Ouray did themselves and their county proud." From Durango, 75 miles south of Ouray, came the *Durango Herald's* opinion that the crime justified the penalty. The *Animas Forks Pioneer,* published in a high-altitude mining hamlet near Ouray, proposed giving each member of the mob a "gold medal."[32]

Other small-town papers were guarded, some hostile. In Lake City, another San Juan mining town, George Betts and James Browning had been lynched in 1882. One of its papers, the *Mining Register,* backed the Ouray vigilantes, arguing that lynching was necessary because bad people gravitated to the border of civilization. But the *Silver World* initially reserved judgment and later called for "a full investigation." The *Rico Record* denounced the lynchers and praised the *Durango Southwest* for also opposing the killings.[33]

Grand Junction's *News,* long at war with David Day, condemned the "masked murderers . . . simply gratifying their spite against society and showing their disregard of law." Silverton, another Ouray rival, lynched Black Kid Thomas and Bert Wilkinson in 1881, but that did not stop the *Silverton Democrat* from concluding, "Ouray is a

STRANGLED!

The Murderers of Mary Rose Mathews Rewarded with Death by the Vigilantes.

Sheriff Rawles' Bullets Faced Without a Flinch by the Determined Mob.

The *Solid Muldoon* Extra gives the following account of the lynching of Michael and Margaret Cuddigan, at Ouray, last Friday night:

Last night a body of armed and evidently determined men approached the Delmonico Hotel, where Cuddigan, his wife and brother-in-law, Carroll, were temporarily confined, in a manner that gave every evidence of perfect organization. Third street contained quite a number of pedestrians at the time, but the vigilantes evaded detection by passing up the parallel alleys on either side of the main street until the hotel was reached.

The first warning of any disturbance was a pistol shot from Sheriff Rawles, who battled nobly and earnestly to protect his prisoners, but the force closed in from behind, grappled, disarmed and threw him on the floor, where he was held by strong arms until others of the party had secured the prisoners and got them well under control. Deputies Vandaver and Woodcock wielded their weapons with more than ordinary nerve, but a brace of loaded Win-chesters wilted them and deeming dis-

4.3 The Rico Record *reported the Cuddigans' lynchings on January 24, 1884. Picture generation, courtesy Christopher Altvater.*

good place for law-abiding people to shun." The *Democrat* placed a bet: "We will wager a four dollar dog that Sheriff Rawles knew of the attack long before it was made and was in sympathy with the mob." Even the *Ouray Times* condemned the killings: "There is no excuse which can paliate [*sic*] the violence of the mob. There are few good citizens who do not deplore the occurrence."[34]

Denver had lynched its share of wrongdoers during its first decade, but except for the 1880 killing of Look Young during a riot, it had not recorded any lynchings since Musgrove's and Duggan's in 1868. Striving for respectability, three of the city's four dailies— the *Republican*, the *Rocky Mountain News*, and the *Times*—condemned the Cuddigan lynchings. Only the *Tribune* supported the vigilantes: "We congratulate the people of Ouray that they conquered sentiment and took the right course."[35]

Caroline Churchill's *Queen Bee*, a Denver weekly, also lauded the lynchers. Churchill, a peppery feminist, could have ranted at the man-filled mob that strangled a defenseless pregnant woman. Certainly, she would have enjoyed embarrassing David Day who once described her as "a happy combination of blight, disappointment, and gall."[36]

But Churchill hated Roman Catholics more than woman killers. The Cuddigans, she asserted, were products of "superstitious humbuggery" without excuse for their actions, "except the following out of savage instinct of animals who have had barbarians for their ancestors for ages." Endorsing "the lynching as the best thing that could have been done under the circumstances," she suggested that Father Servant should also have been hanged.[37]

Antilynchers argued that the hangings were unnecessary. The courts were functioning, the Cuddigans were securely held. Lynchings frightened prospective investors and settlers. Nine days after the Ouray lynchings, vigilantes in Rosita, a mining town southwest of Pueblo, hanged accused murderers John Gray and Frank Williams. That brought the number of January lynchings to four—five if Margaret's unborn baby were counted. Late in the month three horse thieves were captured in southern Colorado, and it appeared they, too, would be killed without benefit of a trial. Pueblo's *Chieftain* warned, "People will not care to take up their residence in a state where human life is valued so lightly."[38]

Other papers blasted the hanging of a woman. "Lynch law," said the *Leadville Daily Herald*, "is rarely, if ever excusable, and surely the administration of law is not so lax in Ouray County that public policy demanded that a mob of strong men should drag a weak defenseless woman out of jail in the middle of the night and choke her to death like they might a dog." The *Herald* continued, "All the world knows that a woman may be coerced by the power of her husband and compelled to do a thing at which she herself would naturally revolt."[39]

David Day tried to deflect criticism with humor: "The amount of free advertising Ouray is enjoying is simply enormous."[40] But flippancy could not protect Ouray, especially after Father Servant boldly rebuked the vigilantes. In a January 27 statement published in Denver newspapers, he revealed that Mary Rose was scarred before going to the Cuddigans: "The wound, so called, that is described as being upon her forehead is a scar of long standing which I and others knew to be on her before leaving Denver." He concluded: "The vigilantes of Ouray, to say the least, acted in a manner not only unlawful, but too hasty. Further developments may even prove the innocence of the Cuddigans, and then those who had a part in their execution will carry with them a burden of self-condemnation."[41] Stung by Servant, the *Muldoon* fumed: "Such religion as he squirts is not safe to rely upon. Let Bishop Machebeuf send that thing down among the Apaches."[42]

Defending the lynchers, the *Muldoon*, the *Denver Tribune*, and other prolynching papers cited the horror of the crime, the slowness of the courts, the cost of trials, the uncertainty of justice. The vigilantes, said the *Muldoon*, were not, as some suggested, made up of rabble: "The Ouray county vigilance committee—and it is a model—is composed of those who are rated as the best, most conservative, prudent and consistent men in the county."[43]

Justifying the killing of a pregnant woman presented a special challenge. Employing rationalizations used to cloak maltreatment of Native and African Americans, some papers stripped Margaret Cuddigan of her humanity and her gender. "Was she worthy [of] the name of WOMAN?" asked the *Animas Forks Pioneer*.[44] She was a female fiend, a devil incarnate, unnatural, an inhuman wretch, a brute, a horrible monster: "A woman so dead to all the feelings of her sex as to torture a poor, little unfriended child into eternity was worse than the man."[45] Killing Margaret was a kindness to her unborn child: "God help the child she would have borne. If she murdered one, she would have murdered the other."[46]

To bolster their case, the *Denver Tribune* and the *Muldoon* charged the Cuddigans with another crime. Mary Rose, they claimed, had been raped. The *Denver Republican* doubted that: "We do not believe it. The doctors who made the post-mortem examination reported no such discovery. It is idiotic to presume that if the child had been outraged the fact would have been kept from the public."[47]

Next the prolynchers played their trump card—the corpse of Mary Rose. Supposedly at the request of her father, they disinterred her body from Ouray's Cedar Hill Cemetery and dispatched it to Denver. On February 1, 1884, a hundred people waited at 7:00 A.M. in front of McGovern's undertaking rooms. For the next fifteen hours an estimated 12,000 gawkers—a quarter of the city's population—filed by Mary Rose, nearly three weeks dead: "Men used to death in every shape shuddered while they gazed earnestly on the little form. . . . Mothers accompanied by their little ones quietly passed around the corpse, giving vent to their feelings."[48] The *Republican* noted that "loafers and all classes" flooded in. "They pushed and jostled for space, and often because of their superior strength managed to crowd back the whimpering women and gain a better sight of little Mary, dead."[49]

The next day Mary Rose was given a funeral Mass at St. Mary's Cathedral and was buried, at Ouray County's expense, in Denver's Calvary Cemetery next to her natural mother. It was her third but probably not her final resting place. Years later many of the bodies at Calvary were moved to the new Catholic cemetery, Mount Olivet, where in 1924 Father Robert Servant was also buried.[50]

Mary Rose was at peace. Ouray was not. James Carroll talked with the *Grand Junction News* in mid-February. He denied that the Cuddigans had tried to keep Mary Rose's death a secret. He explained that the bloodstained rags some thought proved the child's sufferings were sacking he had used to protect his shoulders when he carried slabs of meat. He noted that Mary Rose had a kidney disease that caused her to lose bowel control, leading to wet feet and frostbite.[51]

Carroll told the *News* he recognized some of the lynchers. The paper did not identify the vigilantes, but W. J. Miller, a Grand Junction attorney, acting on Carroll's and Servant's behest, sent Governor James B. Grant a letter naming names. Miller's sloppy penmanship left several of the alleged lynchers' identities open to doubt. Perhaps Miller or Carroll wanted some wiggle room. Arthur Hyde's name is fairly clear, as are Henry Hammond's and Bow Decker's. But was one of the men named Overucan or Overman, and was another Lou Orvis? Census records from 1885 indicate that a Lewis "Oris" lived near one of Michael Cuddigan's brothers and that an "A. Hyde" lived next to Patrick Cuddigan. Some of the Cuddigans' neighbors, it appears, were their lynchers.[52]

If Carroll hoped Governor Grant would smite the murderers of his sister, he was disappointed. In an era noted for its lynching bees, it was unlikely that Grant would offend either David Day, his political ally and an honorary colonel on his staff, or the vigilantes and voters of Ouray County.

Father Servant also learned a hard lesson in Colorado ways. He returned to Ouray on March 4, 1884. He heard rumors that he was to be ordered to leave town. That night Sheriff Rawles and two guards protected him as he slept. After he said Mass the next day, he was told a petition was being circulated asking him to leave. He did. Later, hoping to return to Ouray, he asked Governor Grant for protection. Grant's secretary condescendingly dismissed the priest: "His Excellency makes due allowance for your obvious ignorance of the laws of the state. . . . The proper source to which any citizen who fancies himself in danger of violence should apply is the county in which the danger is apprehended."[53]

One courageous authority, District Judge Melville Gerry, well-known in Colorado for presiding at the trial of the cannibal Alfred Packer, impaneled a grand jury in Ouray to investigate the lynchings. Unfazed by an anonymous threat to lynch him, Gerry told the jurors, "Mob law is simply revolution." His scolding failed to convince them to indict their neighbors. In mid-May 1884 they reported that they could not ferret out the culprits. If Ouray had an adequate jail, the jury surmised, the Cuddigans would have been more fully protected, and their deaths might have been prevented. So the panel recommended that the town build a better jail. That shuffling did not surprise the *Grand Junction News*: "It [is] generally known that there are men on the grand jury of that county who were in the mob of stranglers who murdered the Cuddigans."[54]

Baby Percie went to live with his uncle-in-law, Martin Birtsh; and Patrick, one of Michael's brothers, rented the Cuddigans' farm. Attorneys Lechter and Stewart, who would have assisted in prosecuting Michael and Margaret had they lived, became the attorneys for their estate. David Day, who sanctioned the Cuddigans' deaths, pocketed eight dollars for publishing a notice to their creditors. For his troubles, Father Robert Servant was transferred to another parish. In "that outlandish state," as the *Ottawa* [Illinois] *Republican* called Colorado, it seemed justice was not only blind but also insane.[55] Ouray had lynched a woman, her unborn child, and her husband. Ouray wanted to forget it. The *Denver Tribune* editorialized: "The deed is done, no protestations can bring the dead to life. The people of Ouray County hope to hear no more on the case."[56]

In attempting to forget the Cuddigans, Ouray did not banish lynching, as was the case in some other towns where summary executions marked a place's early history. Leadville's two lynchings came on one night before the town was two years old. In late March 1881 a Durango posse killed its prisoner, Jack Roberts. Less than three weeks later citizens in that young town hanged Henry R. Moorman for killing James K. Polk Pringle. Caroline Romney, editor of the *Durango Record,* approved: "The foully murdered man was avenged ere the day in which the deed was done had flown."[57] Despite that editorial blessing, Durango lynched no more men.

Rosita and Rico hosted double lynchings in the 1880s and then fired Judge Lynch.[58] Del Norte disposed of the Pond brothers in May 1881, then lynched Frank Young in March 1882 and William Blair, known as Coyote Bill, in August 1882, after which it exited the lynching business.[59] Lake City satisfied its lynching itch with the double hanging of George Betts and James Browning on April 29, 1882. Silverton lynched Henry Cleary for murder in August 1879. It then waited two years before lynching an African American, sixteen-year-old Black Kid Thomas, and nineteen-year-old Bert Wilkinson—Wilkinson for killing town marshal David C. Ogsbury and Thomas for accompanying Wilkinson. Historian Allen Nossaman concludes his account of the Thomas-Wilkinson story: "The deed left a bitter taste in most Silvertonians' mouths, and the rope was never again used to mete out justice in San Juan County."[60]

No bad taste lingered in the mouths of people in Ouray, where lynching was made palatable, even tasty, by editor David Day. In 1883 the *Solid Muldoon* advised Gunnison to lynch an accused murderer rather than spend money on a trial.[61] In 1885, little more than a year after the Cuddigan hangings, Blewett Redus murdered Dan MacDonald in Ouray. Some citizens of Ouray, well-versed in extralegal executions, wanted to hang Redus. As Silverton's *La Plata Miner* snidely put it, "Lynching was seriously talked of in that Christian

HIGHER THAN HAMAN.

Williams and Gray Lynched by Citizens of Rosita.

Three Horse Thieves Captured at West Las Animas

Who Are Liable to be Suddenly Hoisted With Hemp.

Virtuous Greeley Makes a Raid On the Gamblers.

Synopsis of Hoar's Bill to Wipe Out the Mormons.

Senator Bowen Appointed Chairman of the Mining Committee.

Two Murderers Lynched.

Special to The News.

SILVER CLIFF, Jan. 28.—This morning about 2 o'clock 100 armed men visited the jail where Frank Williams and John Gray, the murderers of Orion Kurtz, were incarcerated, overpowered the guards and battered down the door and took the prisoners out and hanged them to the corners of a log cabin near by and left their bodies hanging. They were taken down about sunrise this morning and a coroner's inquest was held. The jury's verdict was death from hanging by parties unknown.

The lynchers were all closely masked. Bill Tripp, who was also held as an accessory to the murder, made his escape, but was recaptured at Silver Cliff this evening and is now in jail here.

The body of Kurtz will start for Louisville, Ky., to-morrow morning, accompanied by the widow and a Masonic escort. All quiet at Rosita now.

Another Lynching Probable.

Special to The News.

PUEBLO, Jan. 28.—Sheriff Parsons, of Bent county, assisted by Alf Polk and ten others, yesterday captured the three horse thieves, Elliott, Pegleg and Smoky George, who last

4.4 Shortly after the Cuddigan lynchings, Rosita, southwest of Pueblo, hosted the double lynching of Frank Williams and John Gray. Courtesy, Rocky Mountain News, *January 29, 1884.*

village."[62] Redus was saved in part because Father Edward Ley, Servant's successor, flatly told some of his parishioners that he opposed lynching. They helped guard the jail, and Redus lived.[63]

Such qualms of conscience did not calm the Ouray vigilantes seeking the death of Joseph Dixon, an African American charged with killing a young woman, Ellar Day, on September 13, 1887. Unable or unwilling to force their way into the jail, the avengers soaked the frame structure with coal oil and set it on fire. Offering no apologies for the uncommonly brutal lynching, the *Muldoon* lauded the vigilantes for exercising "the inherent right of social organization to protect itself under the unwritten law of nature."[64] In 1891, Ouray again invoked "the unwritten law of nature" when its citizens killed Lee Quang, a Chinese man, for allegedly attempting to molest a girl. With its typical bravura the *Muldoon* proclaimed, "Our people are always right, and the *Muldoon* is always with them."[65]

The Cuddigans, Dixon, and Quang represented the targets Judge Lynch preferred after the early 1880s. As Colorado grew from fewer than 200,000 people in 1880 to more than 400,000 in 1890 and was knit together by telegraphs, telephones, and railroads, frontier ways passed away. Lynching, the fate of ordinary murderers and horse thieves in the 1860s and 1870s, gradually came to be largely, although not exclusively, reserved for those, like the Cuddigans, accused of serious crimes or those—principally African Americans, Hispanics, and Italians—scorned by the larger society. Between 1885 and 1919, thirty-three men were lynched in Colorado. Of those, four were African Americans, perhaps as many as five were Hispanics, five were Italians, and two were Chinese. Their stories are told in Chapter 6.

Of the remaining nineteen, some—such as Harry Banta, who slew a man in a quarrel over a card game in 1888; Franklin Baker, who killed a trespasser near Cheyenne Wells in 1888; and John Bennett, who was lynched in the remote reaches of Routt County in 1898 for accompanying a murderer—hearkened back to the free and easy lynchings of the 1860s and early 1870s.[66] Many others were men whose misdeeds—murders and sex crimes—so offended society that Judge Lynch could claim to be doing civilization a favor by killing them. One of them, Wilbur D. French, died in Greeley; another, James H. Howe, in Fort Collins—towns that, perhaps because they saw few murders, reacted violently when they found killers in their midst.

4.5 Greeley photographer Frank E. Baker took this picture of Wilbur D. French, lynched in late December 1888. On seeing French hanged, an old lady in the crowd declared "Praise the Lord." Courtesy, Denver Public Library, Western History Collection.

French did not fit the stereotype of the ordinary lynchee. Most reports of those lynched in the 1860s and 1870s failed to mention their age or social status. The impression one gets, however, is that the lynched were mainly young men with little money and scant social standing, whereas the vigilantes in those early years were often described as solid citizens. Those lynchings reflected the distinctions between patricians and riffraff drawn by Owen Wister in his novel *The Virginian* and by historians such as LeRoy Hafen and Carl Rister, who favored the "home-builder" in his war against the "outlaw."[67] French, a prosperous forty-nine-year-old cattleman living in Evans south of Greeley, was neither riffraff nor outlaw. A solid "home-builder," he nevertheless reportedly killed his tenant, Harry Woodbury, because of a dispute over flour. After French's friends testified on his behalf in a preliminary hearing, Woodbury's partisans feared French would not pay for his crime. They broke into the Greeley jail in late December 1888 and hanged French from a nearby tree.

The pioneer-era excuses for lynching—poor judges, flimsy jails, corrupt lawmen, community self-protection—no longer held sway. But as the *Denver Times* reported, the $12,000 Weld County had spent prosecuting French counted heavily against him. With a fortune estimated at $50,000, French might have used his wealth to win acquittal, costing the county additional thousands in the process. In a reversal of the class bias that often disadvantaged the disadvantaged, French's money hurt him. One observer noted, "I think the hanging was done by people who hated to see a rich man tyrannize over a poor man and lord around over other people with bluster and a Colts .44 [*sic*]."[68]

Fort Collins, northwest of Greeley, was, like Greeley, a family-oriented agricultural town—a place Coloradans of the 1880s thought of as staid. James H. Howe—a family man, respected millwright, and mechanic—hardly seemed likely to attract the attention of Judge Lynch. That changed April 4, 1888, when Howe, crazed with drink, repeatedly stabbed his wife Eva who, tired of his cruelty, was preparing to leave him. She staggered to the sidewalk in front of their house, collapsed, and died.

Howe was jailed that afternoon. Sheriff Thomas Davy, aided by a posse, dispersed a crowd of 1,000. At 8:00 P.M. someone cut electric light wires to give cover of darkness to a well-organized mob of 300. Its members broke into the jail, overpowered guards, chiseled through iron door locks, seized Howe, and hanged him near the Larimer County courthouse. Fifty men pulled on the rope "which tightened with a snap and strangled the life out of his worthless body." April 4, 1888, said the *Denver Republican*, was "an exciting day in the staid city of Fort Collins."[69]

Cañon City was not likely to be described as staid. Site of the state penitentiary, it witnessed its share of excitement during the late nineteenth century, including two lynchings in 1876, another in 1883, still another in 1888, and its last in 1900.

Occasional prison breaks also kept the town awake. In a particularly daring escape in May 1874, eight inmates including George Witherill—a young man serving life for murder—overpowered guards and stole supplies, rifles, revolvers, and 2,000 rounds of ammunition.[70] Recaptured, Witherill was closely watched, often shackled, and made to wear a ball and chain. In time he apparently mellowed. "Oh the horror of this life; the living death which seems so endless," he wrote in his diary on December 21, 1884; "patience, patience, weary soul."[71]

In 1887 his patience finally paid off when the legislature mandated that life sentences should be interpreted to mean no more than sixteen years in the penitentiary. Witherill, who had entered the prison in 1871, the year it was established, was released.[72] He remained free until late 1888 when he was arrested for the brutal murder near Cañon City of Charles R. McCain, with whom he had formed an ore-hauling partnership. Witherill denied the crime. Lawmen kept him in Pueblo and Denver for nearly a month, fearful that he would be lynched if returned to Cañon City for trial.[73]

On December 3, 1888, hidden in a railroad baggage car, Witherill was sent from Denver to Cañon City where he was jailed. Before dawn on December 4 a mob overpowered Sheriff Morgan L. Griffith, used "petty tortures" to get the jail keys from the sheriff's son, and gained entry to Witherill's cell. He beat them back with a club fashioned from his bed. They shot, wounded, and handcuffed him. Taken to a telephone pole, he was hanged, let down barely alive, and asked to confess; he refused and was hanged again until dead.[74]

Frank Raynolds, president of the Fremont County Bank, said he had tried "to prevent the affair." But "substantial men of the community" told him "there is no way of talking about preventing this thing, Frank: if Witherill is here he will be hanged. He would get a change of venue if allowed to go to trial, and in some other county would stand a chance of getting off. He is a continual menace to the lives of the citizens of this county and everywhere. He must be put out of the way." Raynolds concluded: "Cañon City has as many law-abiding citizens as any other place, but they recognized the fact that it was necessary this man was out of the way. He was not lynched to punish him, but to rid the world of him." Ouray's vigilance committee sent Cañon City's mayor congratulatory telegrams on Witherill's death, and the *Solid Muldoon* stoutly approved of the lynching, regretting only that Witherill had not been burned to death.[75]

A dozen years later even hotter anger boiled as Cañon City lynched Thomas Reynolds, a convict sentenced to seven years for burglary in 1895. On January 22, 1900, Reynolds and four other prisoners—including eighteen-year-old Antone Wood, sentenced for murder at age eleven—escaped after having killed guard William C. Rooney.[76] By disabling the power generator, the escapees darkened the prison, creating such havoc that town residents feared a mass breakout.[77] Within days the four were captured. Reynolds, apprehended on January 26 at Florence 10 miles southeast of Cañon City, asked one of his captors to shoot him rather than return him to the penitentiary.[78]

4.6 On December 4, 1888, a Cañon City mob lynched George Witherill for allegedly murdering Charles McCain. As the Denver Republican *reported on December 5, "hundreds of men, women, and children went to the scene to view the terrible, but significant sight." Courtesy, Denver Public Library, Western History Collection.*

As Reynolds and his guards entered Cañon City late in the evening of January 26, a mob grabbed him, took him to a telephone pole within sight of the penitentiary, hanged him for a while, then let him down and asked him to make a statement. He requested a cigarette. Hanging him again, some in the assemblage of 500 asked him "if he would be good now." He answered with a kick of his foot.[79] They left his corpse dangling into the morning hours, an "awful warning" to prisoners "not to try a similar escape."[80] Deeming it a "useless expense," the county coroner did not hold an inquiry into Reynolds's death. "It is more than probable that a more orderly mob never gathered any where in the country," said the *Cañon City Record.* "No violence to the guilty man, except the hanging, was permitted."[81]

Reynolds no doubt found it hard to "except the hanging," but compared with Alexander McCurdy, lynched in Golden on June 2, 1894, his treatment appeared gentle. By 1894, Golden, one of northern Colorado's oldest towns, could be described as staid. A quiet, substantial small town, home to the Colorado School of Mines and Jarvis Hall—an Episcopal boys' school modeled on the best schools in England—Golden had not hosted a lynching since the hangings of accused murderers Joseph Seminole and Samuel Woodruff in 1879. Two years later local doctors, thinking Woodruff's huge skeleton would make an impressive display piece, cast a shadow on the town's reputation by unsuccessfully trying to unearth his body.[82] In time the memory of lynchings and ghoulish capers faded as Golden settled into refined routines. Its children at their spelling bees, its women at their quilts, its men brewing beer and talking about the weather— it might have been mistaken for a peaceful New England village if one did not examine the veneer of its civilization too carefully.

That thin layer cracked in June 1894 when some Golden citizens concluded that the law was a weak ass for sentencing McCurdy to only three years for emasculating his stepbrother, who had engaged in "intimate" relations with McCurdy's wife. On June 2, 1894, at 2:00 A.M., twenty men overpowered the jailer at the Jefferson County jail, took McCurdy from his cell, muffled his screams with cloth bound around his head, and emasculated him. Then they hanged him from a railway bridge over Clear Creek, although he may have already bled to death.[83]

Charges of attempted child molestation brought similar punishment to H. F. Allen, a miner, in Montrose in early November

4.7 *The* Rocky Mountain News *on June 2, 1894, reported that Alexander McCurdy admitted "he had been a very wicked man." For his sins he was emasculated and hanged by a Golden mob. Picture generation courtesy Christopher Altvater.*

1904. Fifteen men forced two local doctors to castrate him. When District Judge Theron Field called on a grand jury to investigate, Allen disappeared. District Attorney Hugo Selig reported, "Every effort on the part of the state to find him [Allen] proved unavailing." Selig did not indicate that Allen was killed, but the mob that snatched him from the hospital where he was suffering from blood poisoning, an often fatal condition, may have made certain he would never be found.[84]

As to the death of Lars Leberg, the man who drank Henry Lanvermeyer's blood, there is no question. Leberg—a twenty-two-year-old tramp, formerly an inmate of the Utah state insane asylum—took offense when a farmer northwest of Las Animas refused to let Leberg sleep in his house, offering him instead the use of an outbuilding. He then tried to secure free lodging at Lanvermeyer's but was turned away. In retaliation Leberg torched a haystack. Lanvermeyer captured him and started toward Las Animas with him, planning to jail him there. En route, Leberg secured a hammer, beat Lanvermeyer, unsuccessfully tried to scalp him, slashed his throat, and drank his blood.

Leberg wandered on the prairie, was captured, and was taken to Las Animas. He explained his crime by saying he was an anarchist and that Lanvermeyer was a rich farmer who deserved to die. Told he might be lynched, Leberg reportedly replied: "Let them lynch me if they care to. They are cowards all, and have not the courage to do anything like that."[85]

It was a moment of misstatement that Leberg, albeit briefly, lived to regret. On December 26, 1906, the day of the murder, a mob stormed the jail in an unsuccessful attempt to get him. The next night a better organized group of fifty armed and masked men overpowered Sheriff John D. Brown and two of his deputies; aided by someone skilled at picking locks, they entered Leberg's cell. He went with them calmly to a telegraph pole near the railroad tracks 150 yards from the jail. There he was hanged. In an earlier era Coloradans would have left the body dangling as a lesson to potential evildoers. Those days were gone. Image-conscious citizens insisted that Leberg's corpse be cut down before daylight on December 28, not wanting "the ghastly sight to present itself to passengers on the incoming morning trains."[86]

In 1884 the *Rocky Mountain News* condemned the Cuddigan lynchings.[87] In 1906 it decried Leberg's hanging.[88] In neither case did condemnation bring punishment to the lynchers. Yet Coloradans had changed in the intervening years. Between 1880 and January 1884, the month of the Cuddigans' deaths, Judge Lynch killed thirty-seven, roughly nine a year. From 1884 to 1888 he took more than twenty lives. In the four years before Leberg's death, Colorado had witnessed only one lynching. For thirteen years after he dangled near the tracks in Las Animas, no other accused felon was illegally hanged in the state. By 1906 Judge Lynch was nearly dead, even as an avenger of heinous crimes. Killing him, as Chapter 5 will demonstrate, took his opponents far more time than he spent in taking the lives of Margaret and Michael Cuddigan, Wilbur French, James Howe, George Witherill, Alexander McCurdy, Thomas Reynolds, and Lars Leberg.

5

TUG-OF-WAR

Mob law is dangerous to the very existence of society
itself, and, when once put in motion, no one can tell when
and where it will stop. It is sometimes put into motion
by an honest desire to benefit society, but too often ends
in wanton destruction of life and property.
  —JUDGE MELVILLE GERRY, *SOLID MULDOON,*
                                            MAY 2, 1884

Almost from the moment Judge Lynch first set foot in the
Pikes Peak country, some people recognized that in dallying
with him they were courting a devil. In September 1859,
when Edgar Vanover was lynched for making threats in Golden, some
of that new town's leading citizens objected. After Denver's vigilance
committee killed A. C. Ford, it agonized over his missing gold watch
and scrambled to retrieve it. Coloradans boasted of their civilization in
1863 when they legally executed William Van Horn. Then for a score
of years they preferred lynching to legal executions. Lynching was
usually accounted too useful to be stopped: it eliminated outlaws, it
saved money, it frightened felons away, it helped extract confessions.
It had uses as entertainment, and the threat of it maintained a social, racial, and economic order that solid, white citizens treasured.

Yet proponents and opponents of lynching were always play-ing a game of tug-of-war. From the late 1850s to the mid-1880s the proponents usually won; after that the opponents commanded the field. As early as 1870, L. P. Griswold was prosecuted for lynch-ing James O'Neal near Denver. In 1875 territorial governor John L. Routt considered using federal troops to control vengeful vigilantes in Lake County. In 1880 Edward L. Johnson, U.S. attorney for Colo-rado, traveled more than 500 miles to keep prisoners out of Judge Lynch's hands. In 1891, Salida tried to convict several lynchers. In 1906 two Denver lynchers were sentenced to prison. In the mean-time, officials prevented many illegal hangings, demonstrating that in the land of Pikes Peak, lynching gradually lost the blank check of community acceptance it used to finance its lengthy tenure in the land of Dixie.

From the start, Judge Lynch faced public relations problems— one of the first involved a horse thief's missing gold watch. Per-plexed by a rash of thefts, in early September 1860 a Denver clique decided to kill several of the suspected thieves, including attorney A. C. Ford. Four men abducted Ford as he fled by stagecoach, took him into the prairie grass, and shot him. A few days later his corpse was found minus his gold watch. Seven months later an "unknown person" returned the watch to Ford's widow, Martha.

Forty years later historian Jerome Smiley cleared up much of the mystery of the missing watch. Smiley interviewed the last sur-vivor of the lynching party, a "gentle mannered pioneer" who said he and his associates had left Ford's watch with his body. The next day a man from Denver had left town. The vigilance committee surmised that he had learned of Ford's death, found his body, taken the watch, and fled. They traced him to El Paso, Texas, sent a man after him, and persuaded him to give up the watch.[1]

The vigilantes bore the burden of a 1,600-mile round-trip less out of concern for Ford's widow than out of their need to defend the propriety of Ford's lynching. By secretly killing him they set a dan-gerous precedent, one dishonorable men could use for dishonorable ends. The telltale watch pointed to greed rather than justice as the reason for Ford's death. His killers had to retrieve and return it so they could draw a distinction between their lynching—done, they said, for the public good—and ordinary murders committed by base people for base, watch-stealing motives. Shortly after Ford's death the *Rocky Mountain Herald* warned: "Every man has his right to be tried by a jury of his equals . . . in our proceedings against individuals, however criminal, it would be prudent and judicious not to depart from this principle . . . the violation which today destroys a stranger may tomorrow justify the destruction of ourselves."[2]

Those tomorrows crept in more rapidly and more frequently than Judge Lynch's partisans wanted. Some gold seekers had already narrowly avoided lynching an innocent man. In November 1859 John Pascoe, a miner on Chicago Creek, 35 miles west of Denver, was accused of stealing. A People's Court tried him and acquitted him. George T. Cox and J. C. Jones, victims of the theft, rejected the verdict and persuaded Justice of the Peace A. P. Smith to allow them to threaten Pascoe with hanging to force him to return the money. They promised not to hurt him.

Enjoying an elastic notion of what it meant not to hurt someone, Cox and Jones hanged Pascoe four times, letting him down before he strangled to death. He unwaveringly proclaimed his innocence and after one of his suspensions said, "If you hang me again, hang me dead, for my suffering is indescribable." Finally, his tormentors let him go. Justice of the Peace Smith found him a few hours later, crying, the skin scraped off his neck, unable even to swallow tea. Another witness saw blood oozing from Pascoe's mouth.

"I thought it my duty," said Smith, "to have the parties tried for such wretched cruelty."[3] A six-man jury condemned Cox and Jones and ordered them to pay Pascoe $250. Judge Lynch got his comeuppance. Sometimes tolerated as a community watchdog, he forfeited his mandate when he acted for private ends. The problem was drawing lines and making distinctions. What was to prevent a villain from masking his crime as a lynching?

That was apparently the situation in May 1866, when Bruce Hazlep's body was found hanging in Denver. His death seemed to be a lynching, but Denverites concluded he had been murdered with "an evident design on the part of the murderers to fix their crime upon the Vigilantes."[4] Two years later the *Rocky Mountain News* noted that two other men had been killed at the same time. "Why they were killed and who did it is as yet a mystery," said the paper, which suggested that the dead men were horse thieves who quarreled with others of their ilk.[5] At any rate, the three dead men gave proof to an observation the *News* had made a year earlier: "The necessity for mob law is to be deplored, because it is a means often used by designing men to remove those against whom they may have a personal antipathy. In almost every instance, where this law has existed, it has been thus used."[6]

Personal antipathy seemingly played a role in the death of James O'Neal, found hanged in July 1870 at Brown's Bridge, southwest of Denver. His body bore a message embellished with a drawing of a tree, a rope, a man, and a coffin. Signed "Vigilance Committee," it labeled O'Neal a "cattle thief" and warned Sam Morgan, O'Neal's father-in-law, and his "outfit" to "leave the country in ten days."[7] O'Neal had been arrested on Sunday, July 9, by L. P. Griswold, who had sworn out a warrant charging O'Neal with stealing stock. Early Monday morning Griswold and his partner came into Denver without O'Neal, who they said had been seized "by a large body of men at Brown's Bridge, and they supposed him to be hung."[8]

The story—cattle thief arrested, seized, hanged—was typical. But O'Neal's case was different. Medical evidence suggested he had been strangled before he was hanged. "All day Sunday," said the *News*, "men were seen lurking about Brown's bridge, in the bushes, and from all the facts there can be but little doubt the whole thing is a 'put up' affair, but whether the victim was justly or unjustly hung we cannot say."[9]

"Unjustly" said O'Neal's friends, who agreed with the caption on his tombstone that James O'Neal was "Murdered."[10] A few days after O'Neal's death, Griswold was arrested and charged with murder. He languished in jail for more than a year, one of his trials ironically ending in a hung jury. Then in February 1872 he was killed as he tried to escape.[11]

That crackdown on lynching was short-lived and, for the 1870s, so unusual that it was probably unique. Many Coloradans recognized the dangers of lynching; they simply lacked the will to kick the habit. Consider, for example, their failure to punish the murderers of Judge Elias Dyer.

Feuding factions, split between the friends and enemies of Elijah Gibbs, made Lake County in central Colorado a dangerous place during 1874 and 1875. Gibbs, a rancher accused of an 1874 murder, was given a change of venue and tried in Denver, where he was acquitted. His enemies, who had attempted to lynch him prior to his trial, still thought he was guilty. So they again tried to kill him by setting fire to his cabin, a plot that fizzled because the logs were wet. With a pregnant wife and three children, Gibbs decided to "vamose the ranche."[12] His friends, too, were marked men. In January 1875 the Committee of Safety told Charles Harding, a Gibbs supporter, to leave. He refused. On April 1, 1875, Harding and his dog, the dog's paw in Harding's hand, were found shot to death, evidently victims of the committee.[13] Also in early 1875, Jesse Marion was tortured by the committee, which hanged him three times in an attempt to get him to testify against Gibbs. Marion escaped with his life. The same year two men, stopped by the vigilance committee for questioning, were hanged in an attempt to get them to talk. The torture went too far. According to local lore, both men died.

Probate Judge Elias Dyer also angered the anti-Gibbs men, who accused him of pomposity, among other sins.[14] In July 1875, shortly after he issued warrants for the arrests of sixteen members of the Committee of Safety, he was shot dead in his courtroom in the hamlet of Granite. John Dyer, Elias's father, learned that "while [Elias] Dyer lay weltering in his blood, and in the death agony, John D. Coon, a ringleader of the mob, bent over him, exclaiming with mock concern, 'What a horrible murder!' "[15]

John Dyer, a prominent pioneer Methodist clergyman, demanded that his son's horrible murderers be punished. The newspapers were of two minds: some backed the Committee of Safety; others, such as Central City's *Register*, blamed Lake County sheriff John Weldon—"the sheriff is at the head of the mob."[16] Since local lawmen could not be trusted to enforce the law, the territorial governor, said the *Register*, should send in troops.

Halfheartedly agreeing, Governor Routt asked General William Tecumseh Sherman to dispatch "one company of cavalry under a discreet officer" to Lake County "so that their presence will intimidate the mob and prevent their escape." But, weaseled Routt, he did not want "to make a formal application for troops, as it might provoke a newspaper controversy throughout the country, which would be productive of no good to the territory."[17] Sherman—headquartered in St. Louis, far from the woes of central Colorado—ignored Routt's request, and the lynchers escaped questioning. The Dyer family removed Elias's body from the Granite cemetery and reburied it in Castle Rock south of Denver because John did not want his son interred in a county of murderers. "God's curse," said the old preacher, "was upon them all."[18]

God's curse may have descended on thousands of other lynchers, but man did little to punish them. After a lynching, authorities usually let hangings be bygones, recognizing that prosecuting lynchers would

REV. JOHN L. DYER.

5.1 John L. Dyer, well-known Methodist preacher, unsuccessfully tried to get the Territory of Colorado to prosecute the killers of his son, Judge Elias Dyer. Courtesy, Colorado Historical Society (F10984).

probably be futile and politically unwise. Had Routt openly summoned Sherman's soldiers, he would have alerted the rest of the nation that Lake County was in a state of anarchy at the very moment Colorado was claiming to be a civilized place worthy of admission to the Union. He was willing to trade rank injustice to a couple of ranchers and a dead judge for statehood.

John Dyer chastised Routt: "Governor, if you won't do anything to stop such a state of affairs, I am keen to tell you that I have no use for such a governor, and our country has much less use."[19] Most Coloradans disagreed. They still had use for Routt, making him their first state governor in 1876. In his first message to the legislature he proposed organizing a militia "to protect in case of Indian outbreak, to check mob violence, and to enforce the civil authority when resisted."[20] Perhaps in that mild effort to control Judge Lynch, Routt was glimpsing his own future because years later he was threatened with lynching in Creede.[21]

Routt's failure to punish vigilantes and mobs was typical. Time after time, coroners' juries concluded that the lynched had died at the hands of persons unknown, although often their identities were known. Commenting on the Cuddigan hangings in Ouray, one Denver newspaper sarcastically observed that Sheriff Charles Rawles "neither killed, injured, nor recognized" any of the vigilantes.[22] Seven years later, when Lee Quang was lynched in Ouray, the *Solid Muldoon* reported: "The victim was viewed by a jury Wednesday morning and the usual 'unknown' stereotyped verdict [was] rendered."[23] Asked whether he could identify any of the men who seized George Witherill from the Cañon City jail in December 1888, Sheriff Morgan L. Griffith responded: "No, the night was dark and the confusion great. I could not identify one."[24]

Night blindness also afflicted Larimer County sheriff Thomas R. Davy. He did not identify any of the 300 men—some without masks—who attacked the county jail on April 4, 1888, overpowered Davy and twenty guards, battered down the jail door, grabbed James H. Howe, and hanged him. More than a third of the town's adult males were probably in the mob. Yet the deed was done, said the coroner's jury, "by an infuriated and unknown mob."[25] All the witnesses except one who testified before the Lake County coroner's jury that investigated Judge Dyer's death said they could not identify any of his assailants. One man responded more truthfully, "I am afraid to answer the question for the safety of my life."[26]

Newspapers provided minute details of lynchings except for the names of the lynchers. When George Betts and James Browning were seized by a Lake City mob, the *Silver World* noted that Betts "asked for a chew of tobacco" and Browning "with the strength of a bull plunged into the midst of a flashing circle of revolvers."[27] Who held those revolvers the *Silver World* did not say. The *Fort Collins Courier* reported that it took Howe's lynchers fifteen minutes to break through the jail's iron doors, and the paper knew that a "score" of men pulled on the rope that "shot" Howe "up into the night air like a rocket."[28] Who launched that rocket the *Courier* did not reveal.

By the late 1870s the lynching routine was fairly fixed. Sheriffs opposed disguised vigilantes, who typically operated at night, over-powered guards, then seized and hanged the miscreant. Coroners' juries blamed "parties unknown," and local newspapers praised law-men for bravely resisting mobs whose work the papers sometimes condemned, sometimes approved or at least excused. Good sheriffs, good vigilantes—the ritual allowed them all to be seen as honorable men, each in his own way serving the community. The fact that the common deceit was fooling no one did not seem sufficient reason to abandon it, although Del Norte's *San Juan Prospector* once asked, "Why not tell the truth?"[29]

The answer was obvious. Telling the truth would have embar-rassed a goodly number of local people. It was in communities' interests to officially condemn lynching while unofficially approv-ing it. Openly sanctioning the practice would have frightened pro-spective settlers and investors. Doing something about it would have cost officials votes and towns money.

Tight-fisted town fathers, hesitant to dole out dimes for vital services such as fire departments, only begrudgingly found spare change to pay police and build jails. The professionalization of the police and perfection of the criminal justice system that took hold in parts of the East and Midwest and in California in the late nine-teenth century eventually spread to Colorado, but progress was slow and uneven.[30]

Denver, a city of 65,000 in 1887, made do with 43 policemen, far fewer per capita than New York or Philadelphia.[31] Leadville, a city of nearly 15,000 in 1880, employed 13 policemen during 1879, a year of mushroom growth. In 1880 Mayor William James or-dered officers to raid brothels to snare madams, prostitutes, and some of the city's leading businessmen, whose fines replenished the city's coffers.[32] Montrose, much smaller than Leadville, also hated spending on law enforcement. The *Montrose Messenger* estimated in 1886 that more than half the county's debt of $112,000 had been incurred bringing criminals to justice. The paper observed, "Had

THE FREE AND BOUNDLESS WEST.
A hard road for the honest emigrant to travel.

5.2 Stories about lynchings may have kept some prospective settlers from coming to Colorado, as this August 6, 1881, cartoon from Frank Leslie's Illustrated Newspaper *suggests. Nevertheless, the state's population more than doubled between 1880 and 1890. Courtesy, Clark Secrest and Christopher Altvater.*

---

we chopped off the murderous whelps long ago, what a fund we might have had to use in improving the county's highways."[33]

Denver, according to a story that smacks of legend with a kernel of truth, faced an expensive problem in the early 1860s when Jonathan Leaper refused to vacate the jail after prosecutors dropped charges against him. Leaper, "who took his meat raw, like a beast, and ate more in a day than a dog would in two," evidently enjoyed the free meals, so he vowed he would stay in jail or "burn it down." To get him to leave, the jailer told him a lynching party had been formed and that he had better escape while he could. Leaper fled, only to be shot by some soldiers who assumed he still belonged behind bars.[34]

Unwilling to spend money on adequate prisons, towns suffered numerous jailbreaks, leakage that fostered the cause of lynching. In 1862 thirty-six inmates in the rickety Denver jail rushed the door and forced their way out.[35] Lake City built a log jail in 1876, and that same year an accused murderer dug his way out of it.[36] When two prisoners wiggled through a hole they made in the wall of the Fort Collins jail in 1882, a newspaper correspondent excused them for leaving because "there could not be a much dirtier or filthier place than is the close and miserable pen called 'the cooler' or city jail."[37]

The news from one week in 1885 included jailbreaks in Boulder, La Junta, and Aspen. Three prisoners broke out of the Granite town jail in July 1880, thirteen from Buena Vista in early 1884, and fifteen from Denver in 1887.[38] Arrested for murder in Del Norte in 1881, J. H. Jackson "soon escaped from jail and from his place of concealment announced that he would appear at the proper time and answer; he did not wish to remain in jail until the sitting of the court."[39]

Some places temporarily fumbled along without regular jails. Denver had none until 1861, three years after it was founded. Granada lacked a jail in the early 1870s, so, as one pioneer remembered, "those who violated the law were told to get out. If they refused, they were generally shot, but very few refused the order."[40] Irwin, a mining camp west of Crested Butte, blossomed—as many camps did—into a large town almost overnight. Lacking a jail, it set up a vigilance committee. To show that Irwin was tough on crime, citizens threatened a petty thief with lynching in the summer of 1880 but let him go after he was briefly hanged.[41] Greeley waited half a decade to build a jail. When it did so in the mid-1870s, it rued the cost: "there seems to be no use for it. At one and a half percent a month the interest on the money would now be $180, which would buy Sunday school books to last a generation."[42] With capital so scarce that loans commanded 18 percent interest a year, it is little wonder that taxpayers hated to spend on police, jails, and trials.

Parsimony partially explains the poor state of law enforcement, but other factors—including the temptations to which officers were exposed—also ate away at the fabric of honest police work. Even U.S. marshals, poodles among society's guard dogs, sometimes strayed. Uriah B. Holloway, a marshal in the mid-1860s, was charged with passing counterfeit money obtained from a prisoner. Holloway's successor, Marcus A. Shaffenburg, billed the federal government for the upkeep of nonexistent prisoners. He resided at Shaffenburg Place, a mansion at Eighteenth and Curtis Streets in Denver, until 1877, when he traded his palace for the federal penitentiary in Leavenworth, Kansas.[43]

Lesser lawmen also wandered from righteous paths. Corrupt town officials in Tin Cup, northeast of Gunnison, instructed their police chief to appear to be upholding the law so "tenderfeet might be lured and fleeced."[44] Tin Cup marshals who took their duties seriously often took their leave quickly. Harry Rivers, marshal in 1882, was shot by a saloon keeper. Sam Micky lasted seven months, went insane, and wound up in an asylum where, suffering delusions of limited grandeur, he continued to insist he was still marshal of Tin Cup. Andy Jameson, Micky's successor, enjoyed a few months in office before being shot to death.[45] Such mayhem supposedly appealed to three Irish newcomers who decided to stay "because they liked the lawlessness of the community."[46]

Gunman Port Stockton swaggered as Animas City's marshal until he shot a barber who nicked Stockton while shaving him.[47] Bat Masterson's days as Trinidad's marshal were marred when one of his deputies killed the Las Animas County undersheriff. Telluride's marshal, Jim Clark, a high-altitude Jekyll and Hyde, prevented crime in town but in disguise committed crimes outside of town.[48] Charles Allison, once a Conejos County undersheriff, was later arrested by his boss, Sheriff Joe Smith, for stealing horses.[49]

Honest lawmen were sometimes no better when it came to opposing lynching because they sympathized with the vigilantes. Indeed, they themselves were sometimes vigilantes. In May 1882, when Sheriff John H. Bowman of Gunnison County—who had gone hunting outlaws—was reported dead, grieving citizens organized an elaborate memorial service that became a celebration when he turned up alive. Bowman's popularity did not suffer because of his harsh attitudes toward alleged criminals. When he informed townsfolk that he was still breathing, he told them "will bring no prisoners."

The message was clear, said the *Gunnison Daily Review,* "Judge Lynch will hold court, try, convict and execute the thieves—an action that will save the county a big bill of expense and will be heartily approved by the people of Gunnison county."[50]

Besides saving money, lynching appealed to those who believed the threat of quick hanging prevented crime. In June 1859, Denver's *Rocky Mountain News* warned, "There is a Vigilance Committee, of long standing, in existence here, which is pledged to lynch any man found engaged in giving or selling intoxicating liquor to the Indians, and thus endangering the safety of the settlers."[51] A dozen years later Denver no longer worried much about inebriated Indians, but it still feared outlaws, so vigilantes distributed a handbill picturing five coffins along with a warning to "murderers, thieves and robbers." The admonition worked. The *News* reported, "During the day a good many scalawags that were outside prison bars took time by the forelock and left for other parts. Railway travel was good, and Foot and Walker's line was extensively patronized."[52] Isabella Bird, an English traveler who spent part of 1873 in Colorado, reported that vigilance committees had been formed in Fairplay and Alma: "When men act outrageously and make themselves generally obnoxious they receive a letter with a drawing of a tree, a man hanging from it, and a coffin below, on which is written 'Forewarned.' They 'git' in a few hours."[53] Proof of Bird's observation came in September 1874 when Jack Reynolds, a "notorious character," was hanged by masked men in Alma "until he had just enough breath left to promise to leave town. He left instanter."[54]

Alamosa used similar tactics. After the lynchings of Charles Walrath and James Craft in 1879, a correspondent told the *Rocky Mountain News*: "The 'Committee' here are [*sic*] well organized and last night's proceedings show they can proceed quietly and secretly about their business, and that they are determined to uproot crimes, where the strong arm of the law is powerless."[55] The next year, when "roughs" from Buena Vista disturbed the peace of Alamosa, the town marshal "had a warning printed, hinting at a rope and a tree, and ordering them to leave town." Most of them "skipped out."[56] Another old Alamosa story has it that after a saloon keeper molested a woman, vigilantes hanged the man and posted a note near his body: "Alamosa pertecks her wimmen."[57]

Sometimes threats went beyond words. In early February 1873 several men salted ore near Georgetown to falsely increase its value.

'YOU CAN'T HANG ME BUT ONCE!'

5.3 The notion that "you can't hang me but once" was not true. Vigilantes sometimes tortured suspects by hanging them until they were nearly dead, then letting them down and hanging them again until they confessed. Courtesy, Colorado Historical Society (F6319).

Other miners, objecting to such crookedness, put ropes around two of the salters' necks. "After choking them until they were nearly dead the committee turned the rascals adrift with the strict injunction to 'dust.' And they 'dusted.'"[58] That same month, horse thieves in Larimer County, including "Happy Jack," were taken at gunpoint from the Fort Collins jail and hanged: "They were raised and lowered several times, being suspended by the neck several minutes or until they nearly strangled to death." The others were lowered, but "'Happy Jack' was left suspended in a most unhappy and unpleasant situation." Finally, the vigilantes relented and with effort revived him.[59]

Silver Cliff also scared away undesirables. Once described as "the worst place this side of brimstone and sulphur," the mining town southwest of Pueblo organized a vigilance committee that told the "very bad men" to leave. One who did not was "attached to the business end of a clothes line and fired up towards the blue canopy of heaven. . . . After being let down on trial so to speak, he concluded that walking was only too good for him and took his departure." The result, said the *Rocky Mountain News,* was salutary: "To-day a more orderly city is not to be found east of the Rockies."[60]

A dose of hemp, some thought, served another laudable purpose. Suspects could be threatened with hanging or be hanged and let down before they died, inducing them to confess. A fifteen-year-old boy in Black Hawk, accused of stealing thirty-eight dollars from a butcher, would not admit to the crime. So men took him to a mill, put a noose around his neck, "threw the other end over a beam and commenced to hoist. The boy never squeaked. Once, twice, three times, they raised him off his feet." He refused to confess. "Hang [me] and be d—d," he told them. "All I want you to do is to tell my mother that I was innocent." Again and again they hanged him "until he was black in the face and it took ten minutes to bring him to consciousness." Still he protested his innocence. Finally, facing hanging for the sixth time, the bad boy confessed and was taken to jail.[61]

Like the men of Black Hawk, Mrs. Ekard, keeper of an Animas Forks boardinghouse in southwestern Colorado, probably thought highly of Judge Lynch's persuasive ability. One of her boarders left without paying his bill. Other boarders found him in Silverton. They told him, "You've got to come back and pay your board or give us the money, or we'll hang you." Mrs. Ekard got her money.[62]

African, Chinese, Italian, and Mexican Americans had special reason to fear Judge Lynch, as will be demonstrated in Chapter 6. Labor leaders and those who supported workingmen harbored similar fears. Joseph R. Buchanan, a labor organizer, learned of a plot to lynch him in Denver in 1885. He hired bodyguards, secluded himself for weeks, and paid detective David J. Cook $500 to ferret out the would-be lynchers whose names Buchanan threatened to publish. He advised them "they were proposing a game at which others could play as well as themselves."[63]

Perhaps the mutual realization by management and labor that lynching was a deadly game either side could play prevented its full-blown use in labor disputes. In Idaho Springs, retired merchant W. P. McCormick admonished the antilabor Citizen's Alliance: "When a mob once gets started there is no telling where it will end. I have seen mobs in the South and I know what they come to."[64] The alliance listened to McCormick and decided to banish fourteen strikers rather than lynch them. During Colorado's bloody labor wars union men were killed, kidnapped, and deported; scabs were shot and killed; strikers and their wives and children were killed; a mine manager was assassinated. But neither management nor labor resorted to lynching. Had mine owners done so, they would have made martyrs of union men and risked bad publicity. Had union men done so, they would have courted prosecution and forfeited their hopes of swaying public opinion.

Although capitalists stopped short of lynching, the threat of it remained a useful means of intimidation. Near midnight on June 23, 1894, masked men kidnapped Thomas J. Tarsney—the adjutant general of the State Militia—tarred and feathered him, and left him wandering outside Colorado Springs. They forbore killing him for his sin of siding with labor, but they warned him that he faced death if he returned.[65] In 1904, Victor mine owners pressured Henry Robertson, Teller County's prolabor sheriff, to resign by showing him a coiled rope and telling him that if he did not vacate his office, they would turn him over to a mob to be hanged.[66]

Prized for his usefulness, Judge Lynch was also valued as an entertainer and a teacher. Some lynchings, particularly as practiced by People's Courts, were staged—like medieval morality plays—to teach lessons. Condemned men such as James Gordon were provided with religious counsel and given an opportunity to publicly repent of their evil ways while cautioning others against lives of crime. After Golden vigilantes hanged Joseph F. Seminole and Samuel Woodruff for murdering R. B. Hayward in 1879, the masked men rode to Hayward's widow's home, "each man discharging his revolver in the air and shouting solemnly and loudly, as if in one voice: 'Hayward is avenged.'"[67]

The lesson-teaching aspects of lynching made it attractive to at least some clergymen. George Darley, a Presbyterian minister, admitted that lynching was wrong on "general principles" because it constituted "a breaking of the law," set a "bad example to the rising generation," and gave "an excuse to bad men to take the law into their own hands." But Darley was willing to jettison general principles when it came to special cases such as the 1882 lynchings of George Betts and James Browning in Lake City. Darley explained, "Every man who has seen much of frontier life, will, I think agree with me when I say that hanging is the only thing that will make some men quit their cussedness."[68]

Parson Thomas Uzzell, a Methodist, agreed with Darley. A few hours before the 1879 lynchings of Ed Frodsham and Patrick Stewart in Leadville, one of Uzzell's parishioners asked the parson if he "thought it was wrong to engage in a lynching bee." Uzzell reflected on the town's wildness and lawlessness: "I told him that under the circumstances a lynching might be productive of some good."[69]

Lynchings such as those of Betts and Browning and Frodsham and Stewart, witnessed by large numbers of people, often appealed at least as much to the morbid curiosity, hunger for excitement, and sadism of crowds as they did to the mob's moral instincts. On learning that Frodsham and Stewart were about to be lynched, actor Eddie Foy rushed to the hanging. Nearly half a century later he confessed: "I was thrilled with curiosity to see such a mob in action. . . . I hurried out with the thoughtlessness of youth and ran down the street until I saw the crowd coming. There seemed to be no objection to my joining them, and when they rushed into a large empty warehouse or storeroom, I was swept along with them."[70]

Foy attributed his involvement in the lynchings to "idiotic things [done] in youth." How the lynchers of George Witherill, who cut off his head and put his mustache on display in a Cañon City hotel, explained their actions to themselves is a rationalization lost to history, as are the thought processes of the men who emasculated Alexander McCurdy. Were they, in the economic hard times of the mid-1890s, somehow reacting against their own failures to support themselves and their families? Although Judge Lynch was certainly sadistic enough in those instances, he reserved many of his cruelest barbarisms for the ghoulish pleasure of those participating in some of the racial lynchings detailed in Chapter 6.

People who did not attend lynchings could read graphic accounts in the newspapers. Golden's *Colorado Transcript* let its readers know that before he was hanged, Charles Woodruff maintained a "stolid silence" but that his partner, Joseph F. Seminole, screamed. Readers of the Leadville *Evening Chronicle* got a blow-by-blow description of the abduction of Frodsham and Stewart from the Leadville jail, including the tidbit that Frodsham tried to escape by climbing on top of one of the cells.[71]

Occasionally, newspapers relived the golden days of yesteryear by telling of the People's Courts or reprising other lynchings of the

1860s.[72] Enterprising journalists sometimes peddled tall tales as fact. Such, for example, was the sad saga of "A Woman in Man's Dress" who tried to save her outlaw husband by telling vigilantes she was the culprit. Her noble husband, however, would not allow the sacrifice and told the avengers that the young "man" was "my wife." He was lynched; she was spared. Unfortunately, the *Rocky Mountain News* gives no names, dates, or place; and its florid language smacks of the nucleus of a dime novel.[73]

Even more far-fetched is the spectral tale of the supposed lynching of two men, Langlode and Fillmore, in Empire in 1862. According to a *Rocky Mountain News* story that appeared more than twenty years after the bogus event, Langlode and Fillmore murdered Casper Borgell, intending to blame another man and have him lynched. Casper's ghost took umbrage and warned the innocent man, who in a "who lives by the rope, dies by the rope" twist engineered the lynching of Langlode and Fillmore.[74]

Dime novelists provided their own complement of fictional Colorado lynchings. Sometimes they sided with the vigilantes, as when the town doctor in Juanapolis led citizens in an attempt to kill Desmond the Desparado [*sic*]. Desmond instead was exterminated by an idiot boy before the avengers could act.[75] Colorado Carl, on the other hand, was a good guy, even though he had a "gang" that fought "against the wrong." A group of "vigilants" tried to capture him, but he escaped.[76]

Deadwood Dick Jr., a hero of many dime novels, found Durango an unsavory place, populated by "the true 'border ruffian' and gamblers, thieves and bummers." Nor was its sheriff a nice man. When he and his posse arrived at the ranch of suspected cattle thief Calamity Jane Jr., they found she was not at home. So they decided to lynch her aged, invalid father. "If we keep him here after the girl swings," the sheriff said, "he will be a burden on this glorious community."[77]

Lynching was so popular in many "glorious communities" that antilynchers found it difficult to stop the practice. Those who succeeded sometimes did so by talk, sometimes by trickery, sometimes by travel, sometimes by force. Rarely, Arnold Howard's escape from a Del Norte mob in 1882 a notable exception, did jailed prisoners save themselves. George Witherill's club proved no match for his abductors' guns.[78] L. H. Musgrove flayed away at Denver vigilantes with a pine knot until shots fired over his head subdued him.[79] Bill Hogue, on the other hand, had several advantages when he confronted

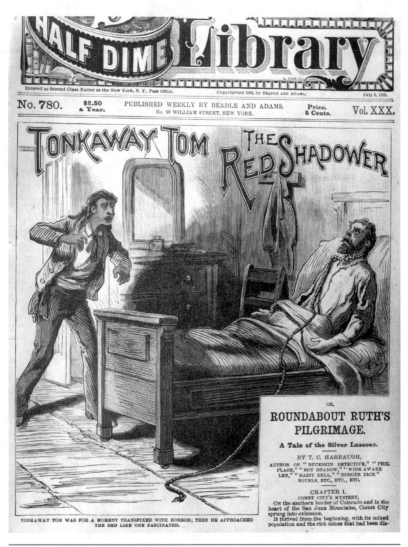

5.4 Dime novels sensationalized an already sensational West by playing up lynchings. Courtesy, Denver Public Library, Western History Collection.

men armed with a rope, intent on hanging him for shooting their friend Thomas Coyne near Creede in June 1892. When they found Hogue, who had not been jailed, he "was armed to the teeth." With his shotgun he clubbed several of his attackers and "held the crowd at bay with a revolver in each hand until he made good his escape."[80]

More commonly, the about-to-die quietly submitted, realizing that resistance would only compound their suffering. Robert Schamle, hanged in a hog pen in Georgetown in late 1877, evidently passively accepted his doom, recorded in a macabre piece of verse, "The Lay of the Vigilantes":

No useless stogas encased his feet
And we saw, as we carefully bound him,
That he stood like a coward, dreading to meet
The shades of his victims around him.[81]

James Howe, the Fort Collins wife murderer, also went meekly to his hanging, "shrinking and terrified with fear and crying for mercy."[82]

On rare occasion friends rescued the doomed. Someone bribed William T. Hadley's guards to allow him to escape from the death sentence imposed by the Denver People's Court in 1860.[83] In 1861 W. W. Clifton avoided hanging in South Park when a man claiming to be a deputy U.S. marshal took charge of Clifton and later let him go.[84]

Escaping before being jailed gave suspects a chance to avoid Judge Lynch. Sometimes the leave-taking was orderly, a word to the wise being sufficient. Dr. C. A. Washington quickly quit La Veta when his wife beating so offended the community that he was told "he must either leave the town forthwith or submit to Judge Lynch['s] adjudication."[85] Years later the evil doctor, reputed to have murdered his own child and a sick girl whom he violated, was lynched in New Mexico. Helmuth Loescher needed no prompting to leave Denver in August 1895, after his reputed failure to tend the boiler at the Gumry Hotel led to a massive explosion that killed twenty-two. Fearing lynching, he speedily fled.[86]

Kindness or at least a modicum of moderation saved a few felons. In Empire an angel of mercy agreed to reimburse the owner of stolen property. Spared from hanging, the thief got forty lashes, and the left side of his beard and mustache as well as the right side of his head was shaved. Then he was ridden out of town on a rail.[87] Moderation of sorts also prevailed at Iowa Gulch near Leadville where tenderhearted men saved a thief from hotheads by opting to give him fifty lashes rather than hang him.[88] Miners in Cañon City, so the questionable story goes, abandoned their plans to lynch a man when a mailman intervened. He did so, he explained, because he had a letter for the condemned man.[89] In late 1879 a persuasive deputy sheriff in Leadville convinced vigilantes, who were torturing an accused murderer by hanging him, to allow the law to take its course. The prisoner, said the *Rocky Mountain News*, "was conducted back to the city jail badly frightened and shook up but none the worse for the visit of the vigilantes."[90]

Common sense helped save a delegation of Ute leaders, including Chief Ouray and his wife, Chipeta, passing through Pueblo on their way to Washington, D.C., in January 1880. A mob of 2,000, itching to avenge the massacre by Utes of Indian Agent Nathan Meeker and others, surrounded the Indians as they changed trains. One man kicked each Ute, some pulled the Indians' hats over their eyes, others pelted them with coal. The crowd yelled, "shoot the murderers, hang the fiends, lynch the red devils." The *Colorado Chieftain* estimated that 500 men armed with revolvers were in the mob; others had shotguns and rifles. Only 10 soldiers protected the Utes: "Had any bad break been made, the soldiers would have been powerless to protect the savages from the fury of an outraged people." Moderate men saved the Utes by telling the crowd that the traveling Indians were not Meeker's murderers. Peacemakers warned that if Pueblo vigilantes killed Utes, then Utes in western Colorado would kill whites.[91]

Talk also benefited an accused horse thief in "eminent [*sic*] danger of being hung" in the mountain town of Frisco when the horse's owner pleaded for the felon's life.[92] Governor John Routt used logic to save himself from an angry assemblage in Creede. Upset about contested land titles, they blustered about lynching him. "Guess you fellows could hang me all right," he told them, "but you would be committing murder and would not get your lots after all."[93]

Often, more than civil discourse was needed. Trickery worked in 1890 when Mark Powers, jailed in Montrose for murder, faced the wrath of men from Delta. District Judge John Bell protected Powers with twenty deputies. While the Delta delegation enjoyed a few prehanging drinks at the Belvedere Hotel, Bell's forces squeezed Powers through a small hole cut in the jail's rear wall, out of sight of the inattentive and inebriated mob. Bell rushed Powers to nearby Fort Crawford. Later he was legally tried before Judge Bell, who ordered him to hang—a sentence eventually set aside.[94]

Charles Allison and members of his horse-thieving gang also owed thanks to wily lawmen. Vigilantes in Alamosa planned to take

Allison and his henchmen out of town on a train and lynch them. Detective Frank A. Hyatt reached the train first and raced away with his prisoners.[95] Later, when Allison had to be returned to Conejos County, Sheriff Joe Smith outfoxed vigilantes by putting dummies in the mail car of the train supposedly transporting Allison. Charles T. Linton, a Denver undersheriff, recalled: "Sure enough, when we arrived at La Veta a crowd was waiting and, as the train stopped, made a break for the mail car and the sheriff had the laugh on them."[96]

Removing prisoners from harm's reach was one of the most effective and most commonly used ways to prevent lynchings. Officers in La Veta sent George McCrum, accused of raping a twelve-year-old girl, to Walsenburg by train. George made it, but his brother, J. D. "Dell" McCrum, charged with the same crime, did not. He was removed from La Veta later in the day by wagon, which made him an easy target for vigilantes who seized him and hanged him from a tree.[97] In 1883 Coony Trethers, a "California Mexican" suspected of murder, was sent from Greeley to Fort Collins to thwart Greeley avengers.[98] On learning that Alfred Packer's first-degree murder conviction had been set aside because of legislative bungling, the *Leadville Democrat* demanded informal justice: "If the Hinsdale County people don't hang the cannibal and two or three members of the legislature they're no good." Lake City wisely packed Packer off to Gunnison.[99] In 1894, when Levi J. Streeter, a shoemaker in Como, murdered Marshal A. E. Cook, authorities whisked Streeter away to Fairplay.[100]

"Whisk" could not describe the arduous journey undertaken by U.S. Attorney Edward L. Johnson in October 1880 to save Indian Agent William Berry and others from angry citizens in south-central Colorado. Johnson's saga had its genesis in late September 1880 when Andrew D. Jackson, a freighter, killed Johnson Shavano, son of Shavano, a Ute chief. The Utes threatened war if Jackson were not punished. As he was being taken to Gunnison, Indians and whites seized him. Soon after, Utes killed him.

Many people in that part of the state approved of whites lynching whites, but they vehemently objected to Utes doing so. Blaming Berry, who was viewed as soft on Indians, and his comrades for failing to protect Jackson, they demanded that the men be turned over to local authorities. Berry and his comrades preferred to place themselves in the hands of Johnson, who promised "to ensure their safety from any mob, which might seek to lynch them." For Johnson, providing safety meant taking his prisoners and a witness from the Los Pinos Indian Agency to Denver, "where no mob was to be feared," by a route calculated to avoid vigilantes.[101]

Shepherded by a "Mexican" guide and later by a Ute, Johnson's party spent a week on horseback negotiating rough trails to reach White River in northwestern Colorado. A few days later they boarded a Union Pacific train at Rawlings, Wyoming, and sped east and south to Denver to complete a trip of more than 500 miles. Arriving late in the evening of October 31, Johnson learned he could not jail his prisoners because "their presence might provoke some violence."[102] Earlier that day, in the city "where no mob was to be feared," a mob had lynched a Chinese man and destroyed practically all of the Chinese businesses. Fortunately for Johnson, who had little stomach left for travel, the lynching frenzy soon faded.[103] The charges against Berry were eventually dropped, a happier ending for him than would have been the case had he been jailed in Gunnison where a vigilance committee had been organized to hang him.

Determined, organized vigilantes often broke into jails, overpowered jailers, and snatched prisoners. Poorly organized mobs fared less well. The 120 cowboys who attacked the Del Norte jail to get Arnold Howard were a disorganized lot, which largely explains his escape.[104] Before Frodsham and Stewart were hanged in Leadville, an impromptu assemblage was unable to get hold of Stewart.[105] A crowd "threatening vengeance" followed officers taking James Howe to jail in Fort Collins, but it was not until late at night that a more carefully orchestrated group actually took vengeance.[106] The first mob that tried to take George Witherill from Cañon City's sheriff Griffith was "bluffed off." Later, "real organized lynchers" succeeded.[107] Soon after Lars Leberg was arrested, a "disorderly leaderless mob" failed to take him from the Las Animas jail. The next night "a thoroughly disciplined body of men under a leader whose commands were obeyed with alacrity" easily overawed Sheriff John D. Brown and other guards.[108]

W. Fitzhugh Brundage, in *Lynching in the New South: Georgia and Virginia, 1880–1930*, divides mobs into four categories "based on size, organization, motivation, and the extent of the ritual." "Small mobs, numbering fewer than fifty participants," says Brundage, "may be separated into two types. They were either terrorist mobs that made no pretense of upholding the law or private mobs that exacted vengeance for a wide variety of alleged offenses." Brundage categorizes a third type of mob as "posses . . . which ranged in size from a few to hundreds of participants." Fourth, there were "mass mobs, numbering from more than fifty to hundreds and even thousands of members, [that] punished alleged criminals with extraordinary ferocity and, on occasion, great ceremony."[109]

With some modifications, Brundage's categories describe Colorado mobs. Small mobs, often referred to as vigilantes, were common, most in the period before the late 1880s, composed of at least some solid citizens intent on punishing crime. Some of the vigilance committees were probably permanent or semipermanent organizations; others were temporary, made up perhaps of members of fraternal organizations. Few were of the terrorist type such as plagued Lake County in the mid-1870s. Lynchings were sometimes witnessed by hundreds, even thousands, but a core group was usually responsible for taking the accused from jail.

Mass mobs, except the large assemblages that watched People's Court executions, were uncommon before the late 1880s, but there were exceptions. Around 2,000 people reportedly aided in the 1880 hanging of Charles Norton in the mountain town of Recen City after Norton had been taken from jail by a smaller group in nearby Kokomo. The killers of Look Young in Denver in 1880 were part of a mass attack on the Chinese that presaged such brutal cast-of-thousands lynchings as those of Italian American Daniel Arata in Denver in 1893 and of African American Calvin Kimblern in Pueblo in 1900, both racially charged hangings treated in Chapter 6.

Organization counted more than size in making lynch mobs successful. Unsurprisingly, posses were among the most effective lynching groups. With no one but the accused to oppose it, a posse dedicated to saving taxpayers'—including its members'—money could easily arrange the death of its prey. The number of hunted men who may have been killed by Colorado posses is impossible to determine. Citizens sworn to uphold the law were not always inclined to trumpet their deviations from that law.

Newspaper reports strongly suggest that some posses had no intention of bringing their prisoners back. After William C. Dubois killed Ed Kinney near Burlington in 1870, Golden's *Colorado Tribune* editorialized: "Our advice is to organize a party for pursuit, and follow the desperado until caught. Then hang him to the nearest tree."[110] That did not happen; the posse shot Dubois instead of hanging him.[111] That same year two "Mexicans" in custody for murder were "taken to Iron Springs and shot."[112] A decade later Jack Roberts was captured and hanged by a Durango posse.[113] H. L. Jeffries, suspected of wife beating, died in a September 1883 shoot-out in Ouray County, preferring that to "being lynched, whipped at the post, or dosed with tar and feathers."[114] As late as 1908, John Bradley, accused of murdering a Denver patrolman, almost became a "posse" victim when police beat him and threatened him with lynching.[115]

Just as the degree of organization among vigilantes increased the probability of a lynching, the degree of resistance to lynching reduced its likelihood. Leadville lawmen put on a show of force in July 1880, posting guards around the county jail, on its roof, and in its corridors to prevent the lynching of Charles Bakewell, accused of mortally wounding a police officer. Bakewell survived.[116] So did Charles Hough, a cattle thief, who was seized by stockmen at Argo Park north of Denver. They had a rope around his neck and were about to hang him when Denver detective James Connor "brought his revolver to bear on the line of the men at the rope." Remarking "'now by God, you had better not,' he looked very much like shooting." Not liking that possibility, the cattlemen left.[117]

More than twenty years later another courageous Denver lawman, John F. Ritchie, faced a crowd of hundreds intent on hanging Albert H. Flood, accused of murder. Ritchie gave his revolver to a trusted friend who guarded Flood. Then, armed with his club, Ritchie waded into the mob to brain anyone who cried "let's hang him." Depriving the rabble of its rousers, Ritchie kept Flood alive.[118]

Preventing lynchings by removing or protecting prisoners saved scores of lives. Prosecution of lynchers after they had killed could not bring the dead to life, but it could deter other lynchers. Authorities usually did not reckon the lesson was worth the economic or political price. Sheriffs and district attorneys, after all, counted vigilantes among their constituents.

Tracing the prosecution of lynchers is even more difficult for the historian than determining the initial fact of a lynching, probably because there were few prosecutions. Most local histories, although they often mention lynchings, say nothing about apprehension of lynchers. Denver newspapers did chronicle the effort to make L. P. Griswold pay for killing James O'Neal in 1870. If one considers Griswold's death while trying to escape a form of just retribution, he was perhaps the only lyncher in Colorado to have been heavily penalized. After Look Young, a Chinese man accused of no crime, was lynched in 1880, Denver prosecuted several men and convicted none.[119] Despite the promptings of Judge Melville Gerry, Ouray did nothing to the Cuddigans' killers. Golden, it seems, was unable to punish those who emasculated and hanged Alexander McCurdy, a bloodletting condemned not so much because McCurdy had been killed but because "the mutilation has shocked the most indifferent."[120]

Salida, too, was shocked by what appeared to some an uncalled-for and overly brutal lynching. In February 1891, Oliver Briley, a nineteen-year-old laborer in the yards of the Denver and Rio Grande Railroad, shot and killed Pat Sullivan, another railroad employee, after Sullivan bashed Briley with a board. Briley was imprisoned in a vacant building that served as the town's makeshift jail. Chained to the floor, he was guarded by ten men who successfully beat back the first attempt of a mob to seize him. On its second try, the mob got Briley. Unable to remove his chains, his abductors shot him, contemplated chopping off his legs, then broke the floor with a sledge-hammer so they could drag him out, chains and all. Again and again they shot him, and twice they hanged him. When he was finally dead, his brother asked for his corpse. A mob member responded, "Here's his brother, let's hang him on the other side." A man who objected to the brutality was warned, "dry up, you G— D— fool, or I'll blow your head off."[121]

Salida bemoaned the rotten press it endured after Briley's death, a "terrible tragedy that has brought our fair city into disgrace."[122] To remove the taint, a grand jury indicted John J. McIvor for his part in the lynching. Convicted of voluntary manslaughter, he appealed, was retried, and was freed. Others accused of the lynching also escaped punishment.[123]

When McIvor was initially judged guilty, the *Salida Mail* speculated that he was the first person convicted of lynching in Colorado, a guess that was probably true. By 1906, when two men were sentenced for their part in the mob killing of a Jewish laborer in Denver, it was clear at last that lynchers risked going to jail.[124] By then lynching was almost dead anyway. Getting rid of it depended far more on a change in attitudes, on resourceful and brave lawmen, than on rare convictions of lynchers.

It was a transformation well under way by the time of Briley's lynching. The fact that Salida vigorously prosecuted its killers suggests that by the early 1890s, Judge Lynch was running out of rope. After Briley's hanging, sixteen more men were lynched in Colorado, most belonging to ethnic groups—African Americans, Italian Americans, and Mexican Americans—easily targeted by lynchers. Race, the leading motif of lynching in the South and, because of the large number of southern lynchings, the major theme in U.S. lynching, became Judge Lynch's last excuse to murder in Colorado.

6

RACE AND LYNCHING

Yesterday's burning at the stake of a negro murderer
in Colorado was attended by circumstances of deliber-
ate ferocity, which make it the most fiendish thing of its
kind ever known in a Northern states [*sic*] . . . it will be
long before a Northern newspaper or politician can again
reproach the South for wrongs to negroes.
—*New York Evening Post*
QUOTED IN THE *Rocky Mountain News*,
NOVEMBER 18, 1900

A t 6:23 P.M. on Friday, November 16, 1900, rancher Robert
W. Frost touched a match to kerosene-soaked lumber piled
at the feet of John Preston Porter Jr., a sixteen-year-old African American accused of raping and murdering Louise Frost,
Robert's twelve-year-old daughter, near Limon, Colorado.[1] Frost,
whose fellow vigilantes had given him the right to name Porter's
torture, said, "I've touched the first match; now boys, you do the
rest."[2]

The fire did the rest. "Wait a minute men. I got something mo'
to tell you," Porter pleaded as the heat rose around him. Soon the
flames burned away the rope that bound his hands to the upright
iron rail to which he was both chained and tied. Slipping one arm
out of its chain, he raised his arms and cried, "Why should I suffer

THE BURNING OF PRESTON PORTER, JR., AT LAKE STATION, COLO.
Sketched by a Times Artist at the Scene of the Ordeal.

6.1 John Preston Porter Jr.'s screams could be heard a mile away when he was burned at the stake at Lake Station near Limon, as depicted in this November 17, 1900, Denver Times *illustration. Picture generation, courtesy Christopher Altvater.*

this?" He asked God to forgive the mob, praying "O Lord have mercy" several times, and told a reporter to tell "papa that I have gone to heaven." Once, when he slipped out of the fire, he begged to be pushed back so he could die quickly. Instead, onlookers heaped wood on his head. He tried to blow the sparks away. "The great crowd," said the *Denver Times,* "shook with pure enjoyment of the situation."[3]

After twelve minutes his moaning ceased and he was presumed dead, although the pyre was kept burning all night, reducing his 105-pound body to charred bones and ash. The iron rail, positioned near the site of Louise Frost's murder, about a mile and a half southeast of Limon, was left standing. The *Rocky Mountain News* proclaimed, "It was there for a purpose that night and it will remain there to answer another purpose, to be a warning."[4]

With more persistence than that stake, the story of Porter's death has remained in Colorado's history, a potent yet largely ignored reminder of the combined power of racism and vigilantism.[5] In less than half a century the 1859 People's Court had devolved into a mob shaking with pure enjoyment as they roasted a human being.

"After 1865," historian Richard Slotkin noted, "vigilantism acquired broader significance as a means of justifying new forms of social violence directed against the 'dangerous classes' of the post-Frontier, urban, and industrial order. As a result, the vigilante ideology itself was transformed from an assertion of a natural and democratic right-to-violence to an assertion of class and racial privilege."[6] Drawing a distinction between the vigilance committees of the Gold Rush days, whose actions were "easily defensible on many good grounds," and the Lincoln County mob, the *New York Times* concluded that Porter's killers were "rebels against civilization, not its forerunners and their deed was without the shadow of justification, even that of mad rage."[7]

Colorado newspapers, true to their notions of white racial superiority, saw it differently. Porter, said the *Rocky Mountain News*, was so calm when he was taken from the train near Limon, so accommodating when his tormentors bound him to the rail, so stoic until the flames began blistering him, that he was obviously "not endowed with human feelings, not human, but animal."[8]

Before Porter was killed, Boulder's *Daily Camera* registered its objection to lynch law, but added that in his case "we relent and almost we consent."[9] After his death the *Camera* pointed to the many allegations of Negroes assaulting whites in the South: "Everyone knows it is in the Negro blood and can only be eliminated, if ever, by the moderating tendencies of climate and society for centuries."[10] Some papers criticized the Lincoln County lynchers for exceeding civilized norms by burning Porter at the stake; others approved of any means the vigilantes cared to use. Many shifted the blame from the lynchers to Colorado lawmakers who had abolished capital punishment a few years earlier. The *Denver Times* faulted "hysterical women" who opposed the death penalty.[11]

"So far Judge Lynch in Colorado has been able to distinguish between the innocent and the guilty. We have no guarantee that this will always be the case," editorialized the *Colorado Springs Gazette* without questioning the circumstantial evidence that led to Porter's arrest or his four days "withstanding the pressure of the 'sweat box'" in the Denver jail, after which—threatened with the lynchings of himself, his father, and his brother—he "broke down and confessed."[12] The fact that he apparently knew the location of Louise Frost's coin purse seemed to implicate him, but the assertion never bore the scrutiny of examination in court because Porter never made it to court.

6.2 *Alva Adams, Colorado's governor from 1897 to 1899, supported repeal of capital punishment laws. Some people blamed the lynchings of Porter and others in 1900 on the state's inability to impose the death penalty. In 1901 the General Assembly restored capital punishment. Courtesy, Colorado Historical Society (F640).*

African Americans in Colorado Springs protested the barbarism in a letter signed by Frank J. Loper, once a slave of Jefferson Davis, president of the Confederate States.[13] In New York, Coloradans were accused of acting as badly as southerners and worse than Indians. Theodore Roosevelt, then New York's governor, declared, "There cannot be the slightest justification for punishing one fiendish crime with another fiendish crime."[14] In Chicago, Methodist ministers asked President William McKinley to investigate the outrage.[15] In Denver, religious leaders called a mass meeting to condemn the mob.

These and other protests did not move Colorado's Georgia-born governor Charles S. Thomas, whose southern roots and grasp of practical politics apparently overrode his commitment to the law.[16] Before the lynching he had failed to protect Porter. After the immolation Thomas reminded Lincoln County sheriff John W. Freeman of his duty to investigate the killing, but the sheriff refused to do so.[17] In word and deed, Freeman certified that lynching still held sway in Colorado as long as Judge Lynch could claim to be doing the work of red-blooded white Americans. "The white people of Colorado," said the *Pueblo Sunday Opinion*, "are fully determined to protect their women and children, and unless the negroes take a tumble in time there will be a wholesale cleaning out."[18]

Maintaining racial dominance meant much to many white people. Preserving that mastery spawned a multitude of sins, including thousands of racially motivated lynchings—most in the South and fewer in places such as Colorado where African Americans were joined by Mexican Americans, Italian Americans, and Chinese Americans in bearing the pain of lynching laced with racism. Given the biases of many Coloradans, it was no accident that before Porter was arrested three "Mexicans," one Native American, and another African American were suspected of killing Louise Frost.[19]

Colorado's people, like those in the rest of the nation, were a mixed lot. Before the 1859 Gold Rush thousands of indigenous people—Utes, Apache, Comanche, Kiowa, Pawnee, Cheyenne, Arapaho, among others—hunted in what would become Colorado. In the first half of the nineteenth century a scattering of non-Indian trappers and traders lived in the region: some, such as William Bent, were scions of old New England families; others, such as Mariano Medina, were representatives of the equally venerable Hispanic families of New Mexico.[20] By the early 1850s the traders had been joined by a few Hispanic settlers in northern New Mexico Territory, land that became part of Colorado Territory in 1861.

That small population was overwhelmed by the human tide that swept into the Pikes Peak country during the Gold Rush. Most of the newcomers, hailing from the North and Midwest, were native-born whites, with about 8 percent foreign-born, mainly from northern Europe. Free blacks numbered only 46 in the 1860 population of 34,277.

Colorado grew slowly in the 1860s to an 1870 population a little shy of 40,000 people. The foreign-born stood at 16.5 percent in 1870, rose to 20.4 percent in 1880, and fell back to 16.9 percent in 1900. Initially, the Germans, Irish, and English were among the most important foreign groups. Later, increasing numbers of Italians and other Southern and Eastern Europeans flowed into the migration stream. The Chinese, numerically insignificant in 1870, saw their population peak in 1890 at nearly 1,400.[21] In 1870, Colorado counted fewer than 500 African Americans, little more than 1 percent of the territory's population. The number grew to more than 11,000 by 1910, when it still made up less than 2 percent of the state's total population of nearly 800,000.[22] Census takers a hundred years ago did not ask people to classify themselves as Hispanic or Latino or Chicano. We can only estimate the number of persons of Hispanic ancestry who lived in Colorado in the late nineteenth and early twentieth centuries. Probably nearly 28 percent of the territory's population was Hispanic in 1870, after which the percentage fell to around 13 in 1880 and to about 10 in 1890.[23]

Colorado's settlers came loaded with cultural baggage, including deep-seated racial biases. Much of the racism was antiblack, so potent that it could be used as a convenient template for racism directed at other groups. Many whites, seeing skin color as the determiner of all things, mocked African Americans' language, appearance, and culture. They did the same with Chinese Americans, Mexican Americans, and Italian Americans. Depending on their whiteness for their status and sense of worth, whites made racial purity a touchstone of their identity.

Believing their self-proclaimed superiority rested on their skin color, whites were especially prone to assert their power in cases in which African Americans or other people of color allegedly stepped across the sexual divide. The attempt, even the accusation of an attempt, by a black man to rape a white woman thrice damned the

African American in the minds of whites because such actions threatened white racial purity and demonstrated as nothing else could that blacks did not know their place. The thought of black men having sex with white women struck primeval chords in the minds of whites who, having classed African Americans as animals, saw in black men powerful sexual competitors. As James H. Madison indicates in *A Lynching in the Heartland: Race and Memory in America*: "Part of this story included the fear of some white men that white women were sexually attracted to black men. Moreover, such a relationship was liable to produce 'mixed' and therefore 'unclean' offspring."[24]

Scott L. Malcomson, in *One Drop of Blood: The American Misadventure of Race*, suggests that the intensity of white racism after the Civil War sprang in part from whites' sense that they were losing mastery in a society increasingly made up of immigrants, increasingly interdependent, increasingly beyond the power of individuals to influence. Whites grasped at any means, including lynching, to maintain their position.

Lynching made clear who held the power. Blacks never lynched whites in Colorado; neither did Chinese Americans or Italian Americans. In the early 1860s the Espinosas, detailed later in this chapter, killed whites in southern and central Colorado until Anglos asserted their power and killed the Espinosas. In Colorado's pioneer era lynching was seen as a necessary evil. In the 1870s and into the 1880s it was excused as a quick, cheap way of disposing of criminals. By 1900 Judge Lynch's main apology for lingering in Colorado, as it was in the rest of the United States, was as an enforcer of white dominance. Historian George Fredrickson noted, "The only way to meet criticisms of the unspeakably revolting practice of lynching was to contend that many Negroes were literally wild beasts, with uncontrollable sexual passions and criminal natures stamped by heredity." White Americans failed to see, as Malcomson pointed out, that in their bestial lynchings of African Americans and other people of color, they became the very animals they accused those darker-hued people of being.[25]

Colorado's racism, less deep than Georgia's or Mississippi's, spawned far fewer racially motivated lynchings. With considerable civic schizophrenia, whites sometimes supported African Americans' rights and sometimes denied them. In 1865, Colorado proposed entering the Union without granting African Americans the vote.[26] In

1873 the Denver School Board backed school integration. In the 1880s state militiamen in Denver tried to rid militia companies of blacks because "the white officers . . . do not wish to associate with colored men even on a war footing."[27] In 1885 Colorado's General Assembly passed a law assuring all citizens, at least in theory, the "full and equal enjoyment of the accommodations, advantages, facilities and privileges of inns, restaurants, churches, barber shops, public conveyances, theaters and other places of public resort and amusement."[28] But if the law did not segregate African Americans, custom and practice often did. In 1900 custom determined African Americans' occupations, limiting them primarily to menial jobs. They also had assigned physical places, mainly older neighborhoods in Denver, Pueblo, and Colorado Springs. In Colorado, as in the rest of the nation, two parallel societies existed side by side—one intent on remaining dominant, the other largely powerless to challenge that dominance.

The separateness of those societies provided African Americans with a degree of safety. In Denver, Pueblo, and Colorado Springs they forged communities that gave them some protection. Few in number, geographically removed from most other Coloradans, and more educated and more prosperous than African Americans in many other parts of the country, Colorado's blacks could—if they were lucky—avoid the extremes of white racism. Still, as the lynching record showed and John Preston Porter Jr.'s burning searingly proved, African Americans lived in a dangerous West.

Colorado's citizens of Mexican heritage faced similar dangers. At the end of the 1846–1848 war between the United States and Mexico, the United States absorbed tens of thousands of persons of Hispanic ancestry into its citizenry. When the conquerors and the conquered—each burdened with centuries-old prejudices against the other—came into contact in Colorado, conflict was certain. That part of the lynching story is covered later in this chapter.

No war marred relations between the United States and China or Italy. Yet the Chinese and the Italians also suffered from racial prejudice. They, like African Americans and Hispanos, were distinguishable from much of the rest of the population and hence presented easy targets. Both groups competed with each other as common laborers, scrambling for footholds on the lower rungs of the economic ladder. Both groups, like Hispanos and African Americans, would suffer the attention of Judge Lynch, who found it relatively easy to kill those who could be exiled from the human family. Denver labor leader Joseph Buchanan proclaimed his belief in the "Brotherhood of Man," but when it came to the Chinese he spoke of the "Brotherhood of Man Limited."[29]

Governor Edward M. McCook, in his 1870 message to the territorial legislature, did not dwell on the humanity of the Chinese. Colorado, he said, needed their labor and should welcome them. Perhaps, admitted McCook, the morals of the "celestials" could stand improvement, but "they are exceedingly muscular: and if we can first avail ourselves of their muscle, we can attend to their morals afterwards."[30] Empire builders, hungry for cheap labor, agreed with McCook. In June 1873, mine owners in Central City brought in forty-five Chinese, in July forty more, and in September another seventeen. Many Coloradans, fearing for their jobs, detested the hardworking newcomers.[31]

When a May 1874 fire destroyed much of Central City, locals blamed the Chinese, and one was threatened with lynching.[32] Other towns needed no pretext to expel the Chinese. That same year several dozen masked men forced Chinese to abandon their jobs at a mill in Nederland west of Boulder.[33] To prevent competition from Chinese in Gunnison, two women went to a Chinese laundry the day it opened. They "proceeded to pound the pair of Chinamen with clubs dealing blows with such vigor and effect that the bewildered 'heathen' retreated at once." The fleeing Chinese fired guns to attract police help. The crowd that gathered blamed the laundrymen for the ruckus and cried, "Hang em! Hang em!" Authorities jailed the Chinese to keep them safe.[34] From Gothic, north of Gunnison, came news in March 1881: "A Chinaman was hung here this afternoon at 5 o'clock by the anti-Chinese organization. He refused to go."[35] Gothic later denied the story, claiming it was a ruse to scare away the Chinese.[36]

Two Chinese restaurateurs in Silverton dallied when they were told to get out, so they were taken away with ropes around their necks.[37] In Rico a mob broke into the homes of eight Chinese, "dragged the inmates from their beds, pounded, kicked and otherwise brutally maltreated them, and robbed and plundered the premises."[38] In 1880, Georgetown toughs, "just for fun," went to a Chinese laundry with a rope and "told the three inmates to prepare to die— they must now be hung." One of the Chinese replied: "You hange me you want to. I no fraid to be hung. You killlee me and many

131

million Chinamen come over and kille ever dam mellican man deader than devil."[39]

A story current in Leadville in the 1880s credited Mrs. Voodoo Brown with ridding that city of its Chinese in 1879. Upset because they were supposedly cutting into her laundry business, she "bewitched the people and caused the disappearance of the moon-eyed Mongolians from the camp. What became of these Chinese nobody ever knew. Some say they were lynched."[40] More believable is the report that in 1878, when mine owners tried to replace "rebellious miners" with Chinese workers, the miners "not only threatened to kill every Chinaman who came to the camp, but were making preparations to lynch the men that would cause them to come."[41] Threats worked. In 1880, Leadville, the second-largest city in Colorado, had no Chinese residents. A decade later more than 5,000 people lived in Aspen and more than 10,000 in Leadville, but neither place tallied a single Chinese person. Of around 1,400 Chinese in Colorado in 1890, nearly 1,000 lived in Denver and most of the rest in Pueblo, El Paso, and Park Counties.[42]

Their concentration and numbers in Denver provided the Chinese with some protection but not always enough. In October 1880, Democrats fanned anti-Chinese sentiment, hoping to defeat Republican presidential candidate James Garfield who, his political rivals charged, favored Chinese immigration. On Sunday afternoon, October 31, anti-Chinese rioters swept through downtown, beating Chinese and destroying their businesses—many of them laundries. Triggered, according to some accounts, by a disagreement between a Chinese laundryman and his customer, the riot raged for hours. When it was over and the homes and laundries of the Chinese lay in ruins, the *Rocky Mountain News*, which had promoted the violence by its attacks on the Chinese, reported, "Chinatown no longer exists. . . . Washee, washee is all cleaned out in Denver."[43] More than that, Look Young, an employee at Sing Lee's laundry, was dead.

Most of the Chinese eluded their pursuers. Some hid in coal bins; some sought sanctuary in the Arapahoe County jail; some took refuge in friendly houses, including that of Denver mayor Richard Sopris. Liz Preston, madam of a brothel—backed by "ten Amazonian beauties" holding stove pokers, champagne bottles, and shoes— frightened off rioters, saving thirty-four Chinese. Gambler Jim Moon used his revolver to persuade part of the mob to leave one Chinese man alone: "This Chinaman is an inoffensive man, and you shant touch him, not a —— one of you."[44]

Sing Hey at first hid in an outhouse but was later found fleeing. "A rope was put around his neck and he was dragged about the ground" until a good Samaritan cut the rope, allowing Hey to live.[45] With the boldness of youth and courage reinforced by his two large six-shooters, one Chinese man stood by a pole: "I say you hang me. I no care."[46]

At Nineteenth and Lawrence Streets the mob "attacked Sing Lee's place with axes, hatchets, stones, etc., and broke in the windows and doors." They found Look Young hiding under a lounge. One of the rioters proclaimed: "Here is one of them, the son of a bitch; we will kill him." They beat Young, took him into the backyard, and beat him again. Then they dragged him—beating him with a large oak stick—to the corner of Nineteenth and Arapahoe Streets, a few hundred feet from where they first found him. They pondered hanging him from a light pole with a clothesline. Deciding against that, they proceeded south on Arapahoe, continuing to beat him. Finally, Dr. Cotton C. Bradbury and others rescued Young.[47] He was taken by wagon to a doctor's office where a *Rocky Mountain News* reporter and others watched him die: "Blood was issuing freely from his mouth and nose. An examination showed a face and neck much swollen, the signs of a rope being visible on the latter. The teeth had been knocked or kicked out. There was a deep wound on the top of the head that had apparently penetrated the skull. There were bruises all over the body, from hand to foot."[48]

The twenty-eight-year-old Young, a man "of unusual good appearance and address," was the sole support of his mother, father, and wife whom he had left behind in a southern Chinese town 80 miles from Canton when he came to the United States in the mid-1870s to make money.[49] Had the Chinese government been successful in pressing claims, Young's family might have gotten something. As it was, U.S. secretary of state James Blaine refused to pay a penny of the more than $50,000 the Chinese had lost. Disgraced by the riot, Denver ferreted out some suspected culprits but failed to convict them.[50] Piling inaccuracy upon injustice, the city's journalists and historians misstated Look Young's name, almost always referring to him as Sing Lee.[51]

The *Denver Republican* blamed the Democrats and the *Rocky Mountain News* for the riot. The *News* blamed the city administra-

6.3 Frank Leslie's Illustrated Newspaper, *November 20, 1880, caught the brutality of Denver's anti-Chinese riot but inaccurately portrayed the city as a mountain town with frame buildings. Courtesy, Colorado Historical Society (F32201).*

tion led by Mayor Richard Sopris, who had angered the rabble by ordering the Fire Department to hose down the mob. Both newspapers saw the killing of Look Young as the work of unruly rioters, and in the accounts of the day the word *lynching* did not figure prominently. In many ways Young's death, although it fit the definition of lynching, did not conform to the pattern of Colorado lynching. He was accused of no crime; the wider community was not in favor of killing him; rioters, not vigilantes, murdered him. Eleven years earlier Sopris had presided over the lynching of Joel Carr in Evans, Colorado. That orderly procedure hearkened back to the People's Court justice of the Gold Rush era.[52] Look Young's death pointed to an ugly future, to gruesome lynchings, and to the racism that would color those killings.

In 1882 Congress passed the Chinese Exclusion Act, a measure severely restricting additional Chinese immigration. Hatred of the Chinese, however, remained strong. In August 1891, when Lee Quang, a laundryman in Ouray, was accused of assaulting eight-year-old Trixie Shaw, a "score or more" of men took Quang from the police "and shot [him] to death under their very noses." After the killing the *Solid Muldoon*, alluding to such well-known lynchings as those of the Cuddigans, bragged: "The town of Ouray has a record for speedy and unwritten justice that is somewhat national in makeup as to notoriety, but it meets with general approval in this section."[53]

Italians also, especially as their numbers increased in the 1880s, were seen as threats by other workers. Only 335 Italians were living in Colorado in 1880. By 1890 the number had grown to nearly 4,000. In Denver they crowded the bottomlands along the South Platte River west of downtown, where they found debris with which to build their shacks, coal and driftwood to supply their stoves.[54] Their children gathered watercress by the river and sold it uptown, where they collected cigar butts they sold in the bottoms. "The majority of the children," a local philanthropist observed, "belong to these dagoes, who would probably follow the same thing if they had thousands of dollars."[55] Other people's children threw stones at the Italians, as they did at the Chinese.[56]

In 1881 a riot in Poverty Flats between "Americans" and Italians led to the total destruction of a house, and in a nearby saloon "all the chairs, tables, and other articles in the rooms in which the fighting occurred had been sent to eternal smash."[57] Tensions between

Hanging of Robert Schamle in a Georgetown Hog Pen, by a Mob.

6.4 Anti-Italian sentiment apparently did not prompt Robert Schamle's December 1877 lynching in a Georgetown pigsty. The lynchings of Daniel Arata in 1893 and of three other Italians in 1895 were motivated in part by hatred of Italians. Courtesy, Denver Public Library, Western History Collection and Phimister Proctor Church, A. Phimister Proctor Museum.

Anglo Americans and Italians had somewhat softened by the flush times of the 1880s. Strong demand for labor kept Colorado wages higher than those in many other parts of the country and assured most workers of employment. Those days ended in the early 1890s when a steep decline in the price of silver hobbled the state's mining industry, throwing thousands of men out of work. Many left mountain towns and came to Denver, where they populated "Camp Relief" on the South Platte.[58] Angry, hungry, and rootless, they had little to do except complain and beg for food.

Daniel Arata, manager of the Hotel D'Italia, a saloon and boardinghouse in the bottoms under the Sixteenth Street viaduct near downtown, was far better off than many of the unemployed. Had he not been Italian and had he not been accused of killing Benjamin Lightfoot, the twenty-eight-year-old Arata might have lived long enough to move into a neat brick house in northwest Denver. Instead Arata, much sooner than he probably expected, wound up occupying a prime burial plot at Riverside Cemetery.

Arata had served Lightfoot, a Civil War veteran, two beers on July 25, 1893. When Lightfoot could not pay five cents for the second one, Arata allegedly brutally beat his sixty-two-year-old customer, then shot and killed him. So drunk when he was arrested that he had to be hoisted into a wagon, Arata was taken to the Arapahoe County jail, a newly constructed fortress housing 500 prisoners near Colfax Avenue and Santa Fe Street.[59]

That evening around 8:00 P.M., a group of unemployed men met at Eighteenth and Market Streets to listen to speeches. Orators dwelt on Lightfoot's murder: "Let the blood of an old soldier be avenged. D— the Dagos, they're no good."[60] The crowd resolved to march the mile to the jail. The throng grew as it coursed through the business district proclaiming, "We're going to lynch the Dago."[61] "Give us the Dago," they demanded when they reached the jail. Officers told them to go away, emphasizing that the jail was strong and the guards resolute. The mob grew to 10,000 and eventually, by some accounts, to 50,000—including women, leading citizens, and many other curious onlookers.

Refused admittance to the jail, the would-be lynchers ineffectually hacked away at the bricks with picks and a crowbar. Guards tried to hose them down with no effect. When the jail lights were turned off, the avengers ripped lamps from passing cable cars and continued beating at the walls. One of the ringleaders, supposedly

6.5 The Arapahoe County jail, completed in 1891 near Colfax Avenue and Santa Fe in Denver, cost $400,000. Its strong doors could not withstand the mob that seized and hanged Daniel Arata on July 26, 1893. Courtesy, Denver Public Library, Western History Collection.

an old soldier, asked Sheriff William K. Burchinell: "Do you want the d— foreigner to escape? Did we fight to save this country for Dagos or for Americans?"[62] Finally, using a street railway rail, the crowd battered down one of the jail doors. Officers fired on them and wounded two, but the mob did not fall back. After a search of the building the attackers found Arata. One of them slashed him across the abdomen with a knife. Bleeding, he was led from the building.

He was taken to a nearby cottonwood tree and hanged, then shot at least four times. When the rope broke, he fell into the gutter. "The crowd laughed and cheered and yelled, 'Burn him; burn him, as they do in Texas.'"[63] A rain that day had soaked everything in sight, so the burning proposal did not catch on. Instead the mob pulled Arata, perhaps already dead, through the streets and rehanged him from a telegraph pole at Seventeenth and Curtis Streets. Souvenir seekers hacked away at the bloody pole until 3:00 A.M., although by then the police had removed Arata's mangled corpse.[64] Later the body was examined by Arapahoe County coroner John M. Chivington, a man well-versed in death, having commanded the troops that massacred Indians at Sand Creek in 1864.

Chivington determined that Arata had died of strangulation, and he surmised that the crowd had acted out of frustration at Governor Davis Waite, who opposed the death penalty and might have stayed Arata's execution had a court sentenced him to die.[65] Some blamed the homeless rabble for the crime; others faulted the police. The *Colorado Catholic*, a Denver weekly, editorialized: "No one will contend that Arata would have met the same fate had he been of a nationality other than Italian."[66]

The lynching shook Denver businessmen, not so much because they considered it brutal but because they feared the homeless poor, realizing the impotence of the police, would steal and loot. Bankers hired guards to protect their vaults, and the Hayward Arms Company kept a dozen armed men in its store.[67] Helpful railroads agreed to transport the out-of-work out of town; bakeries and dairies gave them food for the trip east.[68] County officials calculated the cost of the damage to the jail at $1,000 and reckoned that the mob had saved taxpayers $3,000–$4,000 in trial costs. The lynching, one county commissioner observed, "was a mighty cheap job for the county."[69] Denverites were glad to learn the Italian government could not collect claims because Arata had been born in the United States, making him as much a citizen as those who took his life.[70]

Arata was the third or perhaps the fourth Italian to be lynched in Colorado. Anti-Italian sentiment did not seem to play a part in the hanging of Robert Schamle at Georgetown on December 15, 1877. Variously identified as Swiss-born and as an Italian, Schamle was accused of murdering a German butcher, Henry Thiede. Captured in Pueblo, Schamle was returned to Georgetown. Within hours of being lodged in the jail, he was taken by unmasked men in the dead of night to a nearby pigsty and hanged. Cut down at 9:00 A.M., Schamle's corpse was draped over a cask in which the pigs slept so townsfolk could view it until midday. The hanging, said Georgetown's newspaper, "was, perhaps, a little irregular, but it was only anticipating what should have been the legal act of the sheriff."[71]

"Pete" Theophil, an Italian-speaking railroad laborer, was accused in October 1881 of murdering W. H. Hoblitzell, supervisor of crews building the Denver and Rio Grande through the Black Canyon of the Gunnison River. Theophil was arrested and taken to Gunnison where masked men seized him from the jail, put a rope around his neck, and dragged him through the streets, probably killing him in the process. Finally, they hanged him from a livery stable sign. Whether Theophil would have been lynched had he not been Italian is unclear. Hoblitzell was respected, the crime was serious; anyone who killed Hoblitzell might have been lynched. But being Italian worked against Theophil. Many native-born Americans and immigrants from northern Europe regarded people of color as sinister. After his death the *Gunnison Daily News-Democrat* described Theophil as a "swarthy skinned assassin" and noted, "had he wore [*sic*] his inky locks in a cue at his back he might have been mistaken for a Chinaman. His eyes are almond-shaped and cunning and malicious in expression."[72]

Pepino Tologrino's death apparently had little or nothing to do with his nationality. In May 1891, Tologrino, a truck-gardener in Denver's bottoms near the Twenty-third Street viaduct, got into a row with some boys that led to him shooting and killing Cooney Glance, a sixteen-year-old. Within minutes Tologrino's neighbors coalesced into a mob, secured ropes, and chased him along the South Platte until he plunged in. Unable to swim, he struggled against the swift current, clutching at driftwood. His pursuers tried to save him by throwing him a rope: "When the line came within distance he seemed undecided which to fear the most, the water or those who were trying to save him."[73] The South Platte won. Tologrino's body was found a few miles down the river near Riverside Cemetery.

The *Chicago Tribune* did not list Tologrino among the lynched for 1891.[74] Four years later, as if to compensate for that oversight, the *Tribune* exaggerated the number of Italians lynched in Colorado in 1895, giving a total of five when, in fact, the number was three.

Lorenzo Andinino, Francesco Ronchietto, and Stanislao Vittone were accused of beating saloon keeper Abner J. Hixon to death at Rouse, a coal town southeast of Walsenburg, on March 11, 1895. On March 13–14, 1895, the three Italians were shot to death, presumably by half a dozen of Hixon's friends. The avengers intercepted Vittone and Ronchietto, along with Peitro Giacobini and

Antonio Gobetto, also suspected of killing Hixon, as the Italians were being taken to the Walsenburg jail. A mile southwest of town at the Bear Creek bridge, the vigilantes fired on the wagon, killed the driver Joseph Welsby, killed Vittone, and wounded Ronchietto. Giacobini and Gobetto fled into the frigid night. After the vigilantes rode away, Ronchietto was taken to the Walsenburg jail, where Andinino was already incarcerated. At around 1:00 A.M. on March 14, at least four men shot Andinino and Ronchietto to death. In total, four died that night—Welsby and Vittone at the Bear Creek bridge, Andinino and Ronchietto in the jail.

All of the Italians were citizens of Italy, although Ronchietto and Vittone had declared their intention to become U.S. citizens. In 1891 eleven Italians had been lynched in New Orleans, making the Italian government understandably sensitive to attacks on its nationals. Baron Francesco Fava, Italy's ambassador to the United States, demanded that the Walsenburg lynchers be brought to justice. Colorado governor Albert McIntire offered a $1,000 reward for their apprehension. In Huerfano County, Judge Jesse G. Northcutt overruled the wishes of "the leading citizens" and ordered a grand jury investigation.[75]

The grand jury did not meet until February 1896, nearly a year after the killings. A prisoner, Frank Olk, who was in the Walsenburg jail the night of March 13, had earlier told officials that Walsenburg marshal William Smith and Deputy Sheriff Henry Farr had killed Andinino and Ronchietto. Olk also swore that Ronchietto had told him Farr and Smith had been among the men who killed Welsby and Vittone at the Bear Creek bridge. Olk's testimony was not presented to the grand jury, perhaps because, as a felon, his word was not considered credible. Peitro Giacobini, who escaped at the time of the Bear Creek bridge attack, identified one of the killers, but his testimony evidently was not believed.[76]

As was the norm when either coroners' juries or grand juries investigated lynchings, the jurymen did next to nothing, concluding that the killings had been committed by "unknown persons."[77] Denied justice, Baron Fava won a consolation prize—an indemnity of $10,000 paid by the U.S. government to the families of the dead and to Peitro Giacobini and Antonio Gobetto.

Conrad Woodall, a Colorado State University graduate student who studied the Walsenburg killings, concluded that those murders were "frontier" lynchings, unrelated to the nationality of the victims.

Maybe that was so. But by 1895 frontier lynching—that is, as
Woodall defines it, a lynching "in which the community accepts lawless
revenge in the absence of effective law enforcement mechanisms"—
was exceedingly rare in Colorado, in part because well before the
1890s the state had "effective law enforcement mechanisms."[78] Perhaps the Italians would have been lynched had they been Anglo
Americans, Germans, or Irish; but if race played no part it seems
odd that four of the last fourteen lynching victims in Colorado were
Italians or Italian Americans, three were African Americans, two
were Mexican nationals, and one was Jewish; one wagon driver—
Joseph Welsby—was accompanying the Italian prisoners. Woodall
speculates that the failure to prosecute the lynchers may have reflected the Italians' immigrant status. If so, it seems reasonable to
assume that their immigrant status and their race also contributed
to their deaths.[79]

The *Denver Post* suggested a racial motive for the lynchings when
it editorialized against the practice because it could be used to "work
the purposes of private or class or race vengeance."[80] Denver's *Rocky
Mountain News* reported that after the lynchings about a hundred
"terror-stricken" Italians congregated at a saloon. Evidently, they
saw the racial dimension of the shootings. "No satisfactory motive,"
said the *News*, "for the wholesale killing can be learned except it be
that the Italians are always hated in Western mining districts, and
had added to the ill feeling they incurred during the general strike a
year ago by killing a very popular man without apparent cause or
reason."[81]

Ancient religious prejudices, more than race, help explain the
beating death of Jacob Weisskind on December 25, 1905, a murder
that met the definition of lynching—"an illegal killing at the hands
of a group acting under the pretext of service to justice, race, or
tradition."[82] Ragpickers and junk collectors, many of them Eastern
European Jews living along West Colfax Avenue near downtown
Denver, were often targeted by rock-throwing rowdies.[83] Hooligan-
ism turned deadly on December 25, 1905, when a mob of young
men—offended because Jewish laborers were unloading a freight
car on Christmas Day—attacked the workers, injuring Mendel
Slatkin and Jacob Weisskind. Five weeks later Weisskind died.[84]

Denver papers condemned the crime and demanded that
Weisskind's killers be punished. "There is, of course, absolutely nothing in the foolish attempt of some ill-advised persons to make out

that there was any settled plan of religious persecution at the bottom of this brutality," the *Denver Post* editorialized. Yet in the opinion of Denver assistant district attorney Greeley Whitford, who prosecuted Philip Lind and Philip Keiser, it was obvious that religious hatred figured in Weisskind's death. "The Jew, they [Lind and Keiser] say, was working on Christmas. And they were Christians, and they would avenge the blood of Christ, by shedding the blood of so-called Christ killers."[85]

Would Weisskind have been killed had he not been Jewish? Keiser, a twenty-year-old, led the gang of "about fifteen boys between the ages of 16 and 20." According to the *Denver Post*, "The cry of 'Christ killers' arose from all sides and bricks, stones, sticks and pieces of the very iron the men were unloading began to fly thick and fast towards the two men."[86] Whitford told the jury: "Let us tell the world now: This is one city where a Jew also is allowed the inalienable rights of mankind—life, liberty and the pursuit of happiness."[87]

Denver was shamed by Weisskind's death, but jurors were not prepared to sentence the "boys" to long terms. Lind was convicted of voluntary manslaughter, an offense punishable by one to eight years in the state penitentiary. Keiser was judged guilty of involuntary manslaughter, a crime bearing a sentence of up to one year in the city jail. The other hooligans, it appears, escaped official punishment. A few years later Denver's Jews had a bitter opportunity to reflect on the vagaries of local justice when a Jewish lad, accused of dealing in stolen property, was sentenced to five to ten years in the penitentiary.[88]

At least in jailing Lind and Keiser, Denver distanced itself from the lynching of Weisskind. Such was never the case in the lynchings of Mexican and African Americans. Sheriff Freeman refused to arrest Porter's killers, although they were well-known, because it would "involve Lincoln County in a needless and fruitless litigation against its own citizens."[89] After Calvin Kimblern, an African American, was lynched in Pueblo in May 1900, the coroner decreed that Kimblern "was not a human being" and declined to investigate his death.[90]

The Wallace, Kimblern, and Porter killings accounted for three of Colorado's last nine lynchings. The others, between 1898 and 1919, were Jack Bennett, killed by a small group of ranch hands in remote northwestern Colorado in 1898; Thomas Reynolds, hanged in Cañon City in 1900; the Jewish laborer Jacob Weisskind; the insane

Lars Leberg in Las Animas in 1906; and two "Mexicans," José Gonzales and Salvadore Ortez, in 1919 in Pueblo.[91] Given that African Americans constituted less than 2 percent of the state's population, their numbers among the lynched in the twentieth century were disproportionately large.

The rash of lynchings of African Americans at the turn of the century was unusual for Colorado. Before 1900, five African Americans had been lynched in the state, comprising around 2.5 percent of those lynched. Edward Bainbridge, who killed a man after a card game in 1867, appears to have been the first. Described as a former Mormon who "appeared erratic and fiendish to white men, whenever he got whiskey in him," Bainbridge was seized by vigilantes in Georgetown, thrown from the second story of a building, then hanged in what was for its day a rougher lynching than usual.[92] Whether Bainbridge's race was the deciding factor in his mistreatment would be difficult to prove because whites were also regularly being lynched in the late 1860s. Nor can historians today say with certainty that the unidentified "Negro" lynched in southeastern Colorado in 1874 died because he was African American or because he was accused of stealing horses.[93] Certainly, in the early 1870s many other suspected horse thieves were unceremoniously killed.

The lynching of sixteen-year-old Black Kid Thomas, sometimes known as the "Copper-Colored Kid," in Silverton on August 25, 1881, may have been prompted by Thomas's race, but it also occurred because he was with Bert Wilkinson when Wilkinson killed Silverton's marshal, David C. Ogsbury. Black or white, the chances that Thomas would have been lynched, as Wilkinson was, were great.[94] Bainbridge and the Black Kid's deaths may be seen as part of the ordinary course of lynchings in Colorado.

Denver displayed respect for the law although scant concern for the trappings of civilization as it dealt with Andrew Green, an African American charged with killing Joseph Whitnah, a streetcar driver, during a robbery in late May 1886. After Green was arrested, a mob of 300 marched on the Arapahoe County jail and demanded that Green be given to them. Sheriff Frederick Cramer refused, and the leaderless crowd evaporated. Asked about the propriety of lynching, John M. Chivington, then a Denver undersheriff, saw no reason to lynch Green because it was almost certain he would be legally executed. But, said Chivington, if Green should get off or receive a light sentence, "I am not sure that I would not be willing to help put the rope around the fellow's neck myself and help lynch him."[95]

Extra guards reinforced the jail staff, and Green's trial was hastened so would-be vigilantes would have neither an excuse nor a prolonged opportunity to act. Convicted of the murder, Green was legally hanged on July 27, 1886, before a gathering of 15,000 to 20,000 people. Popcorn and candy vendors worked the crowd, as men and women held children up and jostled one another to get a good view. A visitor, L. Vernon Briggs, who witnessed the macabre carnival, concluded, "socially and morally this place is an enigma to a stranger."[96] Briggs was perhaps unaware that Green's public legal execution was for its time more civilized than vigilante vengeance. Similarly "civilized" was the December 16, 1881, legal execution of Tom Coleman, an African American, in Gunnison, which was witnessed by a large crowd. Later, some of the town's citizens demonstrated that they were less than civilized by hacking off parts of Coleman's frozen body.[97]

Green's and Coleman's executions were more humane than the treatment accorded Joseph Dixon, a black man accused of killing a white woman, Ellar Day, in Ouray in September 1887. Dixon might have been lynched in that lynching-addicted community regardless of his color, but his ancestry likely determined the barbarous nature of his death. According to newspaper reports, Dixon, a pastry chef, blamed nineteen-year-old waitress Ellar Day for causing him to lose his job. He shot her four times and killed her. Taken to the Ouray jail, he was asked if he wanted a gash in his head sewn up. He replied, "no, as that was probably his last night on earth, he did not care to run up a doctor bill."[98] That night masked men surrounded the jail. Unsuccessful in their effort to break in, they drenched the building with coal oil and set it on fire. Dixon died, the Ouray coroner said, from suffocation.[99] The *San Juan Prospector* told of a crueler fate, reporting that "nothing but the scorched remains" were left.[100]

Would Ouray's vigilantes have burned their jail if Dixon had been white? The *Solid Muldoon* asserted that Dixon was "human in form only, devilish by nature and lecherous in disposition, heartless with cruelty and hungry for blood: the assassin of woman's reputation and the would-be slayer of woman's purity: a wild beast of society, slimy with the ooze of moral leprosy and black with the mark of Cain." The *Muldoon* alleged that Day had once received an unsigned note, "which, in substance said that the writer would make her grovel in the mud and bring her to a level with the lowest." Without evidence, the *Muldoon* inferred that it had come from Dixon and on that based its assertion that Dixon was a "would-be slayer of woman's purity."[101] By 1887, Colorado was well on its way to the November 1900 lynching by burning of John Preston Porter Jr.

Calvin Kimblern's gruesome hanging in Pueblo before dawn on May 23, 1900, marked the next stop on that savage line. Press accounts said Kimblern, described as a "mulatto," admitted killing two orphan girls, thirteen-year-old Ethel Straussen and eleven-year-old Jessie Skaggs, and wounding his wife, Hattie, as she tried to stop him. The girls had angered him by accusing him—he maintained falsely—of improper behavior with them.[102]

Returned to Pueblo after he fled to Denver, Kimblern was seized by a mob estimated at 6,000, dragged through the streets, hanged from a telegraph pole at Eighth Street and Santa Fe Avenue—thanks in part to an agile boy who scaled the pole and fixed the rope—and hanged again when the rope broke. The *Rocky Mountain News* reported, "An effort was made to mutilate the man while still alive."[103]

The crowd lowered Kimblern's corpse and "howling and yelling with delight, dragged the body in the dust," abandoning it in the middle of the street.[104] Souvenir hunters ripped off his clothes. A proposal to burn his body was vetoed by citizens anxious that "the good name of the state should not be further blotted." Little concerned about the state's reputation, the mob dragged Kimblern's body back to the pole where they had first hanged him, and there they hanged him again. Obviously worried about the good name of Pueblo, the *Chieftain* claimed: "His sufferings were doubtless few. The lynching was devoid of the slightest thing sensational." The "Negro brute did more than enough to bring such vengeance upon his head."[105]

Governor Charles S. Thomas agreed: "The lynching was a natural outburst of indignation of the people of Pueblo." Thomas observed that because Colorado had abolished the death penalty, Kimblern would have been sentenced to the penitentiary, and "in eight or ten years from now the then governor would be bothered to death by petitions for his pardon, because the 'poor fellow is getting old and he was a soldier in the Philippines.'"[106] Ironically, seven months later Thomas pardoned the cannibal Alfred Packer, who had been spared execution eighteen years earlier.

As had been the case with Thomas Reynolds, lynched in Cañon City in January 1900, and as would be true with John Preston Porter Jr., lynched later the same year, many newspapers blamed Kimblern's torture on the heinous nature of his alleged crime and on the fact that Colorado lacked the death penalty. In 1901 the General Assembly bowed to popular pressure and restored capital punishment.

That did not help Washington H. Wallace. Accused in March 1902 of raping Henrietta Miller, an elderly white woman, in La Junta, Wallace—an army veteran and a railway porter—was arrested in Denver where he lived. He was returned to La Junta on March 25, where he steadfastly denied having committed the crime. He stayed in custody less than a day, spending some of the last moments of his life writing a letter to his wife as a mob stormed the Otero County courthouse: "Mary, My dear wife—I must die to-night for a crime some one did last night. I was arrested and a mob formed and lynched me. You look after the pension. You apply for it as soon as you can. The sheriff will send you my watch and ring and money—about $39. Yours in death, W. Wallace."[107]

Despite objections from leading citizens, the mob, estimated at 4,000, broke every window in the courthouse and battered down its door with a telegraph pole. Wallace—rope around his neck—was dragged out, hustled to a nearby pole, and hanged. "He fought," said the *Rocky Mountain News*, "like a tiger striking the boy who ascended the pole to tie the rope." Shortly after he was hanged, members of the mob riddled his body with bullets.[108] Boulder's *Daily Camera* praised the lynchers for having avoided "such brutal scenes as burning at the stake," adding that the lynching "seems to have been conducted along the best approved lines in such affairs. . . . There seems to be a brutal strain in the negro blood which civilization cannot refine."[109] In Denver the Reverend George R. Vosburg of the First Baptist Church excused the lynchers: "As long as negroes continue to knock down white women and ravish them, we are morally certain that a lynching will follow."[110]

Others objected. The Reverend David N. Beach of Denver's First Congregational Church said, "Such actions are abominable, terrible, unjustifiable."[111] In Grand Junction the *Daily Sentinel* suggested that Wallace might have been innocent: "The perpetrators [of Wallace's killing] should be given the full measure of the law, even if they are white. Anyhow their color should cut no figure whatever."[112]

Color continued to cut a figure in Colorado, but stoic Washington H. Wallace was the last African American lynched in the state. In ten southern states studied by Stewart Tolnay and E. M. Beck, at least 2,500 African Americans were lynched between 1882 and 1930.[113] In the North and the Midwest comparatively few were lynched. Colorado cast its lot with the North and the Midwest largely because most Coloradans originally came from those regions.

That African Americans made up less than 2 percent of the state's population also helps explain why Colorado lynched fewer blacks than did southern states that had far more African Americans.[114] Lincoln County, the site of John Preston Porter Jr.'s death—a 2,500-square-mile expanse—counted fewer than 10 resident African Americans among its 926 citizens in 1900, most of whom came from the Midwest or the North, with some, such as Sheriff John W. Freeman, born in Sweden, hailing from northern Europe.

Small numbers; concentration in Denver, Pueblo, and Colorado Springs; and within those cities concentration in certain neighborhoods probably protected African Americans. But their small numbers and isolation also worked against them. No doubt accepting the myth that African Americans were dangerous sexual predators, Lincoln County was far more ready to believe that a black man—a stranger—killed Louise Frost than that, perchance, the white farm boy next door did.

Nevertheless, the times were changing even in the lynching-prone towns of the Arkansas River Valley. Washington Wallace's lynching in 1902 was followed by the 1906 hanging of the Swede Lars Leberg in Las Animas, 20 miles east of La Junta. Five years later, in early July 1911, La Junta again considered lynching an African American. That time it did not.

On July 4, 1911, Bob Harris, an African American, shot and killed Rocky Ford's police chief, J. B. Craig, and seriously wounded the town's night marshal, Jacob Kipper, who died two weeks later. Because Harris had supposedly caused trouble that day, the two lawmen went to his home at night, broke in without a warrant, and—according to Harris and his aged father—began beating Harris, who shot Craig and Kipper. Harris fled. He was found thirty-six hours later—his loud snoring gave him away—hiding in a Rocky Ford church parsonage. He was taken to the Otero County jail in La Junta and imprisoned along with his father, mother, and sister.

A mob of 200 quickly gathered. Sheriff H. W. Potter quieted them by telling them that justice would be done. "By 1:30 this afternoon," Denver's *Post* reported, "the excitement had died down. If any attack is made at all, it will probably not occur until tonight."[115]

Potter did not wait for night. He telephoned Governor John F. Shafroth, who immediately assured the sheriff of help from the National Guard, a thirty-man company of which was stationed in La Junta. Shafroth also pledged reinforcements from Lamar and Trinidad and told Potter, in a widely publicized telegram, to "use every means at your hands" to prevent Harris's lynching.[116] The announcement that state troops would intervene cooled "the hotheads, who would bring on illegal vengeance."[117]

It also bought Potter some time. Depending more on his wits than on the National Guard, the sheriff stuffed his prisoner in a gunnysack and wrapped it with burlap to disguise it as a package. His assistants took it from the jail and dumped it on the backseat of the sheriff's car. Potter and his deputies sped off. Some suspicious members of the mob rushed to their automobiles. They overtook Potter, but since Harris stayed in his sack they did not see him and concluded that Potter's dramatic exit was a trick designed to get the vigilantes away from the jail. They returned to the courthouse, giving Potter another chance to get away. His fast driving—he covered one 50-mile stretch in a hundred minutes—brought Harris safely to Pueblo, thereby sparing La Junta the embarrassment of a repeat of Wallace's lynching.

In a way, it was simply luck that saved Harris. Had Potter's pursuers looked in that gunnysack, Harris likely would have been lynched.[118] In other ways his life was saved because Sheriff Potter was courageous, smart, and determined and because Governor Shafroth brought the power of the state to bear on La Junta.

In 1900, when Governor Thomas was asked his opinion of the Porter lynching, he responded: "My opinion is that there is one less negro in the world."[119] Coloradans knew in 1900 that they could lynch African Americans with impunity. Governor Thomas told them, in effect, that they had little to risk. Historian James R. McGovern, writing of the South, noted that whites did not lynch blacks "simply because they found them threatening." "Whites," wrote McGovern, "were realistically aware of what they could get away with."[120]

In 1911 Governor Shafroth made it equally clear that whites could not count on getting away with lynching Harris. Sheriff Potter and Shafroth, unlike Governor Thomas and Sheriff Freeman, were willing to pay a political price for protecting an African American. That willingness suggests that they had courage and that they knew many other progressive Coloradans wanted to be rid of lynching. There was a cost for protecting Harris but also one for not protecting him.

At the 1912 Governor's Conference in Richmond, Virginia, Governor Cole L. Blease of South Carolina blatantly defended lynching: "When the Constitution steps between me and the defense of the white women of my state I will resign my commission and tear it up and throw it to the breezes. I have heretofore said 'to hell with the Constitution.'" Governor Shafroth replied: "One mob can do more injury to society than twenty murders, because a lynching permeates the entire community and produces anarchy. The influence of mob rule is most reprehensible."[121]

Twelve years after the hanging of Calvin Kimblern and the burning of John Preston Porter Jr. and a decade after the death of Washington H. Wallace, Colorado was perhaps sufficiently cleansed from its own history of racially motivated lynchings that Shafroth could assume the moral authority to lecture Blease. For some years thereafter, citizens resisted the impulse to lynch. During the anti-German hysteria of World War I, residents of Hugo on the eastern plains threatened to hang a German American and forced him to kiss the U.S. flag. Near Grand Junction a school superintendent was tarred and feathered and told to resign or be hanged because he supposedly used a pro-German book. Yet despite the xenophobia, no Germans were lynched.[122] As the second decade of the twentieth century drew to a close, Coloradans might have been able to congratulate themselves on their civilization had it not been for the work of fifteen men in Pueblo.

Lynching was temporarily revived in Colorado shortly before 10:00 P.M., Saturday, September 13, 1919. That rainy night, masked Pueblo avengers fixed nooses around the necks of José Gonzales and Salvadore Ortez—both citizens of Mexico—tied the other ends of the eighteen-foot-long ropes to the iron railing on the West Fourth Street bridge, and hurled their victims from the bridge to strangle to death over the turbulent waters of the rain-swollen Arkansas River. Less than twenty-four hours earlier Ortez and Gonzales had allegedly killed patrolman Jefferson Evans as Evans attempted to corral them for threatening "to kill every last Negro" in Peppersauce Bottoms, a slum along the Arkansas near the bridge.[123]

There had not been a lynching in the state since Lars Leberg was hanged in 1906. Perhaps that is why police let down their guard and answered a fake riot call. Or, one might guess, the police, who with Evans's death had lost one of their own, sympathized with the lynchers and were happy to abandon their post. With only one jailer to protect them, Ortez and Gonzales were easy marks for the vigilantes. A group of perhaps no more than fifteen entered the jail, put a gun on the guard, knocked both prisoners unconscious, and sped them to the bridge by automobile. After the hanging a thousand people flocked to the bridge, making officials fear the weight would collapse it. Later, Ortez's and Gonzales's corpses were removed to the city morgue where they rested near the body of patrolman Evans.[124] A coroner's jury "failed utterly to reveal the least clue to the identity" of the lynchers.[125]

The *Denver Post* headlined: "Lynching of Two Mexicans Generally Upheld in Pueblo."[126] The *Colorado Springs Gazette* condemned the lynching and praised Governor Oliver Shoup for his promise to go after the lynchers.[127] The *Pueblo Indicator* blamed Shoup for the hangings because he was supposedly soft on crime.[128] Pueblo's *Chieftain* faulted the whole of society, convulsed as it was with lynchings, race riots, and strikes across the United States in 1919. But the *Chieftain* did not let Pueblo's lynchers off the hook: "Under the law their act was a crime, and their offence against their victims was less important than their offence against this community, against the law of this state and against civilization."[129]

Pueblo, preparing to host the annual state fair and looking forward to a visit by President Woodrow Wilson slated for September 25, was shamed. The *Pueblo Indicator* glossed over the tragedy by overlooking the tensions between the United States and Mexico that had marred almost the entire decade. "The men," said the *Indicator*, "would have been lynched no matter whether they had been Americans or foreigners, instead of Mexicans. It was not a matter of nationality at all, but purely one of a mob's idea of meting out justice."[130] Somehow, too, the *Indicator*, in denying the racial overtones of the lynchings, conveniently overlooked six decades of Colorado history during which "Mexicans" frequently died at Judge Lynch's hands. Hundreds of Pueblo's Hispanic residents viewed the corpses of Ortez and Gonzales. Soon after, a policeman was shot at, allegedly by a vengeful Mexican. Recognizing the virulence of old hates between Hispanos and Anglos, the police called on reserves and citizen volunteers to control "any situation that might arise."[131]

The cauldron of tensions between Anglos and Hispanics, so apparent in Pueblo in 1919, had boiled from Colorado Territory's earliest years. On August 2, 1860, the *Western Mountaineer*, a Golden newspaper, reported what was probably the first lynching of a "Mexican" by Anglo Americans in Colorado: "A report from Colorado City received on Tuesday states that a Mexican horse thief who had stolen two horses was executed there on Sunday morning."[132] Three years later Hispanos demonstrated that lynching was a double-edged sword, that Anglos too could suffer at the hands of a group acting outside the law "under pretext of service to justice, race, or tradition."[133]

Vivian, José, and Felipe Espinosa—brothers or perhaps cousins—hated Anglos for having ruined "our family . . . they took everything in our house; first our bed and blankets, then our provisions." Other legends suggest the Espinosas were engaged in a holy war to expiate their father's sins. Whatever their motives, the Espinosas killed by some accounts as many as thirty Anglos. Because the number is slippery and the killings were as much private murders as lynchings, the victims of the Espinosas are not included among the lynched in the list in Table A.1. Thirty or seven, lynched or murdered, the dead Anglos triggered a hunt for the Espinosas.[134]

A posse killed Vivian Espinosa in April 1863. On October 15, 1863, Felipe and sixteen-year-old José were shot by mountain man Tom Tobin, working for the U.S. Army. Tobin and a "Mexican boy" then cut off Felipe's and José's heads. Perhaps Tobin could have spared Felipe because, although he continued to resist, he was badly hurt. A short respite would probably have done him little good because his chances of receiving a fair trial were slight. Denied the opportunity to hang the Espinosas, some of the territory's elite took vengeance by using one of their skulls as a ceremonial drinking cup. As a pioneer member of Denver's Knights Templar recalled, "Sir Knights may have the happy reflection that their 5th libation was taken by the aid of what was left of this murderous chief [Espinosa]."[135]

At least nineteen Hispanics were lynched between 1860 and 1919. The number, although large in absolute terms, was less than 11 percent of all those lynched in Colorado. Before Colorado became a state in 1876, Hispanic Americans constituted at most slightly more than a quarter of the territory's population. During those lynching-filled years they constituted no more than 9 percent of those lynched. From 1880 to 1920 their population probably ranged between 10 and 13 percent of the state total. In those years about 17 percent of all persons lynched were Hispanic.

The reported numbers may not fully reflect the actual number of Hispanos lynched. In southern Colorado, where Anglo American vigilantes in predominantly Hispanic counties feared retaliation, some Mexican Americans may have been clandestinely killed. A slight change in the numbers would dramatically change the percentages. On the other hand, one cannot assume that every lynching of a Hispanic person reflected racial prejudice. Antonius Mestes, who confessed to brutally killing his wife, was seized by a mob, shot, stabbed, and dragged to death in October 1880. Many of those avengers, his neighbors in Huerfano County, were probably Hispanic.[136]

Geography offers some clues to the lynchings of Hispanic Americans. Heavily concentrated in southern Colorado, Hispanos were most often lynched in towns along the Arkansas River—Cañon City, Pueblo, Las Animas. They were also lynched in places farther south—Trinidad, La Veta, Alamosa—but in those communities their lynching rate was much lower than their percentage of the population of the counties in which the towns were located. Until 1848, the Arkansas River marked part of the border between the United States and Mexico. In the late nineteenth century, Arkansas River towns, especially Pueblo, straddled two cultures. At those points of contact, where Anglo Americans held the power, Mexican Americans were more likely to be lynched on a per capita basis than they were in Trinidad and other heavily Hispanic places south of the Arkansas, where their sheer numbers gave them some protection.

In Trinidad, where Mexican Americans could elect sheriffs and other officials, Anglos could not kill with impunity.[137] In fact, interlopers from the eastern United States and northern Europe, although they increasingly exercised economic power, had to watch their step. After Frank Blue killed Pablo Martinez in Trinidad in late 1867, Blue was threatened with lynching, as were his Anglo friends who tried to rescue him from a mob. Barricading themselves in the Colorado Hotel, they held off Hispanos for several days, eventually surrendering and finally being saved by U.S. Army troops. When masked vigilantes lynched two "Mexicans" in Trinidad in 1873 for allegedly killing an Anglo rancher and his wife, Hispanos "took the bodies of the hanged men from the custody of the county coroner; they surged through the streets and vowed vengeance from the house-tops."[138] Prompt action by the sheriff and a hundred deputies prevented a race war, one outnumbered Anglos probably would have lost.

In the nineteenth century few Mexican Americans lived in northern Colorado. Those who did ran a substantial risk in proportion to their numbers of being lynched. Perhaps as many as three Hispanos were killed in or near Colorado City at the foot of Pikes Peak in the early 1860s. In 1871 a "Mexican" accused of horse theft was hanged at Jimmy's Camp on the plains 25 miles northeast of Pikes Peak. In 1866 near Golden, a Mexican man was lynched for supposedly assaulting a woman. Soon after, other Hispanos were forced to leave the area. Commenting on that lynching, the traveler and journalist Bayard Taylor observed that "the improvised code of a new settlement is no longer necessary here, and it seems to exist by virtue of a lingering taste for rude and violent justice."[139] After 1867, vigilantes in northern Colorado apparently lynched no more Hispanos, probably because, until the influx of migrant farmworkers in the twentieth century, few Hispanos lived in northern Colorado.

The taste for lynching, especially when sharpened by racial prejudice, persisted in Colorado for more than half a century after Taylor declared improvised justice no longer necessary. After 1919 the thirst for instant vengeance sometimes reasserted itself. But Coloradans, although they did not know it at the time, were witnessing the last of more than 175 lynchings as Salvadore Ortez and José Gonzales strangled to death over the Arkansas on a rainy September night in 1919. After that, even racial hatred was unable to revive lynching in Colorado.

CONCLUSION

> Lynchings are altogether too frequent in this country.
> They are a reflection on our civilization. They are al-
> most a travesty on our Christianity.
>   —*DENVER POST*, MARCH 15, 1895

William Rathmell, a lad of perhaps sixteen, stopped in Alamosa with his mother in May 1880. On his first day there, he and another boy "went to a bridge that spanned a stream and found, hanging to one of the bridge beams, two men dead." The sight troubled him: "I had left a community whose people made it their business, always in a pursuasive [*sic*] manner, to Christianize and humanize, upgrading the hardened sinner to repentance and re-form, but here they seemed to go about it in a different way." Rathmell returned to his mother and urged her to contact the police. But she told him, "Inasmuch as we are newcomers it would probably be better to let the people of this town settle their differences in their own way."[1]

For six decades Coloradans settled their differences in their own way—a way that often involved lynching. In the beginning the

People's Courts, especially as they functioned in Denver, could claim to be agents of civilization, dealing justice openly and in the only manner practical for isolated Pikes Peakers. Soon, however, some citizens, finding the People's Courts too lenient, resorted to clandestine killings.

Firmly rooted even before Colorado became a territory, lynching, like a hardy weed, proved difficult to eradicate. It was simply too useful, too handy, too exciting for its devotees to be easily stopped. In time Denver, Pueblo, and Leadville worried about their reputations and came to frown on extralegal executions. Those cities could eventually afford to be virtuous because they had made investments in jails, courts, and police forces that allowed them to imprison and try culprits. Smaller towns doubly damned accused criminals—once for committing the crime; a second time for putting the community to the expense of jailing, trying, executing, and burying them. Except for the small cost of a burial, Judge Lynch spared taxpayers that expense.

Lynching in Colorado was practically always prompted by alleged crime. Even in those lynchings with racial overtones, with the exception of the killings of Look Young in 1880 and Jacob Weisskind in 1905, crime or accusation of crime triggered the lynching. Yet crime alone did not explain lynchings. Why were some criminals lynched and others not?

Stewart Tolnay and E. M. Beck, in their careful study of lynching in ten southern states, found that although crime was often the excuse given for lynching, it was not the major cause. Economic considerations, especially fear and distress among poor white southerners who competed with African Americans, were the most significant factors promoting southern lynching. When cotton prices were high and inflation was low, when times were good, lynching declined. When times were hard it increased.[2]

Economic competition does not explain most Colorado lynchings, although Denver's anti-Chinese riot and the killings of Italians were based, in varying degrees, on the dislike of low-paid Chinese and Italian labor. As for the rest, a complex mix of crime and other factors led to their lynchings. Sociologist Roberta Senechal de la Roche, seeing lynching as "social control—a process by which people define or respond to deviant behavior," noted the importance of crime in prompting lynching and suggested four other factors. "Relational distance," that is, the degree to which people are tied together, affects lynching. The less people's lives are intertwined, the more likely it is that lynching will occur. Similarly, the less dependent people are on one another, the more likely lynching is to occur. Position in society plays a part. Lynching is more likely to be used against people of a lower social class than against those of a superior class. Cultural distance also affects lynching, with those removed from the cultural mainstream in more danger.[3]

Each of these factors figured in practically every Colorado lynching, but those elements in themselves do not fully explain the lynchings. The Chinese were always at a considerable relational, functional, cultural, and class distance from much of the rest of society, but obviously not every Chinese person was lynched. Similarly, many accused criminals, although they fit all four categories, evaded Judge Lynch's evil eye. De la Roche's approach provides useful insights. It does not, as she herself points out, pretend to be a full explanation.

In part it was the soil, the social milieu, and the climate of opinion—peculiar to Colorado and, for that matter, to much of the West—that promoted Judge Lynch's career. Frontier communities wanted to save money and to signal that they would not tolerate crime. In their self-reliance these new towns did not scruple "over the method of reaching the right."[4]

The lynched not only received what righteous citizens thought sinners deserved, but the condemned also suffered what the community, or part of the community, could safely get away with giving them. Lynchings flourished not simply because crimes were committed or because lynching saved money. They happened because lynchers knew they would not be punished, that often they would be regarded as community protectors rather than community destroyers.

That was especially true during Colorado's formative years, when pioneer westerners were almost expected to lynch and were given a blank check by easterners to do so. The vigilance committees in California in the 1850s and the Montana vigilantes in the 1860s were viewed from afar as good citizens struggling to establish civilization. As the *New York Times* put it in 1900, Colorado's lynchings during the Gold Rush period were "easily defensible on many good grounds."[5] Western lynchings were so expected that it is not surprising to find Edward Wheeler's dime novel *Deadwood Dick in Leadville*, featuring Deadwood Dick's lynching near that city in July

1879, four months before there was actually a lynching there.[6] Even after easterners and more sophisticated communities in Colorado withdrew their permission to lynch, some places such as Ouray seemed to take perverse pride in their "mind your own business, we'll do it our way" defense of lynching.[7]

It is easier to explain why lynching flourished than it is to fathom why a custom so fashionable before the mid-1880s rapidly fell out of favor. It was not because lynchers were captured, prosecuted, and jailed. That apparently happened only twice before 1906, yet lynching was largely dead by 1906. Nor was it because lawmen became effective at preventing lynching, although some officers' courage thwarted some lynchings. Nor was it because Colorado started executing large numbers of criminals, satisfying its citizens' zeal to crack down on crime. During the 1880s the state legally executed thirteen people and lynched more than four times that number. During the 1890s it executed another dozen and lynched only eleven.

Nor did lynching die because the social fractures delineated by de la Roche healed. Colorado did settle down—compared to its pioneer period—in the early twentieth century, which partly explains lynching's demise. But that alone is not a totally satisfactory reason because some parts of the state remained tumultuous into the twentieth century. Social change and violence, for instance, marked Las Animas County between 1880 and 1920, but the turmoil did not provoke a rash of lynchings.[8]

Newspaper opposition helped curtail lynching, but even as late as the early twentieth century many Colorado papers sanctioned the brutal killing of John Preston Porter Jr. It was not because there was organized, systematic opposition to lynching; there was no organized antilynching movement in the state. William Rathmell's experience provides part of the answer. He was among the tens of thousands who migrated to Colorado from the Midwest and the East, contributing to the tenfold increase in the state's population—from fewer than 40,000 to more than 400,000—between 1870 and 1890. Most of those people, like Rathmell, came from places that usually preferred to Christianize and reform hardened sinners without lynching them.

One of the newcomers, George P. Costigan, born in Ohio in 1848, arrived in Colorado in 1877. Locating in the San Juans, he practiced law in Ouray and Telluride before moving to Denver. One of his sons, Edward Prentiss Costigan—who as a boy may have heard stories of the lynching of Margaret and Michael Cuddigan—went to high school in Denver, graduated from Harvard in 1899, and returned to practice law in Colorado, becoming a leader of the state's Progressives in the early twentieth century. Elected to the U.S. Senate as a Democrat in 1930, he made federal antilynching legislation one of his major, albeit unsuccessful, crusades.

By an odd eddy of fate, Costigan, a son of the lynching-prone San Juans, became a national leader in the effort to end lynching. The lessons lynching was supposed to teach boys were evidently lost on him, unless the lesson was to hate lynching.[9] The new arrivals brought new attitudes with them, and by their sheer numbers—which included far more women, children, and older people than had made up the Gold Rush–era population—they transformed the state. To serve them, entrepreneurs built telegraph and telephone lines and railroads; more than 3,800 miles of track were laid in the state between 1870 and 1888. As Colorado coalesced into a more coherent whole, the region was more fully integrated into the nation. In 1875 General William Tecumseh Sherman and Governor John Routt would have found it difficult to crack down on the lynchers of Judge Dyer in remote Lake County. In 1911 Governor John Shafroth could have called out the National Guard by telephone within minutes to prevent the lynching of Bob Harris in La Junta.

The cords that tied Colorado together physically also bound it together culturally and economically. David Day laughed at the bad press Ouray received for killing the Cuddigans. Behind his forced and studied humor, one senses a forlorn defense of his town's archaic way of doing things. His rhetoric was a Declaration of Independence of the colony, Ouray, against the mother country, Denver, and the other nattering cultural and economic capitals of the East and Midwest. But all Day's sarcasm and even the display of Mary Rose Mathews's body in Denver could not put frontier Colorado and its lynching ways together again.

By the 1880s Ouray and other Colorado places were linked to, similar to, and dependent on the rest of the state and nation. No longer regarded as a frontier territory with special needs, Colorado lost its license to lynch. Realizing that, the citizens of La Junta scrambled to cut down the body of Lars Leberg, lynched in 1906, before his dangling corpse affronted passengers on the morning train. Communities regarded as civilized enjoyed investments and settlement. Those that were not did not.

Many pioneer Coloradans praised lynching, and in the early twentieth century some troglodytes still defended it; but Coloradans never totally approved of it. Mature communities with jails, courts, and police forces had no acceptable excuse for allowing citizens to take the law into their own hands. Initially, illegal killings seemed a way of preserving order. By the early 1880s, however, "the responsible men of the community, the solid real estate owners," often saw them as destructive of law and order—especially since in Denver's anti-Chinese riot, Pueblo's hanging of Phebus and McGrew, and Ouray's killing of Margaret Cuddigan many people concluded that Judge Lynch had gone too far.[10]

Historian Robert Wiebe, in *The Search for Order, 1877–1920*, characterized the progressive movement that colored U.S. politics and thought in the late nineteenth and early twentieth centuries as a search for order in an era made chaotic by rapid industrialization, immigration, and urbanization.[11] The westward movement—especially in its beginning—was destructive of order, for although it may have provided a safety valve in the East, it put pressure on the West. Lynching, a symptom of that pressure, appealed to those anxious to discipline the mishmash citizenry of mining camps, boomtowns, and instant cities. In time Judge Lynch—once applauded as the harbinger of stability and peace—fell victim to the excesses of his henchmen, the defection of his supporters, the removal of his excuses for being, and the criticism of his enemies.

By the late 1880s, lynching was increasingly seen as a foe of civilization, "almost a travesty on our Christianity."[12] Until then lynching's fate hung in the balance. After that the weight of public opinion, lynching's lifeblood, quickly tipped the scales against the practice, except when the weight of racial hatred or a particularly heinous crime was added to lynching's side of the scale. And after 1919 even racial prejudice, of which there was plenty during the state's flirtation with the Ku Klux Klan in the early and mid-1920s, was not sufficient to revive lynching in Colorado.[13]

In April 1934, nearly fifteen years after the hangings of José Gonzales and Salvadore Ortez in Pueblo, the normally staid citizens of Colorado Springs briefly considered resurrecting Judge Lynch after a white college student accused African Americans of attempting to rape her. Five African American suspects were arrested and taken to the Colorado Springs jail. Fearing mob violence, police officials quickly removed the five to the penitentiary at Cañon City.

Other African Americans jailed for minor crimes were sent to Pueblo. When a mob of 500 demanded the prisoners, their representatives were allowed into the jail, where they found no African Americans. "We do not propose to have these five men lynched," said Deputy District Attorney Thomas Purcell.[14] Several weeks later, the two prime suspects were quietly returned to Colorado Springs. In brief court proceedings they pleaded guilty to the assault charges and were sentenced to long penitentiary terms. One was paroled in 1946, the other in 1947.

By 1947 Judge Lynch was truly dead in Colorado. Lynching had become a memory rather than an actuality. The memory, in turn, was less of the actuality than of an idealized Judge Lynch, a stern but fair civilizer who only did what was needed to tame the frontier. He was the noble Judge Lynch of Owen Wister's 1902 novel *The Virginian*, which became part of the national consciousness through various movie versions, rather than the bloodthirsty, mistaken avenger portrayed in Walter Van Tilburg Clark's *The Ox-Bow Incident* (1940).[15]

In his history of Colorado, *The Coloradans*, published in 1976, Robert Athearn, a respected academic historian, reflected Wister's thinking rather than Clark's: "For a brief period during the first days of the gold rush local vigilance committees were obliged to take the law into their own hands on occasion." Such proceedings, he inferred, quickly became a thing of the past. After territorial judges arrived in 1861, "Law had come to Colorado and everybody was happy."[16]

John Preston Porter Jr., burned at the stake in 1900, was not happy. Alexander McCurdy, castrated and hanged in Golden in 1894, was not happy. Law came to Colorado for some but not for all. Generally speaking, until the early 1980s Athearn's and other widely used texts on Colorado history touched lightly, if at all, on Colorado's post-1861 lynching record. Admitting the fact of Porter's lynching without including his name, Athearn noted, "Black lynchings were extremely rare in the state."[17] That alleged rareness was little comfort to lynched African Americans, including Edward Bainbridge, Black Kid Thomas, Joseph Dixon, Calvin Kimblern, and Washington Wallace.

In 1901 Samuel Clemens blasted lynching in a short essay, "The United States of Lyncherdom." He submitted it to his publisher as a possible introduction to a multivolume history of lynching. Several days later he cooled on the idea: "Upon reflection it won't do for me to write that book . . . for I shouldn't have even half a friend left down there [in the South], after it issues from the press."[18] With good commercial sense Clemens hesitated to give offense. Coloradans also would have been angry with him because he twice indicted their state in his essay. John Preston Porter Jr., lynched less than a year before "Lyncherdom" was written, had evidently gotten Clemens's attention.

Not giving offense has also been a hallmark of many Colorado historians. From time to time, a piece of the state's lynching history bobs to the surface like the Loch Ness monster. Many of the town histories listed in the sources to this book contain matter-of-fact accounts of lynchings, particularly the early ones. Articles in *Colorado Magazine* and its successor, *Colorado Heritage*, have sometimes mentioned lynchings. In 1982 the revised edition of Carl Abbott and colleagues' text, *Colorado: A History of the Centennial State*, let readers know of the lynchings of John Preston Porter Jr., Calvin Kimblern, and Washington Wallace.[19] Half a decade later, John H. Monnett and Michael McCarthy, in *Colorado Profiles: Men and Women Who Shaped the Centennial State*, devoted an entire chapter to Porter.[20]

Perhaps most Coloradans will never come to see Judge Lynch as the wolf he was. The sight of Daniel Arata being slashed, hanged, and rehanged and the screams of Margaret Cuddigan are not pleasant to remember. Samuel Clemens recounted a hanging he had witnessed in Nevada in 1868: "I can see that stiff, straight corpse hanging there yet, with its black pillow-cased head turned rigidly to one side, and the purple streaks creeping through the hands and driving the flesh and hue of life before them. Ugh!"[21] Such sickening memories, despite their importance, have a way of being swept to the margins of history, of not being published, of being buried. So has it been with lynching in Colorado.

APPENDIX

COMMENTS ON TABLE A.1: Newspapers often mangled the names of the lynched. For example, the *New York Times* spelled Cuddigan as Cuddihee. I have tried to select the spelling most likely accurate. Dates also represent my best effort to clarify sometimes confusing accounts. I have attributed a lynching to a place even if it was done slightly outside that place. For some obscure places, especially those not more fully identified in the text or not on today's highway maps, I have placed the county name in brackets after the place-name. Most of the places where lynchings occurred are included on the map, which also includes some places such as Grand Junction where apparently no lynchings took place.

The size of lynching parties was often imprecisely reported. I have provided a number in cases in which one was given. In other instances I have estimated. S stands for a small group of 40 or fewer; M for one of medium size—that is, from 41 to 99; L for a large assemblage comprising 100 or more people. I have categorized lynching groups as mobs (M), as posses (P), as People's Courts (PC), as private parties (PP), and as vigilantes (V). Mobs refer to groups acting with some degree of disorder. In the absence of contrary evidence, I have identified as vigilantes those groups that did not act in a frenzied moblike fashion. In general, vigilantes were local citizens of at least some standing in the community and with some community support who acted in an organized fashion, although often their organization was probably temporary. Sometimes vigilantes spearheaded a lynching and mobs joined later. Those cases are described with the abbreviation VM. The private parties category embraces small groups of lynchers apparently acting from private motives rather than from alleged concern for community good. Because contemporary accounts of lynchings are often imprecise, these designations are slippery and should not be assumed to be completely accurate. I have designated cases in which information as to size and composition of the group doing the lynching is unknown with an X.

In the ethnicity column I have included African Americans and persons described as Italian, Chinese, and Mexican. I have not tried to determine the ethnicity of other lynching victims. In the comment column I have indicated some of the instances in which more than one person was lynched. I have also designated cases I consider doubtful by indicating "Weak evidence" to cover instances in which later accounts smack of fabrication and "Definition?" for cases that may not fully meet the definition of lynching.

APPENDIX

Before producing this "final" list, I eliminated at least half a dozen alleged Colorado lynchings because they seemed to be duplicate reports of the same lynching, because although reported as having taken place in Colorado they probably did not, or because they appeared to be private murders committed by one or two people. For example, the murders committed by the Espinosas have not been included because the Espinosas, apparently only two of them operating at a time, cannot be considered a group.

If I have been too generous by including victims of the Lake County Vigilance Committee, all five of whom might be eliminated from the list on the basis of definition, their inclusion likely only partially offsets the exclusion of some who were lynched whose fate was never recorded. The lynched may never rest in peace; the lynching list will never be completely accurate.

TABLE A.1—Colorado Lynching Victims, 1859–1919

Name	Mo	Year	Place	Crime	Mob Size	Ethnicity	Comment
Aitkins, W. W.	2	1860	Missouri City	Assault	M 100		
Andinino, Lorenzo	3	1895	Walsenburg nr.	Murder	V S		With other Italians
Arata, Daniel	7	1893	Denver	Murder	M 10,000	Italian	
Bainbridge, Edward	4	1867	Georgetown	Assault	V	Italian	
Baker, Franklin	4	1888	Cheyenne Wells	Murder	M 50	African American	
Banta, Harry	6	1888	Monarch nr. Salida	Murder	X		
Bartholomew, J. S.	2	1866	Fort Lupton nr.	Theft	V		
Baxter		1863	Fairplay nr.	Theft?	X		
Bell, Arthur	5	1873	Trinidad	Murder	M		a.k.a. Clark
Bennett, John	3	1898	Routt County	Murder acc.	V S		
Berry, S. P.	3	1882	Pueblo nr.	Theft cattle	V 25		With Chastine
Betts, George	4	1882	Lake City	Murder	V M 500		
Bishop, John	7	1861	Apex	Theft horse	X		
Black Hawk	9	1860	Denver	Theft horse	X		
Black Kid Thomas	8	1881	Silverton	Murder acc.	V	African American	With Wilkinson
Black Pete	7	1884	Cebolla	Theft cattle	X		
Blair, William	8	1882	Del Norte	Unknown	X		a.k.a. Coyote Bill
Boice, Mike	8	1873	Hall's Gulch	Threats	V		With Hall
Bonner, J.			Mosquito Gulch	Murder	X		Weak evidence
Briggs, Joseph W.	9	1861	Denver	Theft horse	X		
Briley, Oliver	2	1891	Salida	Murder	M		
Browning, James	4	1882	Lake City	Murder	V M 500		
Carlton, William	9	1869	Colorado City	Threats?	V or PP		a.k.a. Wild Bill

continued on next page

TABLE A.1—*continued*

Name	Mo	Year	Place	Crime	Mob Size	Ethnicity	Comment
Carr, Joel	11	1869	Evans	Murder	PC		
Chastine	3	1882	Pueblo nr.	Theft cattle	V 25		With Berry
Cleary, Henry	8	1879	Silverton	Murder	V 50		
Cleveland, Frank	12	1870	Frankstown nr.	Theft horse	V		With Mason
Coats, Charles	2	1868	Castle Rock nr.	Murder	V 150		With Murrays
Coe, William	4	1868	Pueblo	Theft cattle	U.S. troops		
Craft, James H.	7	1879	Alamosa	Murder	V M 100		With Walrath
Cuddigan, Margaret	1	1884	Ouray	Murder	V		
Cuddigan, Michael	1	1884	Ouray	Murder	V		
Dixon, Joseph	9	1887	Ouray	Murder	V	African American	Burned
Dodge, William	2	1869	Laporte	Theft	V 5–6		
Donahoe, John	5	1869	Bryan	Unknown	X		
Dowling, Henry	7	1883	Maysville	Murder	V 75		With Haggerty
Dubois, Willie	3	1870	Burlington	Murder	P		
Duggan, Sanford	12	1868	Denver	Theft money	V 100		
Dyer, Elias	7	1875	Granite	No crime	PP		
Edwards, Bill	2	1882	Colorado SW	Theft horse	X		Weak evidence
Fillmore, John		1862	Empire	Murder	PC		Weak evidence
Fleming		1860	Divide nr.	Murder	PC		Weak evidence
Ford, A. C.	9	1860	Denver nr.	Theft horse	V S		
French, Wilbur D.	12	1888	Greeley	Murder	V 100		
Frodsham, Edward	11	1879	Leadville	Theft land	V 20		With Stewart
Gonzales, José	9	1919	Pueblo	Murder	V 100	Mexican	With Ortez
Gonzales, Marcus	7	1877	La Veta	Murder	V 75	Mexican	
Gordon, John	10	1860	Denver	Murder	PC		

Name		Year	Place	Crime	Sentence	Ethnicity	Notes
Graham [Major]	10	1875	Wet Mtn. Valley	Theft mine	V L		
Graviel, Juan	1	1880	Alamosa	Theft cattle	V L		
Gray, John	1	1884	Rosita	Murder	V 100	Mexican	
Gredler, Marcus	6	1860	Denver	Murder	PC 3,800		With Williams
Haggerty, Dennis	7	1883	Maysville	Murder	M 75		With Dowling
Hall, Henry	8	1873	Hall's Gulch	Threats	V		With Boice
Harding, Charles	3	1875	Lake [Chaffee] Co.	No crime	V PP		
Haslet	6	1864	Denver	Theft cheating	X		
Hoover, John	4	1880	Fairplay	Murder	VM		
Howe, James H.	4	1888	Fort Collins	Murder	V 300		
Hudson, Frank	6	1868	Fort Lyon	Murder	V 5		With Watson
Indian Charley	1	1874	Frankstown	Murder	X	Indian Mexican	
Jackson, Andrew	10	1880	Cline's Ranch	Murder Utes	X		Definition?
Jackson, Hank	1	1869	Colorado City	Assault	V S		
Kennedy, Solomon	4	1861	Lake Gulch	Murder	PC 3,000		
Kimblern, Calvin	5	1900	Pueblo	Murder	M 6,000		
Latta, James	9	1860	Denver nr.	Theft horse	V S		
Leberg, Lars	12	1906	Las Animas	Murder	V 20		
Madison, Tom	12	1870	Frankstown	Theft cattle	V		With Mason
Magee, Michael	7	1867	Trinidad	Murder	X		
Marion, Joshua	8	1874	Middle Kiowa	Theft horse	V 50		
Marion, Tip	8	1874	Middle Kiowa	Theft horse	V 50		
Martinis, Merijilodo	6	1873	Las Animas	Murder	X		
Mason, Jack	12	1870	Frankstown	Theft cattle	V	Mexican	With Madison
McCrum, Dell	8	1879	La Veta	Rape	V		
McCurdy, Alexander	6	1894	Golden	Mutilation	M 20		

continued on next page

TABLE A.1—*continued*

Name	Mo	Year	Place	Crime	Mob Size	Ethnicity	Comment
McFarland		1860	Tarryall	Theft	X		Weak evidence
McGrew, Jay W.	3	1882	Pueblo	Theft cattle	V 12–20		With Phebus
McIntyre, Jim		1871?	Douglas County	Murder	X		
McLees, James N.		1886	Montrose	Threats	V		
Mestes, Antonius	10	1880	Huerfano County	Murder	M	Mexican	
Moorman, Henry R.	10	1880	Durango	Murder	M		
Morgan, John	4	1881	Monument Creek	Rape	V 9		
Murrays, John	6	1868	Divide nr.	Murder	V		With Coats
Musgrove, L. H.	11	1868	Denver	Theft horse	V M L		
Norton, Charles	7	1880	Recen	Murder	M 2,000		
O'Connor, George	8	1881	Antonito nr.	Theft/threats	V		Weak evidence
Ogden, Charley		1867	Geneva Gulch	Murder	V M		
Ormsby	3	1882	Pueblo nr.	Theft cattle	V M		
Ortez, Salvadore	9	1919	Pueblo	Murder	V 25	Mexican	With J. Gonzales
Perry, John	2	1886	Red Cliff	Murder	V 100		
Phebus, William T.	3	1882	Pueblo	Theft cattle	M 200		With McGrew
Pond, Arthur	5	1881	Del Norte	Theft	V 20		With Silas Pond
Pond, Silas	5	1881	Del Norte	Theft	V 40		
Porter, John	6	1873	Erie	Assault?	V 40		
Porter, John Preston	11	1900	Limon	Murder, rape	PP		Burned
Porter, W. J.	3	1880	Alma	Murder	V		
Quang, Lee	8	1891	Ouray	Rape attempt	V	Chinese	
Reece, Frank	7	1883	Park County	Theft cattle	V		
Reed, Charles	3	1870	Trinidad	Theft horse	X		With Watson
Reynolds Gang #1	9	1864	Parker nr.	Theft money	X		
					U.S. troops		

Name	#	Year	Location	Crime	Code	Ethnicity	Notes
Reynolds Gang #2	9	1864	Parker nr.	Theft money	U.S. troops		
Reynolds Gang #3	9	1864	Parker nr.	Theft money	U.S. troops		
Reynolds Gang #4	9	1864	Parker nr.	Theft money	U.S. troops		
Reynolds Gang #5	9	1864	Parker nr.	Theft money	U.S. troops		
Reynolds, Jack	8	1874	Alma	Threats	V		
Reynolds, Thomas	1	1900	Cañon City	Murder	V 500		
Richards, William	3	1867	Colorado City	Theft horse	V S		With Jackson
Roberts, Jack	3	1881	Durango nr.	Murder	P 15		
Ronchietto, F.	3	1895	Walsenburg nr.	Murder	V 6–8	Italian	With other Italians
Rymer	8	1882	West Las Animas	Murder	V 50		
Salas, Felipe	7	1876	Cañon City	Murder	X	Mexican	With Talmadge
Sanchez, Donacino	1	1871	Saguache	Theft horse	V	Mexican	a.k.a. Santios
Schamle, Robert	12	1877	Georgetown	Murder	V 20	Italian	
Schenck	6	1888	Monarch	Murder	M		
Seminole, Joseph F.	12	1879	Golden	Murder	V 70		With Woodruff
Shear, John	9	1860	Denver nr.	Theft horse	V S		
Smith, Bill	9		Walker's Camp	Murder	V		Weak evidence
Smith, Nickel	9	1880	Pueblo	Rape	X		
Spinner	2	1874	Trinidad	Murder	VM		
Stewart, Patrick	11	1879	Leadville	Theft money	V 20		With Frodsham
Stuffle, John	4	1859	Denver	Murder	PC		
Talmadge, Joe	7	1876	Cañon City	Murder	V		With Salas
"Tex"	8	1870	Pueblo	Theft horse	X		
Theophil, "Pete"	10	1881	Gunnison	Murder	V 20	Italian	
Thompson, Dick	8	1874	Middle Kiowa	Theft horse	V 50		With Marion
"Toby"		1880s?	Unknown	Theft cattle	X		Weak evidence

continued on next page

TABLE A.1—continued

Name	Mo	Year	Place	Crime	Mob Size	Ethnicity	Comment
Toll, William	6	1867	Boulder	Theft horse	V S		
Tologrino, Pepino	5	1891	Denver	Murder	M	Italian	
Trinidad Charley	6	1882	Rico	Murder	X		With Wall
Trujillo, Juan	2	1876	Dry Cimmaron	Murder	X	Mexican	
Unidentified		1859	Cache La Poudre	Murder	X		
Unidentified	7	1860	Colorado City	Theft horse	PC 200		
Unidentified	6	1860	Hangman's Canon	Theft horse	X		
Unidentified		1863	Gold Run/Blue River	Unknown	X		
Unidentified	1	1866	Denver nr.	Theft	X		
Unidentified	1	1866	Denver nr.	Theft	X		
Unidentified	1	1866	Denver nr.	Theft	X		
Unidentified	1	1866	Denver nr.	Theft	X		
Unidentified	1	1866	Fort Lupton	Unknown	V		
Unidentified	1	1866	Fort Lupton	Unknown	V		
Unidentified	1	1866	Fort Lupton	Unknown	V		
Unidentified	2	1866	Denver nr.	Unknown	X		
Unidentified	2	1866	Denver nr.	Unknown	X		
Unidentified	2	1866	Fort Lupton nr.	Unknown	X		
Unidentified	3	1866	St. Vrain Creek	Theft horse	X		
Unidentified	3	1866	Pueblo	Theft horse	V		
Unidentified	6	1866	Golden	Assault	V	Mexican	
Unidentified	2	1868	Denver nr.	Theft horse	X		
Unidentified	2	1868	Denver nr.	Theft horse	X		
Unidentified	7	1869	Iron Springs	Murder	X		
Unidentified		1870s?	Chihuahua	Murder	X		Weak evidence

Unidentified		1870s?	Chihuahua	Murder	X		Weak evidence
Unidentified		1870s?	Chihuahua	Murder	X		Weak evidence
Unidentified		1870s?	Alamosa	Rape	X		Weak evidence
Unidentified		1870	Golden nr.	Unknown	X		Weak evidence
Unidentified		1870	Kit Carson	Murder	X		
Unidentified	7	1870	Pueblo	Theft horse	X		
Unidentified	8	1870	Iron Springs	Murder	X	Mexican	
Unidentified	10	1883	Iron Springs	Murder	X	Mexican	
Unidentified	10	1871	Jimmy's Camp	Theft horse	X	Mexican	
Unidentified	7	1871?	Trinidad	Theft cattle	P		
Unidentified		1873	Trinidad	Murder	X	Mexican	
Unidentified	8	1873	Trinidad	Murder	X	Mexican	
Unidentified	8	1874	Granada	Theft horse	V 4–5	African American	
Unidentified	5	1875	Granada	Theft horse	X		
Unidentified	4	1875	Lake County	None	V PP		
Unidentified		1875	Lake County	None	V PP		
Unidentified	11	1879	Cleora nr.	Murder	X		
Unidentified	7	1880	Cottonwood Pass	Theft horse	X		
Unidentified	10	1883	Rosita	Murder	X	Mexican	
Unidentified		1888	Pueblo	Unknown	X	Mexican	
Unidentified		1888	Pueblo	Unknown	X	Mexican	
Unidentified		1888	Pueblo	Unknown	X	Mexican	
Vanover, Edgar	9	1859	Golden	Assault	M		
Vittone, Stanislao	3	1895	Walsenburg nr.	Murder	V	Italian	With other Italians
Wall, Tom	6	1882	Rico	Murder	X		With Trinidad
Wallace, Washington	3	1902	La Junta	Rape	VM	African American	

continued on next page

TABLE A.1—*continued*

Name	Mo	Year	Place	Crime	Mob Size	Ethnicity	Comment
Walrath, Charles G.	7	1879	Alamosa	Murder	VM 100		With Craft
Ward, Joe	10	1885	Routt County	Murder	M		
Waters, Patrick	12	1860	Denver	Murder	PC		
Waters, T. H.		1881	Frying Pan	Theft horse	X		
Watkins, L. E. "Ed"	8	1883	Cañon City	Theft cattle	V S		
Watson, Charles	6	1868	So. of Fort Lyon	Theft horse	V S		With Hudson
Watson, Ed	7	1883	Park County	Theft cattle	X		With Reece
Weisskind, Jacob	12	1905	Denver	No crime	M S		Died in 1906
Welsby, Joseph	3	1895	Walsenburg	No crime	V S		
White, Bill	10	1872	Pueblo	Theft money	M		
Wilkinson, Burt	9	1881	Silverton	Murder	V		With Black Kid Thomas
Williams, Frank	1	1866	Denver nr.	Theft	V		
Williams, Frank	1	1884	Rosita	Murder	V 100		With Gray
Wilson, Charles	12	1884	Hot Sulphur Springs	Threats	V 15		a.k.a. Texas Charley
Wilson, Jerry	8	1874	Middle Kiowa	Theft horse	V 50		With Marion
Witherill, George	12	1888	Cañon City	Murder	M L		
Woodruff, Samuel	12	1879	Golden	Murder	V 70		With Seminole
Young, Frank	3	1882	Del Norte	Theft cattle	M L		With Howard
Young, Look	10	1880	Denver	No crime	M	Chinese	
Young, Moses	3	1860	Denver	Murder	PC		

TABLE A.2—Colorado Lynchings by Year and Alleged Crime, and Legal Executions, 1859–1919

Year	Lynched	Murder	Stock Theft	Other Theft	Threats/ Assault	Sex Crime	No Crime	Unk.	Legal Executions
1859	3	2	1	—	—	—	—	—	—
1860	13	5	6	—	1	1	—	—	—
1861	3	1	2	—	—	—	—	—	—
1862	1	1	—	—	—	—	—	—	—
1863	2	—	1	—	—	—	—	1	1
1864	6	—	—	6	—	—	—	—	—
1865	0	—	—	—	—	—	—	—	—
1866	16	—	2	—	1	1	—	12	2
1867	5	2	2	—	1	—	—	—	—
1868	10	3	5	1	—	1	—	—	—
1869	6	2	—	1	2	—	—	1	—
1870	11	5	5	—	—	—	—	1	1
1871	4	1	3	—	—	—	—	—	—
1872	1	—	—	1	—	—	—	—	—
1873	7	4	—	—	3	—	—	—	1
1874	8	2	5	—	1	—	—	—	—
1875	6	—	1	—	1	—	4	—	—
1876	3	3	—	—	—	—	—	—	—
1877	3	3	—	—	—	—	—	—	1
1878	0	—	—	—	—	—	—	—	—
1879	9	6	—	2	—	1	—	—	1
1880	10	5	—	3	—	1	1	—	1
1881	9	5	1	3	—	—	—	—	4
1882	13	5	7	—	—	—	—	1	1
1883	6	3	3	—	—	—	—	—	—
1884	6	4	1	—	—	—	—	1	1
1885	1	1	—	—	—	—	—	—	2
1886	2	1	—	1	—	—	—	—	2
1887	1	1	—	—	—	—	—	—	—
1888	9	6	—	—	—	—	—	3	1
1890	0	—	—	—	—	—	—	—	1
1891	3	2	—	—	—	1	—	—	3
1892	0	—	—	—	—	—	—	—	1
1893	1	1	—	—	—	—	—	—	—
1894	1	—	—	—	1	—	—	—	—
1895	4	3	—	—	—	—	1	—	3
1896	0	—	—	—	—	—	—	—	4
1897	0	—	—	—	—	—	—	—	—
1898	1	—	—	1	—	—	—	—	—
1899	0	—	—	—	—	—	—	—	—
1900	3	3	—	—	—	—	—	—	—
1901	0	—	—	—	—	—	—	—	—

continued on next page

Year	Lynched	Murder	Stock Theft	Other Theft	Threats/ Assault	Sex Crime	No Crime	Unk.	Legal Executions
1902	1	—	—	—	—	1	—	—	—
1905	1	—	—	—	—	—	1	—	4
1906	1	1	—	—	—	—	—	—	—
1919	2	2	—	—	—	—	—	—	—

Table A.2 does not include any cases in which the year of lynching was not determinable. It does include those cases listed in Table A.1 in which the evidence is weak or in which the lynching, such as those during the Lake County War, meets only a broad interpretation of the definition of lynching. Half a dozen of the 1866 lynchings designated as unknown in this table were for theft. Sources do not make the type of theft clear.

Most of the sex crimes were rapes or attempted rapes. All the legal executions were for murder. Years with no legal executions are blank. I am indebted to Michael Radelet of the University of Colorado for providing a list of legal executions that confirmed and added to research I had done.

TABLE A.3—Lynching Victims in Selected States, 1882–1903

State	Number Lynched	Annual Rate per 100,000	Average Population
Alabama	244	0.7226	1,534,868
Arizona	28	1.5175	83,871
Arkansas	200	0.8412	1,080,767
California	41	0.6171	302,003
Colorado	64	0.7607	382,425
Dakotas (North and South)	35	0.3420	465,159
Florida	134	1.5362	396,486
Georgia	269	0.6555	1,865,288
Illinois	21	0.0244	3,908,591
Indiana	52	0.1060	2,229,056
Kansas	51	0.1786	1,298,233
Kentucky	167	0.4027	1,884,833
Louisiana	285	1.1297	1,146,720
Mississippi	334	1.1465	1,324,156
Missouri	91	0.1560	2,651,410
Montana	85	2.7246	141,804
Nebraska	56	0.2958	860,453
New Mexico	34	0.9758	158,386
New York	2	0.0015	6,118,313
North Carolina	64	0.1777	1,637,170
Ohio	21	0.0260	3,675,979
South Carolina	117	0.4575	1,162,347
Tennessee	199	0.5091	1,776,831
Texas	324	0.6426	2,291,995
Utah	7	0.1512	210,497
Virginia	91	0.2471	1,674,243
Washington	26	0.3730	316,817
Wyoming	37	2.8688	58,625

The average population was derived from adding the 1880, 1890, and 1900 populations and dividing by three. The annual lynching rate per 100,000 is based on the total lynched, divided by the population, divided by 22, the number of years covered. For example, if a state had an average population of 100,000 and if 22 people were lynched in that state in the 22 years between 1882 and 1903, the annual lynching rate per hundred thousand would be 1.00. The number of persons lynched is taken from James Cutler, *Lynch-Law: An Investigation Into the History of Lynching in the United States* (1969, originally published 1905), 179–180.

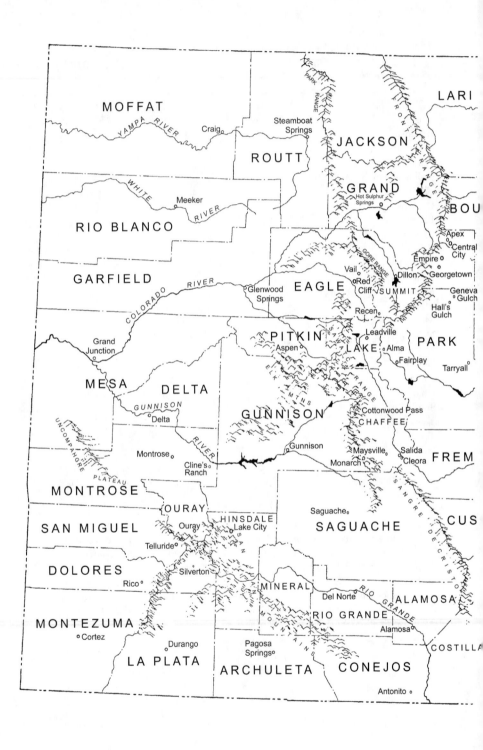

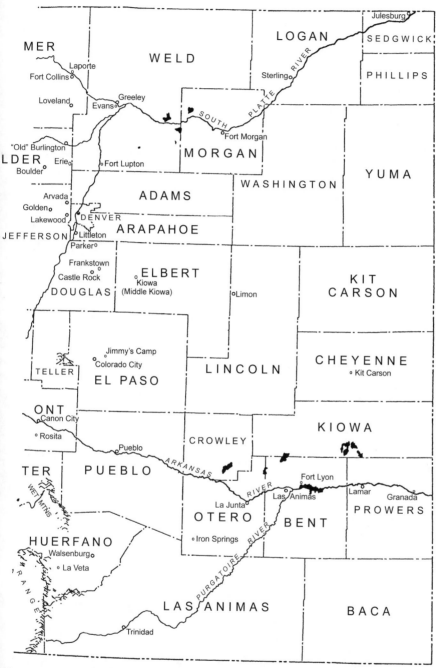

MER
Laporte
Fort Collins
Loveland
"Old" Burlington
LDER   Erie
Boulder
Arvada
Golden
Lakewood
JEFFERSON   Littleton
Parker
Frankstown
Castle Rock
DOUGLAS
ONT
Canon City
Rosita
TER
PUEBLO
HUERFANO
Walsenburg
La Veta
Trinidad

WELD

Greeley
Evans

Sterling

SOUTH

PLATTE

RIVER

LOGAN   SEDGWICK

PHILLIPS

Julesburg

Fort Morgan

MORGAN

ADAMS

DENVER

ARAPAHOE

ELBERT
Kiowa
(Middle Kiowa)

Jimmy's Camp
Colorado City

TELLER

EL PASO

WASHINGTON

Limon

LINCOLN

YUMA

KIT
CARSON

CHEYENNE
Kit Carson

KIOWA

CROWLEY

Pueblo

ARKANSAS

Fort Lyon

RIVER

La Junta

OTERO

Iron Springs

LAS

PURGATOIRE RIVER

ANIMAS

Las Animas

BENT

Lamar

Granada

PROWERS

BACA

This map includes most fo the lynching sites in Colorado. It also includes some places, such as
Grand Junction, Steamboat Springs, and Sterling, that apparently never experienced a lynching.

NOTES

The *Rocky Mountain News*, published in Denver since its 1859 founding, is cited throughout these notes as *RMN*. Other newspapers are cited by name and, if the place is not in the title, by place in brackets after the title. Because Ouray's *Solid Muldoon* is frequently cited, Ouray is not given in brackets. Books are given a full citation the first time they are used. After that they are cited by author's last name and a short title. Allen Nossaman's volumes on Silverton are given full citations in the Sources, as are Jerome Smiley's *History of Denver* (1901) and the *History of the Arkansas Valley*. In the notes, only author, short title, and, if applicable, volume citations are given.

INTRODUCTION

1. *RMN*, December 23, 1863.

2. *Miner's Register* [Central City], October 10, 1863.

3. Ibid., December 23, 1863.

4. Details from an unidentified newspaper clipping in Dawson Scrapbooks, 18:289, in Colorado Historical Society. Lynn I. Perrigo, "Law and Order in Early Colorado Mining Camps," *Mississippi Valley Historical Review* 38 (June 1941), 47, credits Cozens with preventing four lynchings, including one of a man whose crime was that he rejoiced at Lincoln's assassination. Also see ibid., October 20, 1863.

5. Nossaman, *Silverton*, 3:331. Nossaman's volumes will probably long reign as the most exhaustive and carefully written histories of Colorado's smaller towns; *Animas Forks Pioneer*, January 26, 1884.

6. *Denver Times*, November 26, 1900.

7. The murky origins of the word *lynching*, including its incorrect attribution to James Fitzstephen Lynch, a fifteenth-century Irishman, are covered by James E. Cutler in *Lynch-Law: An Investigation Into the History of Lynching in the United States* (New York: Negro Universities Press, 1969, originally published 1905), 13–40. Richard Maxwell Brown, *Strain of Violence: Historical Studies of*

American Violence and Vigilantism (New York: Oxford University Press, 1975), discusses regulators in chapter 3.

8. John P. Reid, *Policing the Elephant: Crime, Punishment, and Social Behavior on the Overland Trail* (San Marino, Calif.: Huntington Library, 1997), 193.

9. Christopher Waldrep, "Word and Deed: The Language of Lynching, 1820–1953," in Michael Bellesiles, ed., *Lethal Imagination: Violence and Brutality in American History* (New York: New York University Press, 1999), 229–256. Patricia Nelson Limerick's essay "Making the Most of Words: Verbal Activity and Western America," in William Cronon, George Miles, and Jay Gitlin, eds., *Under an Open Sky: Rethinking America's Western Past* (New York: W. W. Norton, 1992), 168, notes that western historians have sometimes allowed their thinking to be clouded by "predecessors who did not keep a critical distance between themselves and the written words of the pioneers; this earlier breed of Western historians adopted the terms, the point of view, and the assumptions of the people they studied." To the usual group of suspect words such as *civilization, savagery, frontier*, and *progress*, cited by Limerick, the words *lynch* and *vigilante* should be added.

10. Richard Drinnon, in *Facing West: The Metaphysics of Indian-Hating and Empire-Building* (Minneapolis: University of Minnesota Press, 1980), xii, wrote: "In an imaginative piece in the April 1965 *Speculum* titled 'The Legacy of the Middle Ages in the American Wild West,' Lynn White Jr. easily demonstrated 'our detailed and massive continuity with the European Middle Ages,' including prototypes of the revolver, barbed wire, the windmill, and other paraphernalia for winning the West, down to the rope thrown by lynching parties over a limb of the nearest lone pine. 'In most societies,' White pointed out, 'there are clear rubrics for execution, a tradition of propriety as to the forms of killings committed by the group, which the group feels deeply impelled to follow, perhaps because to follow them makes the past share the guilt of the execution. To know the subliminal mind of a society, one must study the sources of its liturgies of inflicting death' (XL, 199)."

11. W. Fitzhugh Brundage, *Lynching in the New South: Georgia and Virginia, 1880–1930* (Urbana: University of Illinois Press, 1993), 291. Brundage has also edited an excellent selection of scholarly works on lynching, *Under Sentence of Death: Lynching in the South* (Chapel Hill: University of North Carolina Press, 1997). Christopher Waldrep, in "War of Words: The Controversy Over the Definition of Lynching, 1899–1940," *Journal of Southern History* 66 (February 2000), 75–100, treats definitions of lynching.

12. *Denver Post*, December 31, 1903. The story is perhaps legend.

13. Smiley, *History of Denver*, 339–344.

14. Clark Secrest, abstracter, "The 'Bloody Espinosas' Avenging Angels of the Conejos," *Colorado Heritage* (autumn 2000), 10–17.

15. Browne quoted in Stan Hoig, *The Sand Creek Massacre* (Norman: University of Oklahoma Press, 1961), 72.

16. *Denver Republican*, May 27, 1891.

17. Carl L. Hasse, "Gothic, Colorado: City of the Silver Wires" (M.A. thesis, Western State College, Gunnison, 1971), 219–220.

18. Cutler, *Lynch-Law*, 184; *Chicago Tribune*, January 1, 1896.

19. *Denver Republican*, December 5, 1888; *Chicago Tribune*, January 1, 1883. R. R. Maiden's short piece, "Records Show 87 Colorado Lynchings," *Colorado Sheriff and Peace Officer* (May-June 1965), 13, lists around a quarter of Colorado's lynchings, but it omits many and counts some legal executions as lynchings.

20. Undated, unidentified newspaper clipping in Dawson Scrapbooks, 18:233.

21. Ibid., 18:327. The Jenks story smacks of being a tall tale created for eastern consumption.

22. Don L. Griswold and Jean H. Griswold, *History of Leadville and Lake County, Colorado* (Denver: Colorado Historical Society, 1996), 2:1781.

23. Verna Sharp, *History of Montezuma, Sts. John, and Argentine* (Dillon: Summit Historical Society, 1971), 33–34.

24. Cutler, *Lynch-Law*, 1. Lynching is not a practice peculiar to the United States, as Roberta Senechal de la Roche makes clear in "The Sociogenesis of Lynching," in Brundage, ed., *Under Sentence of Death*, 51.

25. Cutler, *Lynch-Law*, 179–180; *Chicago Tribune*, January 1, 1904.

26. Richard White, *"It's Your Misfortune and None of My Own": A History of the American West* (Norman: University of Oklahoma Press, 1991), 332, noted that collective vigilante movements often indicated "larger social conflicts."

27. Undated *Denver Times* clipping in Denver Public Library, Western History and Genealogy Department clipping file.

28. Limerick, "Making the Most of Words," 171.

29. Richard Maxwell Brown, "Violence," in Clyde A. Milner II, Carol A. O'Connor, and Martha A. Sandweiss, eds., *The Oxford History of the American West* (New York: Oxford University Press, 1994), 392–425, presents an overview of western violence, including lynching, and gives a useful, concise bibliography. W. Fitzhugh Brundage, in "Lynching," in Ronald Gottesman, ed., *Violence in America: An Encyclopedia* (New York: Charles Scribner's Sons, 1999), 1:297–303, compares western and southern lynching. A summary of the historiography of studies of western violence is provided by Clare V. McKanna Jr. in *Homicide, Race, and Justice in the American West, 1880–1920* (Tucson: University of Arizona Press, 1997), 5–10.

30. Owen Wister, *The Virginian: A Horseman of the Plains* (New York: Grosset and Dunlap, 1904, originally published 1902), 434.

31. *Denver Post*, Empire Magazine, November 30, 1969.

32. See Chapter 6.

33. *Solid Muldoon*, September 23, 1887.

34. Frederick Jackson Turner, *The Frontier in American History* (New York: Henry Holt, 1920), 254. This collection of Turner's writings includes his original 1893 address on the frontier and various later emanations. The quotation here is not from the 1893 version.

35. LeRoy R. Hafen and Carl Rister, *Western America* (New York: Prentice-Hall, 1950), 440, 451.

36. Ray Allen Billington, *Westward Expansion: A History of the American Frontier* (New York: Macmillan, 1974), 535.

37. Richard Slotkin, *Gunfighter Nation: The Myth of the Frontier in Twentieth Century America* (New York: Atheneum, 1992), 169–183, delves into the significance of *The Virginian*.

38. Hafen and Rister, *Western America*, 442. Joel Williamson, "Wounds Not Scars: Lynching, the National Conscience, and the American Historian," *Journal of American History* 83 (March 1997), 1221–1253, discusses the historiography of lynching with emphasis on southern lynching. Critical examinations of western lynchings are far less common than those of southern lynchings. For a revisionist viewpoint see George W. Hufsmith, *The Wyoming Lynching of Cattle Kate, 1889* (Glendo, Wyo.: High Plains, 1993).

39. Andrew Rolle, *The Immigrant Upraised: Italian Adventurers and Colonists in an Expanding America* (Norman: University of Oklahoma Press, 1968), 174–175.

40. *RMN*, September 14, 1919.

41. John S. Holley, *The Invisible People of the Pikes Peak Region: An Afro-American Chronicle* (Colorado Springs: Friends of the Colorado Springs Pioneer Museum, 1990), 125–127.

42. *The Guardian* [London], September 30, 1999.

43. J. Hector St John de Crèvecoeur, *Letters From an American Farmer*, edited with an Introduction and Notes by Susan Manning (Oxford: Oxford University Press, 1997, originally published 1782), 43–44.

44. David A. Hollinger, *Postethnic America: Beyond Multiculturalism* (New York: Basic, 1995), 1–17.

45. Samuel Clemens, "The United States of Lyncherdom," first published in 1923, rev. version in Ronald Gottesman, Francis Murphy, Laurence B. Holland, Hershel Parker, David Kalstone, and William H. Pritchard, eds., *The Norton Anthology of American Literature* (New York: W. W. Norton, 1979), 276–283.

46. Howard R. Lamar in "Westering in the Twenty-First Century: Speculations on the Future of the Western Past," in Cronon et al., eds., *Under an Open Sky*, 258, points out the felt need for barbarians.

47. Stewart E. Tolnay and E. M. Beck, *A Festival of Violence: An Analysis of Southern Lynchings, 1882–1930* (Urbana: University of Illinois Press, 1995). Works by the other authors have been noted earlier in these notes. Norton H. Moses has compiled an extensive bibliography, *Lynching and Vigilantism in the United States: An Annotated Bibliography* (Westport, Conn.: Greenwood, 1997).

CHAPTER 1:
PEOPLE'S COURTS AND VIGILANCE COMMITTEES, 1859–1861

1. Smiley, *History of Denver*, 349.
2. Ibid., 213.

3. Joan Ostrom Beasley, "Unrealized Dreams: General William Larimer Jr.," *Colorado Heritage* (summer 1996), 8–9, 11; ibid., 213. Beasley indicates that the St. Charles claimants were paid $250 and allowed to share in the new town company.

4. William McKimens, "Letters From Auraria, 1858–1859," *Colorado Magazine* 13 (September 1936), 170.

5. Clark Secrest, *Hell's Belles: Denver's Brides of the Multitudes With Attention to Various Gamblers, Scoundrels, and Mountebanks, and a Biography of Sam Howe, Frontier Lawman* (Aurora, Colo.: Hindsight Historical Publications, 1996), 61.

6. LeRoy R. Hafen, ed., *Pikes Peak Gold Rush Guidebooks of 1859 by Luke Tierney, William B. Parsons, and Summaries of the Other Fifteen* (Glendale, Calif.: Arthur H. Clark, 1941), 175.

7. Secrest, *Hell's Belles*, 72–73. Secrest contends that Stuffle is the correct spelling. Jerome Smiley in *History of Denver* gives Stuffle's last name as Stoefel and says he murdered Thomas Biencroff, not Arthur Binegraff.

8. Smiley, *History of Denver*, 339. Also see Wolfe Londoner, "Vigilance Committees in Colorado," MSS XA Bancroft 401–426, typescript in Colorado Historical Society. Londoner says Stuffle's judge was H.P.A. Smith. The crime took place at the juncture of Ralston and Clear Creeks near what later became Fifty-sixth Avenue and Sheridan Boulevard.

9. James H. Pierce, "With the Green Russell Party," *The Trail* 13 (May 1921), 14; Smiley, *History of Denver*, 305, 306–307, on Wagoner's status. Smiley, *History of Denver*, 527–540, details governance before Colorado became a territory in 1861. *RMN*, March 24, 1872, gives a retrospective account of the trial, as does the *Denver Tribune*, January 11, 1881. The *Tribune* gives the judge's name as H.P.A. Smith, as do several other sources.

10. Smiley, *History of Denver*, 339.

11. *Denver Tribune*, January 1, 1881.

12. Brundage, *Lynching in the New South*, 291. *RMN*, September 16, 1860, used the term *vigies* to describe members of vigilance committees. The term *vigilante* did not come into widespread use until the mid-1860s. See Brown, *Strain of Violence*, 101.

13. Smiley, *History of Denver*, 306, quoting a resolution proposed at an Auraria meeting, April 11, 1859. Calvin W. Gower, "Kansas Territory and the Pike's Peak Gold Rush: Governing the Gold Region," *Kansas Historical Quarterly* 33 (autumn 1966), 289–313, is an excellent account of jurisdictional issues. See also LeRoy Hafen, "Claims and Jurisdictions Over the Territory of Colorado Prior to 1861," *Colorado Magazine* 9 (May 1932), 95–102.

14. Beasley, "Larimer," 14.

15. George M. Willing to Lewis Cass, December 28, 1859, reprinted in "Letters of George M. Willing, 'Delegate of Jefferson Territory,' " *Colorado Magazine* 17 (September 1940), 188.

16. Bassett, despite his short life in Denver, had a street named for him. See Philip Goodstein, *Denver Streets: Names, Numbers, Locations, Logic* (Denver: New Social Publications, 1994), 6, 32.

17. *RMN*, October 27, 1859; Smiley, *History of Denver*, 340. Anne Curtis Knapp, in "Making an Orderly Society: Criminal Justice in Denver, Colorado, 1858–1900" (Ph.D. diss., University of California–San Diego, 1983), 35, indicates that a James Hanna was lynched in May 1859 for horse theft. Smiley does not mention Hanna. Elizabeth Owen, in "Crimes in Denver, 1859–1864," typescript in the Colorado Historical Society, indicates that in May 1859 a James Habna was given fifty lashes and banished for horse stealing.

18. Smiley, *History of Denver*, 340.

19. Ibid., 342; *RMN*, January 6, 1878.

20. Smiley, *History of Denver*, 342.

21. George T. Clark, "Across the Plains and in Denver, 1860: A Portion of the Diary of George T. Clark," *Colorado Magazine* 6 (July 1929), 140.

22. *Western Mountaineer* [Golden], June 28, 1860; *Rocky Mountain Herald* [Denver], June 30, 1860.

23. *RMN*, July 25, 1860.

24. Ibid., August 1, 1860, indicated that Stark had started the fight and had attacked Harrison with a bowie knife. This is in contrast to ibid.

25. J. J. Thomas, "In the Days of the Overland Trail," *The Trail* 2 (May 1910), 7.

26. *RMN*, July 25, 1860. *Western Mountaineer* [Golden], August 2, 1860, gives Wood's name as Carl. Smiley's *History of Denver* gives it as Carroll.

27. *RMN*, August 1, 1860, March 24, 1882, for a reminiscence by Byers.

28. Ibid., August 1, 1860.

29. *Western Mountaineer* [Golden], August 9, 1860; ibid.; Smiley, *History of Denver*, 347.

30. *RMN*, September 5, 1860; *Western Mountaineer* [Golden], August 9, 1860. *RMN*, December 17, 1860, has a scathing denunciation of Purkins who was defending accused murderer Patrick Kelley. Richard Hogan, in *Class and Community in Frontier Colorado* (Lawrence: University Press of Kansas, 1990), 31–32, delves into the societal divisions reflected in the People's Court and in the vigilance committees.

31. *RMN*, September 5, 1860. See *Western Mountaineer* [Golden], July 12, 1860, for an account of a shooting in Denver on July 4, 1860, in which gamblers rescued the miscreant from citizens who tried to arrest him.

32. Smiley, *History of Denver*, 347.

33. Ibid., 347, 765.

34. *RMN*, September 4, 1860. Ibid., 347, says Shear was hauled to a bank of the South Platte River, just above the Larimer Street crossing, and hanged from a leaning cottonwood tree.

35. Smiley, *History of Denver*, 348.

36. *Rocky Mountain Herald* [Denver], September 3, 1860. The *Herald* also named E. W. Wynkoop, S. W. Wagoner, and W. P. McClure, among others, as members of the group intent on controlling thieves.

37. Smiley, *History of Denver*, 350. Smiley says he was told the details of Ford's death by an old pioneer who was a member of the group that killed Ford. Smiley's informant was likely Hiram P. Bennet, named by the *Rocky Mountain Herald* on September 3, 1860, as one of the organizers of the party going after the thieves. Bennet, who later became Colorado's first delegate to Congress, was still alive when Smiley wrote his *History of Denver*. When Bennet died at age eighty-eight, the *Denver Times*, November 11, 1914, noted that he had been a leader in efforts to control desperadoes.

38. *RMN*, September 12, 1860.

39. George F. Willison, *Here They Dug the Gold* (London: Readers Union, 1952, originally published 1931), 94; Stanley W. Zamonski and Terry Keller, *The Fifty-Niners: A Denver Diary* (Denver: Sage, 1961), 151–152; Hogan, *Class and Community*, 32. Jim Latty, the person Williams and others referred to, was likely James Latta, the name used by the *RMN* in 1860. See *RMN*, September 8, 1860, which indicates that James Latta was alive on September 8. Zamonski and Keller report Latty lynched on September 3. The *Western Mountaineer* [Golden], September 13, 1860, says the treasurer of the horse-thieving ring was "a party now on his way to the river." That may have been Latta who, the *RMN* reported September 8, 1860, left Denver that day in the custody of Sheriff William Middaugh bound for Lawrence, Kansas. The *Mountaineer* also says a man named Bentley was captured along with Ford. The fact that Smiley reports neither on Bentley nor Latta nor the five or so other possibly lynched persons may suggest that even forty years after the events Smiley's source had reason to be less than candid. Or it may mean the rumored hangings of September 1860 were rumors and nothing more. That secrecy was likely needed is indicated by the attempt by unknown parties on September 17, 1860, to burn down the *News* office. See *RMN*, September 26, 1860.

40. *RMN*, September 12, 1860.

41. Ibid., September 11, 1860.

42. *Daily Times* [Leavenworth], September 18, 1860.

43. *RMN*, September 24, 1860, has a good account of the Kansas riot. Calvin W. Gower covers Gordon in "Vigilantes," *Colorado Magazine* 41 (spring 1964), 93–104. Pettit called the county "Mountaria." He almost certainly meant "Montana," which was a county carved out of western Arapahoe County by the Kansas legislature. See Gower, "Kansas Territory and the Pikes Peak Gold Rush," 308.

44. *RMN*, October 1, 1860.

45. Ibid.; *Western Mountaineer* [Golden], October 4, 1860.

46. *RMN*, October 10, 1860.

47. *Western Mountaineer* [Golden], October 11, 1860.

48. *RMN*, December 20, 1860.

49. Ibid., December 21, 1860.

50. Thomas Maitland Marshall, "The Miners' Laws of Colorado," *American Historical Review* 25 (April 1920), 438. On Union District's early equal rights stand, see *Rocky Mountain Herald*, July 1912, report on Hugh R. Steele's address to pioneers at Elitch Gardens in files of Colorado Historical Society, Denver.

51. Nolie Mumey, comp., *History and Laws of Nevadaville* (Boulder: Johnson, 1962), 58.

52. *Western Mountaineer* [Golden], November 1, 1860. *Colorado Transcript* [Golden], April 12, 1882, has a retrospective article that differs from the contemporary account in several details.

53. Perrigo, "Law and Order in Early Colorado Mining Camps," 44.

54. *RMN*, September 10, 1859.

55. Libeus Barney, *Letters From the Pikes Peak Gold Rush [or Early Day Letters From Auraria], Early-Day Letters by Libeus Barney, Reprinted From the Bennington Banner, Vermont, 1859–1860* (San Jose, Calif.: Talisman, 1959), 48; *RMN*, September 17, 1859.

56. *RMN*, March 7, 14, 21, 1861.

57. Ibid., April 17, 1861.

58. Transcript of an unidentified newspaper article in the files of the Colorado Historical Society on the Cache la Poudre lynching.

59. Transcript from *Western Mountaineer* [Golden], August 2, 1860, in the files of the Colorado Historical Society; Dorothy Aldridge, *Historic Colorado City: The Town With a Future* (Colorado Springs: Little London, 1996), 13. Several reports of 1860 hangings near Colorado City may stem from only one actual event.

60. *RMN*, July 1, 1884.

61. *Cañon City Times*, July 11, 22, 1861.

62. *RMN*, July 31, 1861; *Colorado Republican* [Denver], July 27, 1861.

63. *RMN*, September 11, 1861. Briggs had supposedly stolen six horses from a Cheyenne Indian named Vermillion.

64. Smiley, *History of Denver*, 349. See also Henry L. Pitzer, *Three Frontiers: Memories and a Portrait of Henry Littleton Pitzer as Recorded by His Son, Robert Claiborne Pitzer* (Muscatine, Iowa: Prairie, 1938), 105.

CHAPTER 2:
MAJOR TOWNS, 1860s–1880s

1. David J. Cook, *Hands Up; or, Twenty Years of Detective Life in the Mountains and on the Plains* (Norman: University of Oklahoma Press, 1958, originally published 1882), 43.

2. Drinnon, *Facing West*, xi–xx, 232–242. Drinnon, xviii, points out that western writers talk of a "Western superculture, or the one true civilization" they distinguished "from so-called primitive cultures."

3. Richard Slotkin, *The Fatal Environment: The Myth of the Frontier in the Age of Industrialization, 1800–1890* (New York: Atheneum, 1985), 135–137, discusses the relationship of the vigilante to the wider society.

4. David A. Johnson, "Vigilance and the Law: The Moral Authority of Popular Justice in the Far West," *American Quarterly* 33 (winter 1981), 573–574, indicates that in California, vigilantism declined rapidly within a few years of the 1849 Gold Rush. In Colorado the decline took longer, in part because new boomtowns, places similar to Denver in 1859, were created constantly throughout much of the late nineteenth century.

5. Cook, *Hands Up*, 39.

6. Owen, "Crimes in Denver, 1859–1864."

7. Today homicide rates are figured per hundred thousand population. So, for example, if a city of 100,000 had 45 homicides in a year, the rate would be 45. Denver's population declined in the early 1860s. To even out some of the distortions caused by using a small population base to determine murder rates, I have figured that the population in each of the years 1861 through 1864 was 4,000. I multiplied that number by four to get 16,000. The number of homicides in those years appears to be 13. Using 16,000 as the base, the rate is 81 per hundred thousand, or about seven times the 1998 rate. Robert R. Dykstra has warned historians against overemphasizing violence in the West in "Field Notes: Overdosing on Dodge City," *Western Historical Quarterly* 27 (winter 1996), 505–514. The homicide numbers for 1859–1864 do not include People's Court executions and other lynchings. If those killings were included the homicide rate would soar. The 1999 numbers are from *RMN*, October 16, 2000. The national murder rate in 1999 was 5.7 per hundred thousand.

8. Irving Howbert, *Memories of a Lifetime in the Pike's Peak Region* (New York: G. P. Putnam's Sons, 1925), 47.

9. A. Z. Sheldon, "History of El Paso County," in Anon., *History of the Arkansas Valley, Colorado* (Evansville, Ind.: Unigraphic, 1971, originally published 1881), 420.

10. B. F. Rockafellow, "History of Fremont County," in Anon., *History of the Arkansas Valley*, 577, describes Baxter as a member of a gang of thieves; *Tri-Weekly Miner's Register* [Central City], May 9, 1863, reports that a guerrilla was hanged near Fairplay. A fourth lynching possibly occurred in this period, but the account of it is noncontemporary. James Rose Harvey, "'Pioneer Experiences in Colorado' Interview With Elizabeth J. Tallman," *Colorado Magazine* 13 (July 1936), 141, includes Tallman's recollection that in late June 1864 "a gambler named Haslet was caught cheating, summarily tried, found guilty, and hanged on a cottonwood tree near our house." I have not been able to find confirmation of this, nor is Haslet mentioned in the crime list Elizabeth Owen compiled for the Colorado Historical Society. Perhaps Tallman was confusing "Haslet" with Bruce Hazlep, killed near Denver in May 1866 by persons who tried to make his death look like a lynching. See *RMN*, May 7, 1866.

11. Ariana Harner, "No Time for a Trial: The Abrupt Fate of the Reynolds Gang," *Colorado Heritage* (autumn 2000), 37–45. Harner notes that there is

some question about the number of Reynolds' gang members killed by the soldiers. It may have been four rather than five. Also see Morris F. Taylor, "Confederate Guerrillas in Southern Colorado," *Colorado Magazine* 46 (fall 1969), 304–323.

12. Hoig, *Sand Creek Massacre*, 70–73. Harner in "No Time for a Trial," 43, quotes Major General S. R. Curtis's October 15, 1864, response to Browne in which Curtis defended the troops, arguing that given "the harsh, summary cruel dictates of the pending trial of war," concern would be more appropriate for "better objects of human sympathy."

13. Hoig, *Sand Creek Massacre*, 147.

14. Ibid., 187.

15. *Weekly Commonwealth and Republican* [Denver], December 30, 1863. The pimp was jailed, escaped, was hunted down years later, "and refusing to be taken was shot by the parties in pursuit," who dumped his body into a well. See *RMN*, January 6, 1869. Although the pimp's death may technically meet the definition of a lynching, he is not counted in this book as having been lynched.

16. *RMN*, October 27, 1865. Charles Young, *Dangers of the Trail in 1865* (Geneva, N.Y.: W. F. Humphrey, 1912), 73, describes Denver in 1865 as "a hotbed of gambling, with murder and lynch law as a secondary pastime." That description seems appropriate for 1866 but not for 1865.

17. Smiley, *History of Denver*, 429–430.

18. Ibid., 429; Frank Hall, *History of the State of Colorado*, 4 vols. (Chicago: Blakely Print., 1889–1895), 1:438–440. Smiley says Williams was hanged on Cherry Creek a short distance southeast of Denver. Hall says the hanging was on the South Platte 4 miles northeast of town. Both sources indicate that years later, a farmer plowed up Williams's bones. Smiley's account, probably derived from interviewing an old pioneer, implies that Williams was lynched in late January. The *RMN* of January 13, 1866, reported that Williams had been hanged on January 4. The *News* article differs from Smiley on other details and does not mention the involvement of Denver citizens in Williams's death.

19. *RMN*, February 1, 1866. Tracks near the Fort Lupton lynching indicated that the lynchers had come from and returned to Denver.

20. Smiley, *History of Denver*, 429.

21. *RMN*, January 20, 1866. See also *RMN*, October 26–27, 1865, for earlier reports on the garroters. The use of the word *vigilantes* in the *News* report of October 26, 1865, was one of the earliest appearances of the term in a Colorado newspaper.

22. Ibid., February 26, 1866.

23. *Daily Mining Journal* [Black Hawk], March 29, 1866; *RMN*, April 3, June 27, 1866.

24. Junius E. Wharton, *History of the City of Denver From Its Earliest Settlement to the Present Time: To Which Is Added a Full and Complete Business Directory, By D. O. Wilhelm* (Denver: Byers and Dailey, 1866); Smiley, *History of Denver*, 428–430, 436.

25. John Evans to Margaret Gray Evans, June 15, 1862, quoted in Harry Kelsey, *Frontier Capitalist: The Life of John Evans* (Denver: State Historical Society of Colorado and Pruett, 1969), 121.

26. William Hepworth Dixon, *New America* (Philadelphia: J. B. Lippincott, 1867), 86–97.

27. The hanging of Bruce Hazlep, which was considered a private murder disguised as a lynching, was reported in the *RMN* on May 7, 1866. Hazlep's body was found in the western part of Denver within the city limits. Perhaps it was visible from some shopkeepers' doors, in which case Dixon was correct.

28. Ibid., May 8, 1867.

29. Ebenezer Cobham Brewer, *Dictionary of Phrase and Fable Giving the Derivation, Source, or Origin of Common Phrases, Allusions, and Words That Have a Tale to Tell, to Which Is Added a Concise Bibliography of English Literature* (Philadelphia: Henry Altemus, 1898; online edition by Bartleby.com). The 1898 dictionary cites Dixon as its authority on the phrase. The sixteenth edition of Brewer's *Dictionary of Phrase and Fable Revised by Adrian Room* (New York: Harper Resources, 1999) does not mention the term *gone up*, which has apparently gone away. For an 1866 use of the term see *RMN*, February 7, 1866: "The thief was caught, and he to use a local phrase, 'has gone up.'" The hanging was near Fort Lupton and may be one of those chronicled by Smiley, or it may be of a different person.

30. *RMN*, May 14, 1868.

31. Ibid., September 22, 1866, quoted in William Hanchett, "'His Turbulent Excellency,' Alexander Cummings, Governor of Colorado Territory, 1865–1867," *Colorado Magazine* 34 (April 1957), 96.

32. James Rusling, *Across America or the Great West and the Pacific Coast* (New York: Sheldon, 1874), 59, 61, 62.

33. Cook, in *Hands Up*, spells Duggan's name "Duggan," and that is the spelling adopted in this book. Smiley in *History of Denver*, 436, indicated that Duggan's first name was Sam.

34. Cook, *Hands Up*, 39–65, has considerable detail. Smiley, *History of Denver*, 437, confuses the sequence of events.

35. Cook, *Hands Up*, 54; *RMN*, November 23, 1868.

36. *RMN*, November 23, 1868.

37. Ibid., November 24, 1868.

38. Cook, *Hands Up*, 59.

39. Ibid., 60; *RMN*, November 23, 1868, July 11, 1911.

40. *RMN*, December 2, 1868; *Central City Register*, December 3, 1868.

41. *RMN*, November 24, 1868.

42. Ibid.

43. *Central City Register*, December 3, 1868.

44. Taft A. Larson, *History of Wyoming* (Lincoln: University of Nebraska Press, 1978), 60–61; ibid., November 22, 25, 1868. D. Claudia Thompson, "Driven From Point to Point: Fact and Legend in the Bear River Riot," *Montana*

46 (1996), 24–37, takes a revisionist look at the Bear River City troubles. Whatever the merits of the Bear River City rioters, Denver's solid citizens saw the events there as an uprising of outlaws against the better people.

45. Paul H. Giddens, "Letters of S. Newton Pettis, Associate Justice of the Colorado Supreme Court, Written in 1861," *Colorado Magazine* 15 (January 1938), 9.

46. Dawson Scrapbooks, 35:7.

47. Wilbur F. Stone, ed., *History of Colorado* (Chicago: S. J. Clarke, 1918), 1:734.

48. Ibid.

49. James Owen, "Reminiscences of Early Pueblo," *Colorado Magazine* 22 (May 1945), 104.

50. John D.W. Guice, *The Rocky Mountain Bench: The Territorial Supreme Courts of Colorado, Montana, and Wyoming, 1861–1890* (New Haven: Yale University Press, 1972), 70.

51. Ibid., 65.

52. *RMN*, April 25, September 20, 1866.

53. Guice, *Rocky Mountain Bench*, 70.

54. *RMN*, May 25, 1866.

55. Ibid., November 23, 1868.

56. Morris F. Taylor, "The Coe Gang: Rustlers of 'Robbers Roost,' " *Colorado Magazine* 51 (summer 1974), 199–215.

57. *Colorado Chieftain* [Pueblo], December 28, 1871.

58. *RMN*, April 16, 1868.

59. *Colorado Chieftain* [Pueblo], August 4, 1870.

60. Cook, *Hands Up*, 257–267; *RMN*, October 30, November 2, 1872.

61. *RMN*, September 15, 1880.

62. *Colorado Chieftain* [Pueblo], April 1, 1882.

63. Ibid., April 6, 1882.

64. Ibid.

65. Ibid.

66. *RMN*, April 1, 1882.

67. *Colorado Chieftain* [Pueblo], April 6, 1882.

68. Ibid.

69. *Colorado Springs Gazette*, April 1, 1882.

70. *Colorado Chieftain* [Pueblo], April 6, 1882.

71. Ibid., January 24, 1882.

72. Ibid., April 1, 1882.

73. William Vickers, *History of the City of Denver, Arapahoe County, and Colorado* (Chicago: O. L. Baskin, 1880), 218. Vickers spelled Duggan's name "Dugan."

74. Smiley, *History of Denver*, 437.

75. Griswold, *Leadville*, 1:351.

76. Ibid., 1:345.

77. Ibid., 1:160.

78. Ibid., 1:346; Sherrill Warford and Nancy Manly, "The View From Both Sides of the Badge: Edward Frodsham Patrick A. Kelly," *Mountain Diggings* 18 (1988), 21–35. Frodsham's first name is sometimes given as Edwin; his last name is variously spelled in the press.

79. Griswold, *Leadville*, 1:349. Stewart's name is sometimes given as Stuart.

80. *RMN*, November 21, 1879. Ibid., 1:353, quotes a passage from the memoirs of the actor Eddie Foy who witnessed the lunching. Foy indicates that a third person was hanged that night, "a boy of no more than fourteen or fifteen years." The Griswolds question Foy's account.

81. Griswold, *Leadville*, 1:954–957. Wilde might have held a grudge against Leadville because, as local legend has it, as he started his lecture with "I give myself to Leadville," a stagehand accidentally hit the curtain in front of which Wilde stood, propelling him into the orchestra pit.

82. Ibid., 1:807–809. The weighted hanging machine used in Denver's 1886 public execution of Andrew Green led to Green's slow strangulation. That spectacle, witnessed by around 15,000 persons, prompted a state law providing that executions be conducted at the penitentiary. See William M. King, *Going to Meet a Man: Denver's Last Public Execution, 27 July 1886* (Niwot: University Press of Colorado, 1990).

83. Oscar Wilde, *The Soul of Man Under Socialism* (London: Arthur L. Humphreys, 1912), 35–36.

84. Edward L. Wheeler, *Deadwood Dick in Leadville; or, a Strange Stroke for Liberty, Volume II, Number 23* (New York: Arthur H. Westbrook, March 15, 1899, originally published June 24, 1879). Deadwood Dick turned himself in and allowed his pursuers to lynch him with the plan of being revived later. Another view of Leadville's lack of law and order is given by Italian visitor Giovanni Vigna Dal Ferro in *Un Viaggio Nel Far West Americano*, portions of which, translated and edited by Frederick G. Bohme, were reprinted in *Colorado Magazine* 35 (October 1958), 290–302.

85. Griswold, *Leadville*, 2:1776.

86. *Denver Tribune Republican*, September 21, 1886.

87. *Colorado Chieftain* [Pueblo], April 6, 1882.

88. Colorado City, founded in 1859, was later absorbed into Colorado Springs, which was established in 1871. See Aldridge, *Historic Colorado City*. Perhaps as many as five people were lynched in or near Colorado City between 1860 and 1869.

CHAPTER 3:
THE HINTERLAND

1. John Ophus, "The Lake County War, 1874–1875," *Colorado Magazine* 47 (spring 1970), 124.

2. *RMN*, May 17, 1869.

3. *Colorado Chieftain* [Pueblo], July 15, 1869.

4. *RMN*, October 25, 1870.

5. *Daily Central City Register,* August 2, 1870.

6. *Las Animas Leader,* May 8, 1874.

7. *Cañon City Times,* April 22, 1875, quoted in *Pueblo Chieftain,* December 1, 1960.

8. *RMN,* July 6, 1880.

9. Ibid., June 27, 1866, October 25, 1870, July 15, 1871; *Colorado Chieftain* [Pueblo], August 28, 1873; Rockafellow, "Fremont County," 587; *Buena Vista Democrat,* November 1, 1883; Elizabeth Cairns, "Interview With J. H. Maxey, December 12, 1933," Civil Works Administration Interviews, Pueblo County, CWA 344/3, 11, typescript in Colorado Historical Society. Cairns reports that she came to Pueblo in 1888 and in a walk about town saw the bodies of three Mexican men near Eleventh and Santa Fe "hanged to trees by means of lassos of baling wire." The *Pueblo Chieftain,* August 29, 1873, reported an unconfirmed rumor that an unidentified Mexican woman had been killed in Trinidad in retaliation for having turned in two men accused of murder. The woman's death, being unconfirmed and perhaps not meeting the definition of lynching, is not counted as a lynching in this study.

10. *Silver World* [Lake City], August 7, 1875.

11. *Tri-Weekly Miner's Register* [Central City], May 5, 1866. The *Miner's Register* pointed out that until 1863 the law had allowed horse thieves to be punished by death or by not less than twenty years' imprisonment. In 1863 the law was softened to make the prison term up to twenty years' or death. According to the *RMN,* July 25, 1860, a horse thief, Samuel K. Dunn, was sentenced, evidently by a People's Court, "to receive 25 lashes in public this evening and [was] ordered to leave the country."

12. *RMN,* June 29, 1867. Transcript from *Boulder Tribune,* April 3, 1908, in Colorado Historical Society.

13. Griswold, *Leadville,* 1:87, quoting the diary of John Lawrence. Another horse theft was attributed to Sanchez after he was arrested for the two thefts.

14. *RMN,* October 2, 1867.

15. Ibid., June 5, 1868; *Colorado Chieftain* [Pueblo], June 1, 1868. Pueblo's *Chieftain* reported this lynching in its first issue, just as Denver's *RMN* had reported the hanging of John Stuffle in its first issue.

16. *Colorado Chieftain* [Pueblo], June 1, 1868. The reference is to the impeachment of President Andrew Johnson, which concluded in mid-May 1868, shortly before the hangings of Watson and Hudson.

17. Frankstown later became known as Franktown.

18. Transcript from *Daily Central City Register,* December 4, 1870, in Colorado Historical Society.

19. *RMN,* September 9, 1874. Middle Kiowa was later renamed Kiowa.

20. *Colorado Chieftain* [Pueblo], January 8, 9, 1880. The *Chieftain* reported that the men who overpowered the sheriff did not wear masks.

21. *Chicago Tribune,* January 10, 1880.

22. *Denver Republican*, September 28, 1881.

23. Laura Manson-White, "Reminiscences of Uncle John B. Heilman Retold by Laura Manson-White," *San Luis Valley Historian* 16(2) (1984), 23. Heilman said he was among the crowd at the jail, as were Hank Dorris and Tom McCunnif. Such admissions, even years later, of participation in lynchings are rare. The *Denver Tribune Republican*, April 15, 1885, reported that in 1868, Howard had been part of the Musgrove horse stealing gang. See also *San Juan Prospector* [Del Norte], August 19, 1882. Arnold Howard is not to be confused with George Howard, another "bad man" living in southwestern Colorado until he was killed while resisting arrest in 1882.

24. Newspaper clipping from unidentified and undated Del Norte newspaper in files of Colorado Historical Society, Denver.

25. *RMN*, August 5, 1884. Cebolla was 17 miles west of Gunnison.

26. Dodge may also have been involved in stagecoach robberies in the Laporte area. See ibid., March 1, 2, 1869. In support of the inference that he was lynched for more than stealing $250, see ibid., July 25, 1872.

27. Muriel Sibell Wolle, *Stampede to Timberline: The Ghost Towns and Mining Camps of Colorado* (Chicago: Swallow, 1974), 279; Joanne West Dodds, *Custer County: Mountains, Mines, and Ranches* (Denver: Colorado Endowment for the Humanities, 1992), 7; A. W. Monroe, "Interview With Robert M. Ormsby, December 11, 1933," Civil Works Administration Interview, CWA 357/64, in Colorado Historical Society.

28. Anon., *Southern Colorado Historical and Descriptive* (Cañon City, Colo.: Binckley and Hartwell, 1879), 103.

29. Ramon F. Adams, comp., *Six Guns and Saddle Leather: A Bibliography of Books and Pamphlets on Western Outlaws and Gunmen* (Norman: University of Oklahoma Press, 1969), covers LeRoy in entries 202, 541, 1065, 2454. Adams notes that some authors have confused LeRoy with Billy the Kid. For identification of the Pond brothers, see *Denver Republican*, June 7, 1881.

30. *San Juan Prospector* [Del Norte], May 28, 1881.

31. Ibid.; *RMN*, May 25, 1881.

32. *Denver Tribune*, July 22, 1881.

33. *RMN*, July 23, 1881. The slaughterhouse was outside Antonito.

34. Robert Black III, *Island in the Rockies: The History of Grand County, Colorado, to 1930* (Granby, Colo.: Country Printer, 1977), 220–224.

35. *RMN*, October 10, 1886.

36. Sybil Downing and Robert E. Smith, *Tom Patterson: Colorado Crusader for Change* (Niwot: University Press of Colorado, 1995), 47.

37. Carolyn H. Wright and Clarence Wright, *Tiny Hinsdale of the Silvery San Juan* (Denver: Big Mountain, 1964), 125.

38. *Denver Weekly Tribune*, November 5, 1873.

39. Alfred A. Look, *Unforgettable Characters of Western Colorado* (Boulder: Pruett, 1966), 231.

40. *Alamosa Journal*, May 1, 1884.

41. *Denver Republican*, March 9, 1891.

42. Sam Howe Scrapbook, 1896, entry 11448, clipping probably from the *Denver Republican*, January 8, 1896, in Colorado Historical Society.

43. *Denver Post*, December 31, 1905.

44. Ervan F. Kushner, *Alferd G. Packer, Cannibal! Victim?* (Frederick, Colo.: Platte 'N Press, 1980), 163. Colorado historians enjoy debating the spelling of Packer's first name, which is sometimes given as Alfred and at others as Alferd. "Memorandum From Agnes Wright Spring to Judge Hickey, February 18, 1959," typescript in files of Colorado Historical Society, gives a short history of the legalities surrounding the legal mess created by the Colorado legislature in the early 1880s when, in an effort to make it easier to impose the death penalty, it accidentally repealed the law against first-degree murder. It did not repeal the statute against manslaughter. Packer was resentenced for five counts of that crime, giving him a total sentence of 40 years.

45. *Denver Republican*, March 30, 1897; *Denver Post*, February 6, 1905.

46. "List of Inmates at the Colorado State Penitentiary," Colorado State Archives, Denver.

47. *San Juan Prospector* [Del Norte], September 25, October 16, 1886; *Solid Muldoon*, October 1, 1886.

48. *Solid Muldoon*, October 8, 1886.

49. Griswold, *Leadville*, 1:1245, quoting *Evening Chronicle* [Leadville], September 1, 1883. The Griswold account is confused. The date may be September 11, 1883.

50. *Colorado Tribune* [Golden], August 7, 1867.

51. William A. Bell, *New Tracks in North America* (Albuquerque: Horn and Wallace, 1965, originally published 1870), 91–92.

52. *Weekly Transcript* [Golden], May 1, 1867.

53. Ibid.; *RMN*, May 2, 1867. Transcript of an article identified as having appeared in the Georgetown *Courier* in either September or October 1940 in Colorado Historical Society gives the location of Dr. Aduddel's offices as Central City. Also see "Randall Clippings," 2:242, June 1907, in Colorado Historical Society, for transcript of what is evidently an article in a Georgetown newspaper.

54. John W. Irion, "Lynching of Hull's Slayers," *The Trail* 2 (April 1910), 23.

55. *RMN*, February 25, 1868; *Colorado Tribune* [Golden], February 19, 1868; Jonathan Shinn, *The Memoirs of Capt. Jonathan Shinn* (Greeley, Colo.: Weld County Democrat, 1890), 79–83; Vauna S. Schulz, "Pioneer Justice in Douglas County," *Colorado Magazine* 24 (May 1947), 125. Schulz does not give the names of the men, and she places the event in 1867. She is likely writing a confused account of the deaths of Murrays and Coats. She says the skeleton was burned when the school burned in the 1880s.

56. *RMN*, November 8, 1869.

57. Richard B. Townshend, *A Tenderfoot in Colorado* (Norman: University of Oklahoma Press, 1968, originally published 1923), 114–116.

58. Charles T. Linton, "An Early Western Experience," *Sons of Colorado* 1 (May 1907), 37–38.

59. Townshend, *Tenderfoot*, 127–128.

60. Alonzo Allen, "Pioneer Life in Old Burlington, Forerunner of Longmont," *Colorado Magazine* 14 (July 1937), 155.

61. Dodds, *Custer County*, 7; Gail Bederman, *Manliness and Civilization: A Cultural History of Gender and Race in the United States, 1880–1917* (Chicago: University of Chicago Press, 1995), 45–76.

62. *RMN*, February 18, 1874. Nearly forty years later *Field and Farm*, a Denver publication that often took liberties with the truth, reworked Spinner's lynching. Moll Howard became a stagecoach passenger "who said her name was Molly Brown." Spinner became a man named Henson who killed Brown with a rock after she refused to pay him for carrying her luggage. Women then lynched him. See *Field and Farm*, February 17, 1912.

63. *RMN*, July 23, 1876; Rockafellow, "Fremont County," 587.

64. *RMN*, November 23, 1877.

65. Ibid., July 8, 1879; *Denver Republican*, July 7, 1879.

66. Cook, *Hands Up*, 103.

67. Ibid., 73–103; transcript of *Colorado Transcript* [Golden], December 31, 1879, in Colorado Historical Society.

68. *RMN*, September 3, 5, 1879; Nossaman, *Silverton*, 2:227–278. Cleary was buried in an unmarked grave in Silverton's Hillside Cemetery, thereby costing San Juan County fifteen dollars. Freda C. Peterson, comp., *The Story of Hillside Cemetery, San Juan County Burials, 1873–1988* (Oklahoma City: n.p., 1989), 108.

69. *Silver World* [Lake City], April 29, 1882.

70. Ibid.

71. Ibid.

72. *RMN*, March 30, 1878.

73. Ibid., July 29, 1877.

CHAPTER 4:
THE CUDDIGAN AND OTHER LYNCHINGS, 1884–1906

1. *Denver Tribune*, January 25, 1884; *Grand Junction News*, February 16, 1884, for time of lynching. Mary Rose Mathews's age was sometimes reported as eleven and her name given as Rose. The 1880 census, taken June 5, 1880, lists her name as Mary and her age as six. See U.S. Census Bureau, 1880 Census, Colorado, Arapahoe County, Denver, 294, microform in Western History and Genealogy Department, Denver Public Library.

2. Morris F. Taylor, *Trinidad, Colorado Territory* (Pueblo: O'Brien, 1966), 135, reports the killing of the Hispanic woman as a fact, but the August 29, 1873, report of the event in Pueblo's *Chieftain*, upon which Taylor relied, says the report was a rumor and "this rumor needs confirmation."

3. *Daily Register* [Central City], January 26, 1884; *Grand Junction News*, January 26, 1884; *Gunnison Review-Press*, February 1, 1884. See also *Summit*

County News [Breckenridge], January 26, 1884; *Colorado Springs Weekly Register*, January 26, 1884; *Denver Times*, January 20, 1884, for reports that this lynching was unusual, perhaps the first of a woman. The *New York Times*, January 20, 1884, said Margaret was the first woman to be lynched in Colorado. The *White Pine Cone* [White Pine, Gunnison County], January 25, 1884, cited an earlier case of a woman being lynched in Kansas but gave neither name nor date. The lynching of Juanita is covered in Hubert Howe Bancroft, *Popular Tribunals* (San Francisco: History, 1887), 586.

4. George A. Crofutt, *Crofutt's Grip-sack Guide of Colorado, Volume II, 1885* (Golden, Colo.: Cubar, 1966, originally published 1885), 126.

5. Ernest Ingersoll, *The Crest of the Continent* . . . (Glorieta, N. Mex: Rio Grande, 1969, originally published 1885), 278.

6. *Solid Muldoon*, January 4, 1884.

7. Ibid., January 13, 1882, reprint of *Denver Republican* annual edition article for description of Dallas; also Crofutt, *Grip-sack Guide*, 86.

8. Crofutt, *Grip-sack Guide*, 126.

9. *Solid Muldoon*, April 20, 1883.

10. Ibid., December 7, 1883, January 11, 1884.

11. Crofutt, *Grip-sack Guide*, 127.

12. *Solid Muldoon*, January 25, 1884, quoting *Denver Republican*.

13. *Denver Tribune*, January 27, 1884. *Delta Chief*, January 23, 1884, has a good recapitulation of Denver papers' reports on Charles Mathews; *Grand Junction News*, February 16, 1884, published an interview with Father Servant and James Carroll in which Servant told of Rose's mistreatment by her own parents.

14. *Delta Chief*, January 24, 1884.

15. U.S. Census Bureau, 1880, La Salle County, Illinois, Township of Manlius, Village of Crotty [Seneca], household 154, lists Kate Carroll, a widow, and her family including Maggie, then age seventeen.

16. *Solid Muldoon*, February 2, 1884.

17. Colorado State Census, 1885, Ouray County, microfilm in Western History and Genealogy Department, Denver Public Library. In 1885, Colorado conducted a special census. It listed three adult male Cuddigans—Henry, age thirty-eight; Patrick, age thirty-five; and William, age thirty-six—living in the same area of Ouray County as Michael had. All, with little doubt, were Michael's brothers. Near William lived "M. Baitch," probably a mistaken rendering of the name Martin Birtsh, and with him lived his mother-in-law, Margaret Cuddigan, likely the mother of the other Cuddigans and also likely the mother of "Maggs," the wife of Martin Birtsh. William Cuddigan was household thirty-one; M. Baitch, Maggs Baitch, and M. Cuddigan were number thirty-two; P. Cuddigan, number 133. P. Cuddigan was then living on the farm that had belonged to Michael. Listed among his children was P. Cuddigan, age two, likely young Percie. Henry Cuddigan was at household 146. Michael Cuddigan Estate Records, "Administrator's Bond January 22, 1884," in Ouray

County Probate Court Records, Box 3341, Colorado State Archives, Denver, lists Henry Cuddigan as the administrator of the estate, with the document appointing him signed by Martin Birtsh, Patrick and William Cuddigan, and H. S. Holaday. The estate records are available at the Colorado State Archives, Denver. The *Solid Muldoon*, January 25, 1884, reported that Margaret and Michael had been buried in an enclosure on the farm of H. S. Holiday [*sic*]. The census report shows Holaday as household 24, not far from William Cuddigan and M. Baitch [Birtsh].

18. *Denver Tribune*, January 25, 1884, February 1, 1884.

19. Ibid., January 27, 1884.

20. Ibid.

21. Ibid., January 25, 1884, has details other papers lack. *Grand Junction News*, February 16, 1884; *Solid Muldoon*, January 18, 1884; *Denver Tribune*, February 1, 1884.

22. *Solid Muldoon*, January 18, 1884.

23. Ibid.

24. Ibid.

25. *Animas Forks Pioneer*, January 26, 1884; *Grand Junction News*, February 16, 1884.

26. *Denver Tribune*, February 1, 1884; Michael Cuddigan Estate Records.

27. *Solid Muldoon*, January 18, 1884.

28. *Animas Forks Pioneer*, January 26, 1884; *Denver Republican*, January 30, 1884.

29. *Denver Tribune*, January 27, 1884; *Solid Muldoon*, February 1, 1884.

30. *Grand Junction News*, February 16, 1884; *Denver Tribune*, January 25, 1884.

31. *Grand Junction News*, February 16, 1884.

32. *Fairplay Flume*, January 24, 1884; *San Juan Prospector* [Del Norte], January 26, 1884; *Dolores News* [Rico], January 26, 1884; *Durango Herald* quoted in *Denver Tribune*, February 3, 1884; *Animas Forks Pioneer*, January 26, 1884. The *Denver Republican*, February 5, 1884, lists twenty-two antilynching Colorado papers. The *Denver Tribune*, February 3, 1884, provides press excerpts, many favoring the lynching.

33. *Mining Register* [Lake City], quoted in *Denver Tribune*, February 3, 1884; *Silver World* [Lake City], January 26, February 2, 1884: *Rico Record*, January 31, 1884.

34. *Grand Junction News*, January 26, 1884; *Silverton Democrat*, January 26, 1884. See reprint of *Ouray Times* article in *Silverton Democrat*, February 9, 1884.

35. *Denver Tribune*, January 22, 1884.

36. *Solid Muldoon*, April 20, 1883.

37. *Queen Bee*, January 30, February 7, 1884.

38. *RMN*, January 29, 1884; *Colorado Chieftain* [Pueblo], February 7, 1884.

39. *Leadville Daily Herald*, January 22, 1884.

40. *Solid Muldoon,* January 25, 1884.

41. *Denver Tribune,* January 27, 1884; *Denver Republican,* January 27, 1884.

42. *Solid Muldoon,* February 1, 8, 22, 29, 1884; quotation from February 22 edition.

43. Ibid., January 25, 1884; *Denver Tribune,* February 1, 1884.

44. *Animas Forks Pioneer,* April 19, 1884.

45. *Denver Tribune,* January 22, 1884.

46. Ibid.

47. Ibid., January 28, 1884; *Solid Muldoon,* February 1, 1884; *Denver Republican,* January 29, 1884.

48. *Denver Tribune,* February 2, 1884.

49. *Denver Republican,* February 2, 1884.

50. *Solid Muldoon,* February 8, 1884; *RMN,* April 20, 1924.

51. *Denver Tribune,* January 27, 1884; *Grand Junction News,* February 16, 1884.

52. W. J. Miller to James B. Grant, February 28, 1884, in James B. Grant Papers, Box 26689, Colorado State Archives, Denver.

53. Robert Servant to James Grant, February 9, 1884, in James B. Grant Papers, Box 26689, Colorado State Archives, Denver; *Solid Muldoon,* March 21, 1884. Day delighted in the governor's response to Servant.

54. *Solid Muldoon,* May 9, 1884; *Grand Junction News,* May 10, 1884.

55. Ouray County, Probate Court Records, Box 3341, Colorado State Archives, Denver; *Ottawa* [Illinois] *Republican,* January 25, 1884.

56. *Denver Tribune,* January 25, 1884.

57. Quoted in *Durango-Cortez Herald,* February 22, 1976. In a March 20, 1934, interview conducted by A. L. Soens, Dr. W. C. Folsom recalled that Moorman had intended to shoot out the lights in a Durango saloon, "but not being accustomed to double action six shooters killed a man by accident." Civil Works Administration Interviews, CWA 362/40, typescript in Colorado Historical Society.

58. On the June 1882 Rico lynchings of Trinidad Charley and Tom Wall see Carl F. Mathews, "Rico, Colorado—Once a Roaring Camp," *Colorado Magazine* 28 (January 1951), 43; *La Plata Miner* [Silverton], December 31, 1882.

59. *San Juan Prospector* [Del Norte], August 19, 1882, presented a retrospective account of the career of Arnold Howard with incidental information on Frank Young. On William Blair see *RMN,* August 18, 1882.

60. Nossaman, *Silverton,* 2:88.

61. *Solid Muldoon,* August 8, 1883, said of the Gunnison trial: "The cost of prosecution will reach far into the thousands. Here in civilized Ouray, Judge Lynch officiates in complicated cases of a capital nature, and does so very economically." Made four months before the Cuddigan lynchings, the first lynchings I have found recorded in Ouray, the *Muldoon* statement implies there were other, unrecorded or as yet unearthed illegal executions in that mountain town.

62. *La Plata Miner* [Silverton], April 4, 1885.

63. *Silverton Democrat-Herald,* April 11, 1885.

64. *Solid Muldoon,* September 16, 1887; *San Juan* [Silverton], September 15, 1887. The Dixon case is more fully treated in Chapter 6.

65. *Pueblo Chieftain,* August 26, 1891; *Solid Muldoon,* August 28, 1891.

66. On Banta see George G. Everett and Wendell F. Hutchinson, *Under the Angel of Shavano* (Denver: Golden Bell, 1963), 413–414; *Daily Register-Call* [Central City], April 17, 1888, on Baker; Diana A. Kouris, *The Romantic and Notorious History of Brown's Park* (Greybull, Wyo.: Wolverine Gallery, 1988), 86–90, on Bennett.

67. See the Introduction for a fuller account of Wister's, Hafen's, and Rister's work.

68. *Denver Republican,* December 30, 1888; *Denver Times,* December 29, 1888. *Greeley Tribune,* July 20, 1960, tells of the razing of the jail from which French was taken. The site became a parking lot.

69. *Fort Collins Courier,* April 5, 1888; *Denver Republican,* April 5, 6, 1888.

70. Transcript from *Denver Tribune,* May 28, 1874, in Colorado Historical Society. Witherill's name has been spelled numerous ways.

71. *Denver Times,* January 3, 1889.

72. Kenneth Jessen, *Colorado Gunsmoke: True Stories of Outlaws and Lawmen on the Colorado Frontier* (Boulder: Pruett, 1986), 183.

73. *Denver Times,* November 5, 1888.

74. *Denver Republican,* December 5, 1888. Witherill was also suspected in the murder of Marinus Jansen in the autumn of 1887.

75. Ibid. Fred M. Mazzulla, "Undue Process of Law—Here and There," in Francis B. Rissari, ed., *Brand Book of the Denver Westerners* (Boulder: Johnson, 1965), 264–269, has a picture of Witherill's head on a pole and information on the disposition of souvenirs, including Witherill's lip and walrus mustache. See *Solid Muldoon,* December 7, 1888, for Ouray's approval of Witherill's lynching.

76. Sam Howe Scrapbooks, Murder Book, 366; *Trinidad Chronicle News,* January 23, 1900.

77. *Cañon City Record,* January 25, 1900.

78. Unidentified newspaper clipping ca. January 26, 1900, in Western History and Genealogy Department, Denver Public Library.

79. *Trinidad Chronicle News,* January 27, 1900.

80. Unidentified newspaper clipping ca. January 26, 1900, in Western History and Genealogy Department, Denver Public Library.

81. *Cañon City Record,* February 1, 1900.

82. *RMN,* May 24, 1959, retrospective on the lynchings said the doctors gave up when they found the coffin too heavy to move.

83. *Denver Times,* June 2, 1894. McCurdy's brother-in-law lived through his ordeal.

84. Hugo Selig, *Early Recollections of Montrose, Colorado* (Montrose: Reprinted from the Montrose Daily Press, 1939), 22–23. This rare book is at the

Colorado Historical Society. See also *Montrose Press*, November 25, 1904; *Montrose Enterprise*, November 4, 11, 1905.

85. *RMN*, December 27, 1906.

86. Ibid., December 28, 1906. I am indebted to Ellen Slatkin who suggested the "moment of misstatement" line.

87. Ibid., January 23, 1884.

88. Ibid., December 29, 1906.

CHAPTER 5:
TUG-OF-WAR

1. Smiley, *History of Denver*, 347–348; *RMN*, September 20, 1860, on comments in Denver regarding the missing watch; *RMN*, March 15, 1861, on the return of the watch. Some inconsistencies are found between contemporary accounts and Smiley's account. Smiley's informant may have been Hiram P. Bennet, who the *Rocky Mountain Herald* [Denver], September 3, 1860, inferred was among the party that went after horse thieves. Bennet's obituary, *Denver Times*, November 11, 1914, credited him with helping rid the region of outlaws. A typescript of an interview with Richard Sopris, in the files of the Colorado Historical Society, suggests that the watch was not recovered in El Paso, Texas, but on the "Heufranan" River and that the man who took it was killed. Heufranan may be a misspelling of the Huerfano River in southern Colorado.

2. *Rocky Mountain Herald* [Denver], September 15, 1860.

3. Transcript from the *Western Mountaineer* [Golden], January 25, 1860, in Colorado State Historical Society.

4. *RMN*, May 5, 1866.

5. Ibid., May 14, 1868.

6. Ibid., June 30, 1865.

7. Ibid., July 12, 1870. On July 20, 1870, the *News* carried a message from the self-styled vigilance committee that accused O'Neal of burning two ranches. Brown's Bridge was on the South Platte between present-day Quincy and Belleview Avenues.

8. Ibid., July 12, 1870.

9. Ibid.

10. O'Neal was probably first buried at Mount Prospect, which later became Denver's Cheesman Park. His modest tombstone is now at Denver's Fairmount Cemetery to which some of the bodies at Mount Prospect were moved.

11. *RMN*, December 12, 1871, February 25, 1872.

12. Ibid., January 29, 1875.

13. That dog may not have been the only animal lynched in Colorado. Many years ago I found a report of a trained bear killing a human opponent in a wrestling match, which resulted in both the bear and its owner, an African American named Pete Burns, being lynched. The case has not been included in this book because I cannot find the original source.

14. Griswold, *Leadville*, 1:117.

15. John L. Dyer, *The Snow-Shoe Itinerant: An Autobiography of the Rev. John L. Dyer, Familiarly Known as Father Dyer, of the Colorado Conference, Methodist Episcopal Church* (Cincinnati: Cranston and Stowe, 1890), 314. Dyer is quoting *RMN*, July 5, 1875.

16. Ophus, "Lake County War," 130, quoting *Central City Register*, July 8, 1875.

17. Ibid., 131. The Ophus article is the best of many accounts of the Lake County war. A few years after Dyer's death Chaffee County, scene of most of the anti-Gibbs strife, was separated from Lake County, so histories of Chaffee County such as June Shaputis and Suzanne Kelly, comps. and eds., *A History of Chaffee County* (Marceline, Mo.: Walsworth, 1982), also contain accounts of the feud.

18. Quoted in Ophus, "Lake County War," 133. In 1883 Grand County factions warred over the location of the county seat, leading to five deaths, including one suicide. That fracas, unlike the Lake County War, was not marked by the trappings of lynchings such as vigilance committees and hangings; nor has it been viewed as a lynching by Grand County's leading historian, Robert C. Black III. See Black, *Island in the Rockies*, 186–205.

19. Dyer, *Snow-Shoe Itinerant*, 290.

20. Ophus, "Lake County War," 134.

21. Albert B. Sanford, "John L. Routt, First State Governor of Colorado," *Colorado Magazine* 3 (August 1926), 84.

22. *Denver Republican*, January 30, 1884.

23. *Solid Muldoon*, August 28, 1891.

24. *Denver Republican*, December 5, 1888.

25. Transcript from *Colorado Topics* [Hyde, Washington County, Colo.], April 13, 1888, in Colorado Historical Society; Ansel Watrous, *History of Larimer County, Colorado* (Fort Collins: Courier, 1911), 117. In 1890, Fort Collins had a total population of 2,011. If one makes the generous assumption that 1,000 were males over eighteen, then a mob of 300 constituted about one-third of the adult males.

26. Ophus, "Lake County War," 132.

27. *Silver World* [Lake City], April 29, 1881.

28. *Fort Collins Courier*, April 5, 1888.

29. *San Juan Prospector* [Del Norte], September 5, 1886.

30. Johnson, "Vigilance and the Law," 562.

31. Stephen J. Leonard and Thomas J. Noel, *Denver: Mining Camp to Metropolis* (Niwot: University Press of Colorado, 1990), 66.

32. *Leadville Herald-Democrat*, March 27, 1902. Griswold, *Leadville*, 1:445, paints a less grim picture of Leadville's law enforcement establishment, indicating that in late 1879 the city had twenty police officers and eight other law enforcers, including detectives, prison and jail guards, and a city marshal. Policemen were paid $100 a month.

33. *San Juan Prospector* [Del Norte], October 16, 1886, quoting the *Montrose Messenger.*

34. Rockafellow, "Fremont County," 580–585. The Leaper story may be one of those legends bedeviling western history.

35. *RMN*, March 1, 1862.

36. Wright and Wright, *Tiny Hinsdale*, 124.

37. *RMN*, June 16, 1882.

38. *Mountain Mail* [Salida], July 21, 1880; *Animas Forks Pioneer*, February 2, 1884; *RMN*, July 4, 1887.

39. *Gunnison Daily Review*, May 30, 1882. J. H. Jackson was the uncle of Andrew Jackson, the freighter killed by Utes in retaliation for the killing of the Ute Johnson Shavano in 1880.

40. Unidentified, undated newspaper clipping in George A.H. Baxter Scrapbook, Colorado Historical Society.

41. Henry C. Cornwall, "My First Years in the Gunnison Country," ed. Duane Vandenbusche, *Colorado Magazine* 46 (summer 1964), 238–239.

42. Transcript from *Greeley Tribune*, June 16, 1875, in Colorado Historical Society.

43. *RMN*, February 16, 28, April 4, 1877.

44. William B. Thom, "Early Day Marshals of Tin Cup," *Colorado Magazine* 10 (July 1933), 143.

45. Ibid., 143–144.

46. Nolie Mumey, *History of Tin Cup, Colorado (Virginia City), an Alpine Mining Camp Which Refused to Become a Ghost Town* (Boulder: Johnson, 1963), 159.

47. Maxine Benson, "Port Stockton," *Colorado Magazine* 43 (winter 1966), 27.

48. Cyrus W. Shores, *Memoirs of a Lawman*, ed. Wilson Rockwell (Denver: Sage, 1962), 192.

49. *RMN*, June 15, 1882.

50. *Gunnison Daily Review*, May 13, 1882.

51. *RMN*, June 18, 1859.

52. Ibid., August 27, 1871.

53. Isabella Bird, *A Lady's Life in the Rocky Mountains* (New York: Ballantine, 1973, originally published 1879), 166.

54. Transcript of *RMN*, September 7, 1874, in Colorado Historical Society. It is unclear from the article whether Reynolds died from his hanging or merely got the message and left alive. The story says he "met a sudden and tragic fate at Alma," which implies that he died.

55. Ibid., July 8, 1879.

56. Ibid., July 16, 1880.

57. Ronald K. Inouye, "Alamosa, Colorado: Some Highlights of Its Early History," *San Luis Valley Historian* 19(1) (1987), 29.

58. *RMN*, February 14, 1873.

59. Ibid.

60. Ibid., August 13, 1880. Also see ibid., November 3, 1870, February 14, 1873, August 12, 1877; *Pueblo Chieftain,* July 22, 1879, for other examples of lynching threats.

61. *RMN,* July 14, 1874.

62. A. L. Soens interview with John Davis [undated, ca. February 1934], Civil Works Administration Interviews, CWA 362/2, typescript in Colorado Historical Society.

63. Joseph R. Buchanan, *The Story of a Labor Agitator* (New York: Outlook, 1903), 188.

64. Carroll D. Wright, *A Report on Labor Disturbances in the State of Colorado From 1880 to 1904,* Senate Executive Document No. 122, 58th Congress, 3d Session (Washington, D.C.: Government Printing Office, 1905), 153.

65. Ibid., 85; *Colorado Transcript* [Golden], June 27, 1894.

66. Wright, *Labor Disturbances,* 249.

67. Transcript from *Colorado Transcript* [Golden], December 31, 1879, in Colorado Historical Society.

68. George M. Darley, *Pioneering in the San Juan: Personal Reminiscences of Work Done in Southwestern Colorado During the "Great San Juan Excitement"* (Chicago: Fleming H. Revell, 1899), 198.

69. William C. Ferril, *Sketches of Colorado . . .* (Denver: Western Press Bureau, 1911), 1:108.

70. Griswold, *Leadville,* 1:353.

71. Typescript from *Colorado Transcript* [Golden], December 31, 1879, in Colorado Historical Society; *Evening Chronicle* [Leadville], November 20, 1879, quoted in Griswold, *Leadville,* 1:348.

72. *RMN,* August 16, 1871, January 29, 1874, January 6, 1878.

73. Ibid., October 22, 1884.

74. Ibid., March 3, 1884.

75. A. W. Aiken, *Cool Desmond; or the Gambler's Big Game, a Romance of the Regions of the Lawless* (New York: Beadle's Half Dime Library 8[186], February 1881).

76. Anon., *Colorado Carl; or, King of the Saddle* (New York: Harry E. Wolff, May 8, 1918), Pluck and Luck, 1040.

77. Edward L. Wheeler, *Deadwood Dick, Jr. in Durango; or, "Gathered In"* (New York: Beadle and Adams, June 10, 1890), 3.

78. *Colorado Springs Gazette,* December 8, 1888; *Denver Republican,* December 5, 1888.

79. *RMN,* November 23, 1867; Cook, *Hands Up,* 67.

80. *Creede Candle,* June 24, 1892.

81. Cook, *Hands Up,* 220. Stogas were heavy boots or shoes.

82. *Fort Collins Courier,* April 5, 1888.

83. Smiley, *History of Denver,* 342; *Western Mountaineer* [Golden], June 28, 1860.

84. Dawson Scrapbook, 18:333, undated clipping from *Georgetown Courier.*

85. *Huerfano Herald* [La Veta], January 6, 1881.

86. Smiley, *History of Denver,* 930; Dick Kreck, *Denver in Flames: Forging a New Mile High City* (Golden: Fulcrum, 2000), 82. Smiley says Loescher's first name was Helmuth; Kreck says Elmer.

87. Wolle, *Stampede to Timberline,* 141.

88. Griswold, *Leadville,* 1:701, quoting *Evening Chronicle* [Leadville], July 28, 1880.

89. Alfred A. Look, *Sidelights on Colorado History: A Glance at Colorado History Without Depth, Details, or Direction* (Denver: Golden Bell, 1967), 3. Look and Wolle are not above repeating old stories.

90. *RMN,* December 13, 1879.

91. *Colorado Chieftain* [Pueblo], January 8, 1880; *Chicago Tribune,* January 10, 1880.

92. *RMN,* December 30, 1880.

93. Sanford, "John L. Routt," 84. Routt was Colorado's last territorial governor and its first state governor (1877–1879). He served again as governor from 1891 to 1893.

94. Wilson Rockwell, *Uncompahgre Country* (Denver: Sage, 1965), 73–74.

95. Jessen, *Colorado Gunsmoke,* 140.

96. Charles T. Linton, "An Experience With Horse Thieves," *The Trail* 1 (September 1908), 27.

97. *RMN,* August 5, 1879.

98. *Buena Vista Democrat,* October 18, 1883.

99. Kushner, *Alferd G. Packer,* 169. Kushner spells Packer's first name as Alferd.

100. *RMN,* April 7, 1894. See also Olivia Spalding Ferguson, "A Sketch of Delta County History," *Colorado Magazine* 5 (October 1928), 164, for the story of mob action against William Radcliffe and his employees at Grand Mesa in 1896. Other examples, among many, of threatened lynchings include that of John Bradley in Denver, *RMN,* August 26, 1908; of Thomas Stimson in Cañon City in 1890, in Sam Howe Scrapbooks, 1894–1895, item 1127; of Joe "Arizona Charley" Wolfe in 1895 at Gillett, in Perry Eberhardt, *Guide to the Colorado Ghost Towns and Mining Camps* (Chicago: Sage, 1970), 446; of Henry Dillman in Brighton in 1900, *Denver Post,* October 14, 1900; of a tramp in Littleton in 1896, Sam Howe Scrapbooks, item 11715; of Thomas Thomas in Florence in 1907, *RMN,* January 3, 1907; of Gilbert Nicholson in Cheyenne Wells in 1905, *RMN,* November 11, 1905; and of Robert Scott in 1890, *Denver Times,* January 23, 1890.

101. Edward L. Johnson to Charles Devens, November 11, 1880, in Letters Received by the Attorney General, 1871–1884 [Microform], Western Law and Order, Colorado, Reel II (Bethesda, Md.: University Publications of America, 1996), in Western History and Genealogy Department, Denver Public Library.

102. Ibid.

103. Jerome W. Johnson, "Murder on the Uncompahgre," *Colorado Magazine* 43 (summer 1966), 209–224.

104. Manson-White, "Reminiscences," 23.

105. Griswold, *Leadville*, 1:348.

106. Watrous, *History of Larimer County*, 117; *Denver Republican*, April 5, 1888.

107. *Denver Republican*, December 5, 1888.

108. *Colorado Transcript* [Golden], January 3, 1907.

109. Brundage, *Lynching in the New South*, 18–19.

110. Transcript of *Colorado Tribune* [Golden], March 3, 1870, in Colorado Historical Society.

111. Augusta H. Block, "Old Burlington," *Colorado Magazine* 19 (January 1942), 17; ibid.; Dorothy Large, *Old Burlington: First Town on the St. Vrain 1860–1871* (Longmont, Colo.: St. Vrain, 1984). The Burlington of the 1860s was a precursor town to Longmont, north of Denver, not the Burlington in eastern Colorado.

112. *RMN*, October 25, 1870.

113. Nossaman, *Silverton*, 3:30.

114. *Solid Muldoon*, September 15, 1883.

115. *RMN*, August 26, 1908.

116. *Leadville Daily Herald*, July 24, 1880.

117. *RMN*, July 10, 1882.

118. *Denver Post*, September 12, 1902. Flood was tried and sentenced to a year in jail. He was later pardoned. I am indebted to Ramona Percarek for finding this information.

119. *RMN*, February 19, 1881.

120. Ibid., June 2, 1894.

121. *Denver Republican*, February 25, 1891; Ruby G. Williamson, *Down With Your Dust: A Chronicle of the Upper Arkansas Valley, Colorado, 1860–1893* (Gunnison, Colo.: B&B, 1979), 101–102. Briley's brother was not lynched.

122. *Denver Republican*, March 1, 1891, quoting the *Salida Mail*.

123. Williamson, *Down With Your Dust*, 102.

124. Ida L. Uchill, *Pioneers, Peddlers, and Tsadikim: The Story of the Jews in Colorado* (Boulder: Quality Line, 1979), 158.

CHAPTER 6:
RACE AND LYNCHING

1. *Denver Times*, November 17, 1900. Porter's name was variously given by the newspapers. The *Denver Times* called him John Porter; the *RMN* used Preston Porter Jr.

2. *RMN*, November 18, 1900.

3. *Denver Times*, November 17, 1900. Some estimates put the mob size at 300, some of the onlookers having come to Limon by train from Colorado Springs.

4. *RMN*, November 18, 1900. The lynching was extensively covered in Denver papers. The information and quotations are from the *RMN*, November 18, 1900, and the *Denver Times*, November 18, 1900. The *Denver Times*, November 17, 1900, said the lynching took place "half way between Lake and Limon, not far from the railroad track and about a hundred yards from the wagon road." Lake Station is about 3 miles east of Limon.

5. John H. Monnett and Michael McCarthy devote a chapter to Porter in *Colorado Profiles: Men and Women Who Shaped the Centennial State* (Evergreen, Colo.: Cordillera, 1987).

6. Slotkin, *Gunfighter Nation*, 173–174.

7. *New York Times*, November 19, 1900.

8. *RMN*, November 18, 1900.

9. *Boulder Daily Camera*, November 16, 1900.

10. Ibid., November 17, 1900.

11. *Denver Times*, November 19, 1900, has a sampling of press comment from around the state, including the "hysterical women" quotation from the *Leadville Herald-Democrat*.

12. *Colorado Springs Gazette*, November 18, 1900; *Daily Sentinel* [Grand Junction], November 15, 1900.

13. *Denver Times*, November 23, 1900. The letter was also signed by several other people. On Loper see Carl Abbott, Stephen J. Leonard, and David McComb, *Colorado: A History of the Centennial State* (Niwot: University Press of Colorado, 1994), 214. Part of the Davis family moved to Colorado Springs in the late nineteenth century, and Loper remained loyal to them.

14. *New York Times*, November 21, 1900.

15. *Denver Times*, November 20, 1900.

16. Stephen J. Leonard, "Swimming Against the Current: A Biography of Charles S. Thomas, Senator and Governor," *Colorado Heritage* (fall 1994), 29.

17. *Denver Times*, November 22, 23, 26, 1900.

18. *Pueblo Sunday Opinion*, quoted in ibid., November 19, 1900.

19. *Denver Times*, November 9, 1900. Russell Lohshe, in "The Burning of Preston John Porter," a paper done December 5, 1994, for a senior seminar class at Metropolitan State College in Denver, makes the point regarding the other arrests.

20. *Denver Post*, May 5, 2001, for article on Mariano Medina.

21. All figures unless otherwise noted are from Colin P. Goodykoontz, "The People of Colorado," in LeRoy R. Hafen, ed., *Colorado and Its People: A Narrative and Topical History of the Centennial State*, 4 volumes (New York: Lewis Historical Publishing, 1948), 2:75–120. The Chinese statistics are from the U.S. Department of Commerce, Bureau of the Census, *Thirteenth Census of the United States Taken the Year 1910, Volume II, Population 1910, Alabama–Montana* (Washington, D.C.: Government Printing Office, 1913). Other census numbers are from the various decennial censuses conducted by the U.S. Census Bureau.

22. Jesse T. Moore Jr., "Seeking a New Life: Blacks in Post–Civil War Colorado," *Journal of Negro History* 78 (summer 1993), 166–187, includes much information, as does Abbott, Leonard, and McComb, *Colorado*, 187, 220.

23. Colorado's 1870 census has been indexed. That year there were approximately 418 persons with the common Hispanic surnames of Martines, Martinez, and Sanchez. Practically all of them lived in the southern Colorado counties of Conejos, Costilla, Huerfano, Las Animas, and Saguache. That same year the 559 persons in the territory with the non-Hispanic surnames of Miller and Smith were overwhelmingly found in Colorado counties outside the southern counties. Clearly, that year the southern counties were heavily Hispanic, and the rest of the territory was heavily non-Hispanic. Those southern counties comprised 28 percent of the territory's population in 1870. The 1880 census has also been indexed, and it shows the same high concentration of Hispanic population. That year the above-named southern counties plus Rio Grande, carved in 1874, mainly from Conejos, constituted 13 percent of the state's population. Probably by 1890, the number of Hispanics in Colorado dipped to less than 10 percent, a percentage that probably also applied to 1900. These figures are merely informed estimates. There were, for example, 5 persons named Sanchez in Pueblo County in 1870. The undercount in Hispanos for some Colorado counties, such as Pueblo, however, is offset by an overcount of Hispanos in southern counties such as Huerfano and Las Animas, which even in the 1860s had some non-Hispanos and gained—especially after 1880—increasing numbers of foreign-born coal miners. See Genealogical Society of Weld County, *1870 Colorado Territory Census Index* (Greeley: Weld County Genealogical Society, 1977); Ronald V. Jackson, ed., *Colorado 1880 Census Index* (Bountiful, Utah: Accelerated Indexing Systems, 1980).

24. James H. Madison, *A Lynching in the Heartland: Race and Memory in America* (New York: Palgrave, 2001), 14.

25. Scott L. Malcomson, *One Drop of Blood: The American Misadventure of Race* (New York: Farrar, Straus & Giroux, 2000), 352; George M. Fredrickson, *The Black Image in the White Mind* (New York: Harper and Row, 1971), 276.

26. Eugene H. Berwanger, "Hardin and Langston: Western Black Spokesmen of the Reconstruction Era," *Journal of Negro History* 64 (spring 1979), 101–115.

27. *RMN*, March 13, 1884; Abbott, Leonard, and McComb, *Colorado*, 214–216.

28. Colorado State General Assembly, *Laws Passed at the Fifth Session of the General Assembly of the State of Colorado, Convened at Denver on the Seventh Day of January, A.D. 1885* (Denver: Collier and Cleaveland, 1885), 132–133.

29. Buchanan, *Story of a Labor Agitator*, 278.

30. Colorado Territory, Legislative Assembly, Council, *Council Journal of the Legislative Assembly of the Territory of Colorado Eighth Session, Convened at Denver, January 31, 1870* (Central City: David R. Collier, 1870), 21–22.

31. Gerald E. Rudolph, "The Chinese in Colorado, 1869–1911" (M.A. thesis, University of Denver, 1964), 14–16. *Denver Republican*, March 10,

1891, reports the February 8, 1891, birth of what the *Republican* said was the first Chinese baby born in Denver.

32. Caroline Bancroft, *Gulch of Gold: A History of Central City, Colorado* (Denver: Sage, 1958), 260–261.

33. Transcript from *Boulder County News*, April 3, 1874, in Colorado Historical Society.

34. *RMN*, September 23, 1881.

35. *Denver Tribune*, March 6, 1881.

36. Hasse, "Gothic, Colorado," 220–221.

37. *Denver Times*, May 14, 1902.

38. Transcript of *Ouray Times*, May 20, 1882, in files of the Colorado Historical Society.

39. *RMN*, November 5, 1880. The spelling is that in the original news article.

40. Griswold, *Leadville*, 2:1683, quoting *Carbonate Chronicle* [Leadville], November 7, 1885. Some Leadville news reports were clearly fictitious. The story of Voodoo Brown, which includes an account of her cat being cut in half, "whereupon the tail half of the cat ran in one direction and the head half in the other," appears to be a tall tale.

41. *Chicago Tribune*, January 2, 1884.

42. U.S. Department of Commerce, *Bureau of the Census, Thirteenth Census*, 235. The 1910 census included statistics from earlier years.

43. *RMN*, November 1, 1880.

44. Roy T. Wortman, "Denver's Anti-Chinese Riot, 1880," *Colorado Magazine* 42 (fall 1965), 283, quoting the *Times* [London], November 19, 1880.

45. *RMN*, November 1, 1880.

46. *Denver Times*, November 1, 1880.

47. U.S. Department of State, *Papers Relating to the Foreign Relations of the United States . . . 1881* (Washington, D.C.: Government Printing Office, 1882), 327.

48. *RMN*, November 1, 1880.

49. *Denver Times*, November 1, 1880; Department of State, *Foreign Relations, 1881*, 323–324.

50. Wortman, "Denver's Anti-Chinese Riot," 286, 291.

51. Smiley, *History of Denver*, 472, erroneously reports that the mob's "only" victim was an old man hanged on Seventeenth Street. The correct name of the victim is supplied in Department of State, *Foreign Relations, 1881*, 321.

52. Linton, "Early Western Experience," 37–38.

53. *Solid Muldoon*, August 28, 1891; *Denver Times*, August 26, 1891.

54. Goodykoontz, "The People of Colorado," 2:83.

55. *RMN*, August 11, 1884.

56. Ibid., March 11, 1884, reported that four boys, including a sixteen-year-old and a fifteen-year-old, had received suspended sentences for throwing stones at "a Chinaman and a Dago on Saturday."

57. Ibid., December 27, 1881.

58. *Denver Republican,* July 28, 1893.

59. *RMN,* July 26, 1893.

60. *Denver Times,* July 27, 1893.

61. Ibid.

62. *Denver Republican,* July 27, 1893.

63. *Colorado Springs Gazette,* August 3, 1893.

64. *Denver Times,* July 27, 1893

65. *Denver Republican,* July 28, 1893.

66. *Colorado Catholic* [Denver], February 15, 1894.

67. *Denver Republican,* July 28, 1893.

68. *Colorado Springs Gazette,* August 3, 1893.

69. *Denver Times,* July 27, 1893.

70. Ibid.

71. *Colorado Miner* [Georgetown], December 15, 1877. See also Cook, *Hands Up,* 216–221.

72. *Gunnison Daily News-Democrat,* October 29, 1881; George A. Root, "Gunnison in the Early Eighties," *Colorado Magazine* 9 (November 1932), 204.

73. *Denver Republican,* May 27, 1891.

74. *Chicago Tribune,* January 1, 1892.

75. Jesse G. Northcutt to Albert W. McIntire, October 17, 1895, quoted in Conrad L. Woodall, "The Italian Massacre of Walsenburg, Colorado, March 1895" (M.A. thesis, Colorado State University, 1989), 115. The McIntire Papers are at the Colorado State Archives, Denver. Woodall's thesis carefully details the lynchings and their aftermath. He clears up much of the considerable confusion that surrounded these lynchings at the time and that has been misrecorded in the history books.

76. Ibid., 69–79. Smith and Farr's possible involvement is suggested by other evidence presented to the grand jury, especially the testimony of a local hotel keeper who said two prisoners from the jail had been housed in his hotel earlier in the evening of March 13. The lynchers may have wanted to get potential witnesses out of the jail that night. Olk, who had initially offered to testify if he were pardoned and given a reward, later evidently told his story without promise of release. He was then in the Colorado State Penitentiary and risked retaliation by naming Farr and Smith.

77. Ibid., 3.

78. Ibid., 1.

79. Ibid., 3–8, reviews the inaccurate reports of the lynchings. He notes that historian John Higham, in *Strangers in the Land: Patterns of American Nativism, 1860–1925* (New York: Atheneum, 1973), 91, incorrectly says 6 Italians were lynched. There were 23 Italians in Huerfano County in 1890 and 163 in 1900 (Woodall, 39). As a growing immigrant group, the Italians, like the Chinese in the 1870s, were regarded as a threat by other laborers.

80. *Denver Post*, March 15, 1895.

81. *Colorado Chieftain* [Pueblo], March 21, 1895, quoting the *RMN*.

82. Brundage, *Lynching in the New South*, 17.

83. Uchill, *Pioneers, Peddlers, and Tsadikim*, 156–164, covers the "forms of hatred" directed against Denver's Jews.

84. *Denver Post*, April 29, 1906.

85. Ibid., April 28, 1906.

86. Ibid., December 26, 1905.

87. Ibid., April 28, 1906.

88. Uchill, *Pioneers, Peddlers, and Tsadikim*, 159. In January 1907 two men, described as part of "the Jew-baiting gang of West Colfax," killed two Jews in a fight. The circumstances that led to the crime were unclear, and the two men were not a "group"; hence it seems the killings of Teve Bosker and Max Weissblei were not lynchings. See *RMN*, January 20, 1907.

89. *Denver Times*, November 26, 1900.

90. *Denver Republican*, May 24, 1900.

91. Most of these lynchings have been treated elsewhere in this text. On Bennett, see Kouris, *Romantic and Notorious History*, 86–90. The *Denver Times*, January 10, 1900, reported the killing of "French Joe" in Fremont County as a lynching, but it was probably an ordinary murder. French Joe's surname was probably Grandorge.

92. *Colorado Transcript* [Golden], May 1, 1867.

93. *RMN*, May 12, 1874.

94. Nossaman, *Silverton*, 3:83–88. Nossaman includes a picture of the lynched Black Kid Thomas. A man named "Black Pete," supposedly a horse thief, was lynched in 1884. Sketchy newspaper reports do not make his race clear. See *RMN*, August 5, 1884.

95. *RMN*, May 28, 1886.

96. L. Vernon Briggs, *Arizona and New Mexico, 1882, California, 1886, Mexico, 1891* (Boston: privately printed, 1932), 138.

97. Belle Cassidy, "Recollections of Early Denver," *Colorado Magazine* 29 (January 1952), 55, confuses the legal execution of Green with the lynching of Daniel Arata, demonstrating the dangers of oral history. On Coleman, see Duane Vandenbusche, *The Gunnison Country* (Gunnison, Colo.: B&B, 1980), 182.

98. *San Juan* [Silverton], September 15, 1887.

99. *Solid Muldoon*, September 16, 1887.

100. *San Juan Prospector* [Del Norte], September 15, 1887. The *Prospector* said, "Dixon's face and hands were burned, but he undoubtedly died of suffocation."

101. *Solid Muldoon*, September 16, 1887.

102. *Pueblo Chieftain*, May 23, 1900.

103. *RMN*, May 23, 1900.

104. Ibid.

105. *Pueblo Chieftain*, May 23, 1900. Other papers excusing the mob included the *Colorado Springs Gazette*, May 24, 1900; the *Denver Republican*, May 24, 1900; the *Daily Sentinel* [Grand Junction], May 23, 1900; and the *Salida Mail*, May 25, 1900. The *Boulder Daily Camera*, May 23, 1900, however, said the lynching was "an uncalled for deed" and added that Pueblo was "in disgrace."

106. *Denver Republican*, May 24, 1900.

107. *RMN*, March 29, 1902. Frances B. Keck, in *Conquistadors to the 21st Century: A History of Otero and Crowley Counties, Colorado* (La Junta: Otero, 1999), 349, says Wallace "was convicted of the crime." In fact, he was lynched the same day he was returned to La Junta. There was no trial.

108. *RMN*, March 26, 1902. The *Leadville Herald-Democrat*, March 26, 1902, said Wallace did not resist.

109. *Boulder Daily Camera*, March 26, 1902.

110. *RMN*, March 30, 1902.

111. Ibid.

112. *Daily Sentinel* [Grand Junction], May 28, 1902.

113. Tolnay and Beck, *Festival of Violence*, ix.

114. Bruce A. Glasrud, "Enforcing White Supremacy in Texas, 1900–1910," *Red River Valley Historical Review* 4 (fall 1979), 65, notes that in 1910, 690,049 blacks were living in Texas, about 18 percent of the population.

115. *Denver Post*, July 6, 1911. I am indebted to David Lutter, a student at Metropolitan State College of Denver, who told me about this failed lynching.

116. Ibid.

117. Ibid.

118. In 1902, Otero County sheriff George Barr had tried to take Washington Wallace from La Junta, but railroad officials refused to operate a train with Wallace on it. Barr then tried to get Wallace to Pueblo by horse-drawn carriage but was intercepted southeast of Fowler. Wallace was taken back to La Junta to die. *Leadville Herald-Democrat*, March 26, 1902, reprinting an article from the *Pueblo Chieftain*. Also see *RMN*, March 26, 1902.

119. *Boulder Daily Camera*, November 17, 1900.

120. James R. McGovern, *Anatomy of a Lynching: The Killing of Claude Neal* (Baton Rouge: Louisiana State University Press, 1982), 151.

121. *New York Times*, December 6, 1912.

122. Lyle W. Dorsett, "The Ordeal of Colorado's Germans During World War I," *Colorado Magazine* 51 (fall 1974), 277–293.

123. *Pueblo Chieftain*, September 14, 1919, gave the mob size at 100 to 1,000. Other estimates were much lower. Press accounts indicate that only a few men participated in the kidnapping of Ortez and Gonzales from the jail. Others probably arrived at the Fourth Street bridge after the two men were hanged. *Denver Post*, September 14, 1919.

124. *Denver Post*, September 15, 1919.

125. *RMN*, September 20, 1919.

126. *Denver Post*, September 15, 1919.

127. *Colorado Springs Gazette*, September 15, 1919.

128. *Pueblo Indicator*, September 20, 1919.

129. *Pueblo Chieftain*, September 15, 1919.

130. *Pueblo Indicator*, September 20, 1919.

131. *Pueblo Chieftain*, September 15, 1919.

132. Transcript from *Western Mountaineer* [Golden], August 2, 1860, in files of Colorado Historical Society.

133. Brundage, *Lynching in the New South*, 291.

134. Secrest, "Bloody Espinosas," 11–25.

135. William D. Todd et al., *Souvenir: Dedication of the Masonic Temple, Denver, Colorado, July 3, 1890, A.L. 5890* (Denver: W. F. Robinson, 1890), 89.

136. *RMN*, October 16, 1880.

137. R. R. Maiden's list of county sheriffs indicates that between 1864 and 1888, Hispanic-surnamed persons occupied the sheriff's office in Las Animas County for 11 years, in Huerfano for 12 years, in Conejos for 10 years, and in Costilla for 9 years. R. R. Maiden, "Sheriffs of Colorado Counties, 1871–1965," *Colorado Sheriff and Peace Officer* (February-March 1965), 61–66.

138. Taylor, *Trinidad*, 134. A few months earlier, in a Trinidad lynching without racial overtones, citizens did not bother with masks when they carried out the daylight lynching of Arthur Bell. See *RMN*, May 25, 1873.

139. Bayard Taylor, *Colorado: A Summer Trip*, ed. William W. Savage Jr. and James H. Lazalier (Niwot: University Press of Colorado, 1989, originally published 1867), 51. Taylor's letter of June 23, 1866, appeared in the *RMN*, September 7, 1866. See also *RMN*, June 26, 30, 1866.

CHAPTER 7:

CONCLUSION

1. William Rathmell, "A Brief History of Ouray Co., Colo.," typescript in Western History and Genealogy Department, Denver Public Library. Rathmell may have confused his dates. James H. Craft and Charles Walrath were hanged from a bridge near Alamosa in July 1879.

2. Tolnay and Beck, *Festival of Violence*, 239–258.

3. De la Roche, "Sociogenesis of Lynching," 48–76.

4. Turner, *Frontier in American History*, 254.

5. *New York Times*, November 19, 1900.

6. Wheeler, *Deadwood Dick in Leadville*, 30–31.

7. Malcolm J. Rohrbough, "The Continuing Search for the American West: Historians Past, Present, and Future," in Gene M. Gressley, ed., *Old West/New West Quo Vadis?* (Worland, Wyo.: High Plains, 1994), 123–146, sees westerners' questioning of authority as one attribute defining westerners.

8. McKanna, *Homicide, Race, and Justice*. McKanna notes that vendetta killings, particularly among Italians, occurred in Las Animas County. Although

they had aspects of lynchings, they belonged at least as much, if not more, to old world customs than to the American tradition of lynching. Hence they have not been included among the lynchings in this book. If they had been, the number of lynchings would increase substantially, for more than twenty vendetta homicides took place in Las Animas County alone between 1880 and 1920.

9. Fred Greenbaum, *Fighting Progressive: A Biography of Edward P. Costigan* (Washington, D.C.: Public Affairs, 1971), 160–175; Benjamin P. Draper, "Manuscripts in the Bancroft Library Relating to Colorado," entry on George P. Costigan in Volume 1, in Western History and Genealogy Department, Denver Public Library.

10. *Colorado Chieftain* [Pueblo], April 6, 1882.

11. Robert H. Wiebe, *The Search for Order, 1877–1920* (New York: Hill and Wang, 1967).

12. *Denver Post*, March 15, 1895.

13. Robert Goldberg, in his carefully researched *Hooded Empire: The Ku Klux Klan in Colorado* (Urbana: University of Illinois Press, 1981), does not report a single Klan lynching in Colorado in the 1920s, although Klansmen sometimes resorted to lesser forms of violence.

14. *Denver Post*, April 17, 1934; Holley, *Invisible People*, 123–129.

15. For a comparison of Wister's and Clark's works, see J. Bakker, "The Role of the Mythic West in Some Representative Examples of Classic and Modern American Literature: The Shaping Force of the American Frontier," Volume 13 in *Studies in American Literature* (Lewiston, N.Y.: Edwin Mellen, 1991), 157–175.

16. Robert Athearn, *The Coloradans* (Albuquerque: University of New Mexico Press, 1976), 57–58.

17. Ibid., 217.

18. L. Terry Oggel, "Speaking Out About Race: 'The United States of Lyncherdom' Clemens Really Wrote," *Prospects: An Annual of American Cultural Studies*, Volume 25 (New York: Cambridge University Press, 2000), 129.

19. Carl Abbott, Stephen J. Leonard, and David McComb, *Colorado: A History of the Centennial State* (Boulder: University Press of Colorado, 1982), 208.

20. Monnett and McCarthy, *Colorado Profiles*, 205–214.

21. Oggel, "Speaking Out," 131, quoting Clemens writing as Mark Twain in *Chicago Republican*, May 31, 1868.

SOURCES

Practically all of the material cited here is in either the Denver Public Library or the Colorado State Historical Society's collections. The Historical Society has a particularly rich selection of Colorado newspapers. Some newspapers listed here may no longer be extant. Some lynching items were transcribed from newspapers at the Colorado Historical Society and now exist as typed copies in the society's files. Other items were republished by other newspapers. I consulted many sources not cited here. They in some instances gave me negative evidence that a lynching had probably not occurred in a particular place or provided such sketchy information that I decided to cite better sources.

BOOKS AND PAMPHLETS

Abbott, Carl, Stephen J. Leonard, and David McComb. *Colorado: A History of the Centennial State.* Niwot: University Press of Colorado, rev. ed., 1982; 3d ed., 1994.

Adams, Ramon F. *Six Guns and Saddle Leather: A Bibliography of Books and Pamphlets on Western Outlaws and Gunmen.* Norman: University of Oklahoma Press, 1969.

Aiken, A. W. *Cool Desmond; or the Gambler's Big Game, a Romance of the Regions of the Lawless.* New York: Beadle's Half Dime Library 8(186), February 1881.

Aldridge, Dorothy. *Historic Colorado City: The Town With a Future.* Colorado Springs: Little London, 1996.

Anon. *Colorado Carl; or, the King of the Saddle.* New York: Harry E. Wolff, May 8, 1918. Pluck and Luck, 1040.

Anon. *History of the Arkansas Valley, Colorado.* Evansville, Ind.: Unigraphic, 1971, originally published 1881.

Anon. *Southern Colorado Historical and Descriptive*. Cañon City, Colo.: Binckley and Hartwell, 1879.

Athearn, Robert. *The Coloradans*. Albuquerque: University of New Mexico Press, 1976.

Bair, Everett. *This Will Be an Empire*. New York: Pageant, 1959.

Bakker, J. "The Role of the Mythic West in Some Representative Examples of Classic and Modern American Literature: The Shaping Force of the American Frontier." Volume 13 in *Studies in American Literature*. Lewiston, N.Y.: Edwin Mellen, 1991.

Bancroft, Caroline. *Gulch of Gold: A History of Central City, Colorado*. Denver: Sage, 1958.

Bancroft, Hubert Howe. *History of Nevada, Colorado, and Wyoming, 1540–1888*. San Francisco: History, 1890.

———. *Popular Tribunals*. San Francisco: History, 1887.

Barney, Libeus. *Letters From the Pikes Peak Gold Rush [or Early Day Letters From Auraria]: Early-Day Letters by Libeus Barney, Reprinted From the Bennington Banner, Vermont, 1859–1860*. San Jose, Calif.: Talisman, 1959.

Bederman, Gail. *Manliness and Civilization: A Cultural History of Gender and Race in the United States, 1880–1917*. Chicago: University of Chicago Press, 1995.

Bell, William A. *New Tracks in North America*. Albuquerque: Horn and Wallace, 1965, originally published 1870.

Billington, Ray Allen. *Westward Expansion: A History of the American Frontier*. New York: Macmillan, 1974.

Bird, Isabella. *A Lady's Life in the Rocky Mountains*. New York: Ballantine, 1973, originally published 1879.

Black, Robert C., III. *Island in the Rockies: The History of Grand County, Colorado, to 1930*. Granby, Colo.: Country Printer, 1977.

Brewer, Ebenezer Cobham. *Dictionary of Phrase and Fable Giving the Derivation, Source, or Origin of Common Phrases, Allusions, and Words That Have a Tale to Tell, to Which Is Added a Concise Bibliography of English Literature*. Philadelphia: Henry Altemus, 1898, online edition by Bartleby.com.

Briggs, L. Vernon. *Arizona and New Mexico, 1882, California, 1886, Mexico, 1891*. Boston: privately printed, 1932.

Brown, Richard Maxwell. *Strain of Violence: Historical Studies of American Violence and Vigilantism*. New York: Oxford University Press, 1975.

Brown, Robert L. *An Empire of Silver: A History of the San Juan Silver Rush*. Caldwell, Idaho: Caxton, 1965.

Brundage, W. Fitzhugh. *Lynching in the New South: Georgia and Virginia, 1880–1930*. Urbana: University of Illinois Press, 1993.

———, ed. *Under Sentence of Death: Lynching in the South*. Chapel Hill: University of North Carolina Press, 1997.

Buchanan, Joseph R. *The Story of a Labor Agitator*. New York: Outlook, 1903.

Burrows, John Rolfe. *Where the Old West Stayed Young*. New York: William Morrow, 1962.

Bury, Susan, and John Bury, comps. and eds. *This Is What I Remember: By and About the People of White River Country.* Meeker, Colo.: Rio Blanco Historical Society, 1972.

Callaway, Llewellyn L. *Montana's Righteous Hangmen: The Vigilantes in Action.* Norman: University of Oklahoma Press, 1982.

Caughey, John W. *Their Majesties the Mob.* Chicago: University of Chicago Press, 1960.

Clark, Walter Van Tilburg. *The Ox-Bow Incident.* New York: Vintage, 1940.

Cook, David J. *Hands Up; or, Twenty Years of Detective Life in the Mountains and on the Plains.* Norman: University of Oklahoma Press, 1958, originally published 1882.

Cooley, Dale, and Mary L. Owen, comps. *Where the Wagon Rolled: The History of Lincoln County and the People Who Came Before 1925.* Arriba, Colo.: Southwestern Institute of Colorado, 1982.

Crèvecoeur, J. Hector St John de. *Letters From an American Farmer,* edited with an Introduction and Notes by Susan Manning. Oxford: Oxford University Press, 1997, originally published 1782.

Crofutt, George A. *Crofutt's Grip-sack Guide of Colorado, Volume II, 1885.* Golden, Colo.: Cubar, 1966, originally published 1885.

Cronon, William, George Miles, and Jay Gitlin, eds. *Under an Open Sky: Rethinking America's Western Past.* New York: W. W. Norton, 1992.

Cutler, James E. *Lynch-Law: An Investigation Into the History of Lynching in the United States.* New York: Negro Universities Press, 1969, originally published 1905.

Darley, George M. *Pioneering in the San Juan: Personal Reminiscences of Work Done in Southwestern Colorado During the "Great San Juan Excitement."* Chicago: Fleming H. Revell, 1899.

Dimsdale, Thomas J. *The Vigilantes of Montana, or Popular Justice in the Rocky Mountains.* Norman: University of Oklahoma Press, 1953, originally published 1866.

Dixon, William Hepworth. *New America.* Philadelphia: J. B. Lippincott, 1867.

Dodds, Joanne West. *Custer County: Mountains, Mines, and Ranches.* Denver: Colorado Endowment for the Humanities, 1992.

Dodge, Joseph V. *Killers of Judge Dyer, Granite, Colorado Territory, 1875.* Cañon City, Colo.: Rocky Mountain Books, 1975.

Downing, Sybil, and Robert E. Smith. *Tom Patterson: Colorado Crusader for Change.* Niwot: University Press of Colorado, 1995.

Drinnon, Richard. *Facing West: The Metaphysics of Indian-Hating and Empire-Building.* Minneapolis: University of Minnesota Press, 1980.

Dyer, John L. *The Snow-Shoe Itinerant: An Autobiography of the Rev. John L. Dyer, Familiarly Known as Father Dyer, of the Colorado Conference, Methodist Episcopal Church.* Cincinnati: Cranston and Stowe, 1890.

Eberhart, Perry. *Guide to the Colorado Ghost Towns and Mining Camps.* Chicago: Sage, 1970.

Elliot, Donald R., comp., and Doris L. Elliot, ed. *Place Names of Colorado: A Genealogical and Historical Guide to Colorado Sites.* Denver: Colorado Council of Genealogical Societies, 1999.

Etulain, Richard, ed. *Writing Western History: Essays on Major Western Historians.* Albuquerque: University of New Mexico Press, 1991.

Everett, George G., and Wendell F. Hutchinson. *Under the Angel of Shavano.* Denver: Golden Bell, 1963.

Ferril, William C. *Sketches of Colorado: Being an Analytical Summary and Biographical History of the State of Colorado as Portrayed in the Lives of the Pioneers, the Founders, the Builders, the Statesmen, and the Preeminent and Progressive Citizens Who Helped in the Development and History Making Colorado.* Denver: Western Press Bureau, 1911.

Fredrickson, George M. *The Black Image in the White Mind.* New York: Harper and Row, 1971.

Genealogical Society of Weld County. *1870 Colorado Territory Census Index.* Greeley, Colo.: Weld County Genealogical Society, 1977.

Goldberg, Robert A. *Hooded Empire: The Ku Klux Klan in Colorado.* Urbana: University of Illinois Press, 1981.

Goodstein, Philip. *Denver Streets: Names, Numbers, Locations, Logic.* Denver: New Social Publications, 1994.

Greenbaum, Fred. *Fighting Progressive: A Biography of Edward P. Costigan.* Washington, D.C.: Public Affairs, 1971.

Greenleaf, Lawrence N. *King Sham and Other Atrocities in Verse.* New York: Hurd and Houghton, 1868.

Gregory, Doris H. *History of Ouray: A Heritage of Mining and Everlasting Beauty.* Ouray, Colo.: Cascade, 1995.

Griswold, Don L., and Jean H. Griswold. *History of Leadville and Lake County, Colorado.* 2 vols. Denver: Colorado Historical Society, 1996.

Guice, John D.W. *The Rocky Mountain Bench: The Territorial Supreme Courts of Colorado, Montana, and Wyoming, 1861–1890.* New Haven: Yale University Press, 1972.

Hafen, LeRoy R., ed. *Pikes Peak Gold Rush Guidebooks of 1859 by Luke Tierney, William B. Parsons, and Summaries of the Other Fifteen.* Glendale, Calif.: Arthur H. Clark, 1941.

Hafen, LeRoy, and Carl Rister. *Western America.* New York: Prentice-Hall, 1950.

Hall, Frank. *History of the State of Colorado.* 4 vols. Chicago: Blakely, 1889–1895.

Higham, John. *Strangers in the Land: Patterns of American Nativism, 1860–1925.* New York: Atheneum, 1973.

Hogan, Richard. *Class and Community in Frontier Colorado.* Lawrence: University Press of Kansas, 1990.

Hoig, Stan. *The Sand Creek Massacre.* Norman: University of Oklahoma Press, 1977.

Holley, John S. *The Invisible People of the Pikes Peak Region: An Afro-American Chronicle.* Colorado Springs: Friends of the Colorado Springs Pioneer Museum, 1990.

Hollinger, David A. *Postethnic America: Beyond Multiculturalism.* New York: Basic, 1995.

Horner, Jack W. *Silver Town.* Caldwell, Idaho: Caxton, 1950.

Howbert, Irving. *Memories of a Lifetime in the Pike's Peak Region.* New York: G. P. Putnam's Sons, 1925.

Hufsmith, George W. *The Wyoming Lynching of Cattle Kate, 1889.* Glendo, Wyo.: High Plains, 1993.

Ingersoll, Ernest. *The Crest of the Continent: A Record of a Summer's Ramble in the Rocky Mountains and Beyond.* Glorieta, N. Mex.: Rio Grande, 1969, originally published 1885.

Jackson, Ronald V., ed. *Colorado 1880 Census Index.* Bountiful, Utah: Accelerated Indexing Systems, 1980.

Jessen, Kenneth. *Colorado Gunsmoke: True Stories of Outlaws and Lawmen on the Colorado Frontier.* Boulder: Pruett, 1986.

Jocknick, Sidney. *Early Days on the Western Slope of Colorado.* Denver: Carson-Harper, 1913.

Keck, Frances B. *Conquistadors to the 21st Century: A History of Otero and Crowley Counties, Colorado.* La Junta: Otero, 1999.

Kelsey, Harry. *Frontier Capitalist: The Life of John Evans.* Denver: State Historical Society of Colorado and Pruett, 1969.

King, William M. *Going to Meet a Man: Denver's Last Public Execution, 27 July 1886.* Niwot: University Press of Colorado, 1990.

Kouris, Diana A. *The Romantic and Notorious History of Brown's Park.* Greybull, Wyo.: Wolverine Gallery, 1988.

Kreck, Dick. *Denver in Flames: Forging a New Mile High City.* Golden: Fulcrum, 2000.

Kushner, Ervan F. *Alferd G. Packer, Cannibal! Victim?* Frederick, Colo.: Platte 'N Press, 1980.

Large, Dorothy. *Old Burlington: First Town on the St. Vrain 1860–1871.* Longmont, Colo.: St. Vrain, 1984.

Larson, Taft A. *History of Wyoming.* Lincoln: University of Nebraska Press, 1978.

Leonard, Stephen J., and Thomas J. Noel. *Denver: Mining Camp to Metropolis.* Niwot: University Press of Colorado, 1990.

Logan, James K., ed. *The Federal Courts of the Tenth Circuit.* Denver: U.S. Court of Appeals, 1992.

Look, Alfred A. *Sidelights on Colorado History: A Glance at Colorado History Without Depth, Details, or Direction.* Denver: Golden Bell, 1967.

———. *Unforgettable Characters of Western Colorado.* Boulder: Pruett, 1966.

Lord, John. *Frontier Dust.* Hartford: Edwin Valentine Mitchell, 1926.

Madison, James H. *A Lynching in the Heartland: Race and Memory in America.* New York: Palgrave, 2001.

Malcomson, Scott L. *One Drop of Blood: The American Misadventure of Race.* New York: Farrar, Straus & Giroux, 2000.

McGovern, James R. *Anatomy of a Lynching: The Killing of Claude Neal.* Baton Rouge: Louisiana State University Press, 1982.

McGrath, Roger D. *Gunfighters, Highwaymen, and Vigilantes: Violence on the Frontier.* Berkeley: University of California Press, 1984.

McKanna, Clare V., Jr. *Homicide, Race, and Justice in the American West, 1880–1920.* Tucson: University of Arizona Press, 1997.

Mocho, Jill. *Murder and Justice in Frontier New Mexico, 1821–1846.* Albuquerque: University of New Mexico Press, 1997.

Monnett, John H., and Michael McCarthy. *Colorado Profiles: Men and Women Who Shaped the Centennial State.* Evergreen, Colo.: Cordillera, 1987.

Moses, Norton H., comp. *Lynching and Vigilantism in the United States: An Annotated Bibliography.* Westport, Conn.: Greenwood, 1997.

Mumey, Nolie. *History of Tin Cup, Colorado (Virginia City), an Alpine Mining Camp Which Refused to Become a Ghost Town.* Boulder: Johnson, 1963.

———, comp. *History and Laws of Nevadaville.* Boulder: Johnson, 1962.

Nash, Gerald. *Creating the West: Historical Interpretations 1890–1990.* Albuquerque: University of New Mexico Press, 1991.

Nossaman, Allen. *Many More Mountains: An Illustrated History of Silverton and the High San Juans From the Opening of the 1880s Through the Outlaw Period and the Construction of the Railroad to the Beginning of the Red Mountain Excitement.* Denver: Sundance, 1989–. 3 volumes to 1998. Volume 1: *Silverton's Roots;* Volume 2: *Ruts Into Silverton;* Volume 3: *Rails Into Silverton.*

Parkhill, Forbes. *The Law Goes West.* Denver: Sage, 1956.

Peterson, Freda C., comp. *The Story of Hillside Cemetery, San Juan County Burials, 1873–1988.* Oklahoma City: n.p., 1989.

Pitzer, Henry L. *Three Frontiers: Memories and a Portrait of Henry Littleton Pitzer as Recorded by His Son, Robert Claiborne Pitzer.* Muscatine, Iowa: Prairie, 1938.

Raine, William MacLeod. *Guns of the Frontier: The Story of How Law Came to the West.* Boston: Houghton Mifflin, 1940.

Raper, Arthur F. *The Tragedy of Lynching.* New York: Negro Universities Press, 1969, originally published 1933.

Rawick, George P., ed. *The American Slave: A Composite Autobiography.* Supplement Series I, Volume 2. Westport, Conn.: Greenwood, 1977.

Reid, John P. *Policing the Elephant: Crime, Punishment, and Social Behavior on the Overland Trail.* San Marino, Calif.: Huntington Library, 1997.

Richardson, Albert D. *Beyond the Mississippi: A Complete History of the New States and Territories, From the Great River to the Great Ocean.* Hartford: American, 1867.

Rockwell, Wilson. *Sunset Slope: True Epics of Western Colorado.* Denver: Big Mountain, 1955.

———. *Uncompahgre Country.* Denver: Sage, 1965.

Rohrbough, Malcolm J. *Aspen: The History of a Silver Mining Town 1878–1893.* New York: Oxford University Press, 1986.

Rolle, Andrew. *The Immigrant Upraised: Italian Adventurers and Colonists in an Expanding America*. Norman: University of Oklahoma Press, 1968.

Rusling, James. *Across America, or the Great West and the Pacific Coast*. New York: Sheldon, 1874.

Secrest, Clark. *Hell's Belles: Denver's Brides of the Multitudes With Attention to Various Gamblers, Scoundrels, and Mountebanks, and a Biography of Sam Howe, Frontier Lawman*. Aurora, Colo.: Hindsight Historical Publications, 1996.

Selig, Hugo. *Early Recollections of Montrose, Colorado*. Montrose: Reprinted from Montrose Daily Press, 1939.

Sharp, Verna. *History of Montezuma, Sts. John, and Argentine*. Dillon, Colo.: Summit Historical Society, 1971.

Shinn, Jonathan. *The Memoirs of Capt. Jonathan Shinn*. Greeley, Colo.: Weld County Democrat, 1890.

Shores, Cyrus W. *Memoirs of a Lawman*, ed. Wilson Rockwell. Denver: Sage, 1962.

Slotkin, Richard. *Fatal Environment: The Myth of the Frontier in the Age of Industrialization, 1800–1890*. New York: Atheneum, 1985.

———. *Gunfighter Nation: The Myth of the Frontier in Twentieth Century America*. New York: Atheneum, 1992.

Smiley, Jerome. *History of Denver*. Evansville, Ind.: Unigraphic, 1971, originally published 1901.

Smith, Duane. *Rocky Mountain Boom Town: A History of Durango*. Niwot: University Press of Colorado, 1992, originally published 1980.

Stone, Wilbur F., ed. *History of Colorado*. 6 vols. Chicago: S. J. Clarke, 1918–1919.

Taylor, Bayard. *Colorado: A Summer Trip*, ed. William W. Savage Jr. and James H. Lazalier. Niwot: University Press of Colorado, 1989, originally published 1867.

Taylor, Morris F. *Trinidad, Colorado Territory*. Pueblo: O'Brien, 1966.

Todd, William D., et al. *Souvenir: Dedication of the Masonic Temple, Denver, Colorado, July 3, 1890, A.L. 5890*. Denver: W. F. Robinson, 1890.

Tolnay, Stewart E., and E. M. Beck. *A Festival of Violence: An Analysis of Southern Lynchings, 1882–1930*. Urbana: University of Illinois Press, 1995.

Townshend, Richard B. *A Tenderfoot in Colorado*. Norman: University of Oklahoma Press, 1968, originally published 1923.

Turner, Frederick Jackson. *The Frontier in American History*. New York: Henry Holt, 1920.

Uchill, Ida L. *Pioneers, Peddlers, and Tsadikim: The Story of the Jews in Colorado*. Boulder: Quality Line, 1979.

Vandenbusche, Duane. *The Gunnison Country*. Gunnison, Colo.: B&B, 1980.

Vandenbusche, Duane, and Duane A. Smith. *A Land Alone: Colorado's Western Slope*. Boulder: Pruett, 1981.

Vickers, William. *History of the City of Denver, Arapahoe County, and Colorado*. Chicago: O. L. Baskin, 1880.

Watrous, Ansel. *History of Larimer County, Colorado.* Fort Collins: Courier, 1911.

Wharton, Junius E. *History of the City of Denver From Its Earliest Settlement to the Present Time: To Which Is Added a Full and Complete Business Directory, by D. O. Wilhelm.* Denver: Byers and Dailey, 1866.

Wheeler, Edward L. *Deadwood Dick in Leadville; Or, a Strange Stroke for Liberty, Volume II, Number 23.* New York: Arthur Westbrook, March 15, 1899, originally published June 24, 1879.

————. *Deadwood Dick, Jr. in Durango; or, "Gathered In."* New York: Beadle and Adams, June 10, 1890.

White, Richard. *"It's Your Misfortune and None of My Own": A History of the American West.* Norman: University of Oklahoma Press, 1991.

White, Walter. *Rope and Faggot: A Biography of Judge Lynch.* New York: Arno, 1969, originally published 1929.

Wiebe, Robert H. *The Search for Order, 1877–1920.* New York: Hill and Wang, 1967.

Wilde, Oscar. *The Soul of Man Under Socialism.* London: Arthur L. Humphreys, 1912.

Williamson, Ruby G. *Down With Your Dust: A Chronicle of the Upper Arkansas Valley, Colorado 1860–1893.* Gunnison, Colo.: B&B, 1979.

Willison, George F. *Here They Dug the Gold.* London: Readers Union, 1952, originally published 1931.

Wister, Owen. *The Virginian: A Horseman of the Plains.* New York: Grosset and Dunlap, 1904, originally published 1902.

Wolle, Muriel Sibell. *Stampede to Timberline: The Ghost Towns and Mining Camps of Colorado.* Chicago: Swallow, 1974.

Wright, Carolyn H., and Clarence Wright. *Tiny Hinsdale of the Silvery San Juan.* Denver: Big Mountain, 1964.

Wynar, Bohdan S., ed. *Colorado Bibliography.* Littleton, Colo.: Libraries Unlimited, 1980.

Young, Charles. *Dangers of the Trail in 1865.* Geneva, N.Y.: W. F. Humphrey, 1912.

Zamonoski, Stanley W., and Terry Keller. *The Fifty-Niners: A Denver Diary.* Denver: Sage, 1961.

CHAPTERS IN BOOKS

Brown, Richard Maxwell. "Violence," in Clyde A. Milner II, Carol A. O'Connor, and Martha A. Sandweiss, eds., *The Oxford History of the American West.* New York: Oxford University Press, 1994: 392–425.

Brundage, W. Fitzhugh. "Lynching," in Ronald Gottesman, ed., *Violence in America: An Encyclopedia.* New York: Charles Scribner's Sons, 1999, 1:297–303.

Clemens, Samuel. "The United States of Lyncherdom," first published in 1923, revised version in Ronald Gottesman, Francis Murphy, Laurence B. Holland, Hershel Parker, David Kalstone, and William H. Pritchard, eds., *The Norton Anthology of American Literature.* New York: W. W. Norton, 1979: 276–283.

De la Roche, Roberta Senechal. "The Sociogenesis of Lynching," in W. Fitzhugh Brundage, ed., *Under Sentence of Death: Lynching in the South.* Chapel Hill: University of North Carolina Press, 1997: 48–76.

Goodykoontz, Colin P. "The People of Colorado," in LeRoy R. Hafen, ed., *A Narrative and Topical History of the Centennial State,* 4 vols. New York: Lewis Historical Publishing, 1948: 2:75–120.

Lamar, Howard R. "Westering in the Twenty-First Century: Speculations on the Future of the Western Past," in William Cronon, George Miles, and Jay Gitlin, eds., *Under an Open Sky: Rethinking America's Western Past.* New York: W. W. Norton, 1992: 257–274.

Limerick, Patricia Nelson. "Making the Most of Words: Verbal Activity and Western America," in William Cronon, George Miles, and Jay Gitlin, eds., *Under an Open Sky: Rethinking America's Western Past.* New York: W. W. Norton, 1992: 167–184.

Mazzulla, Fred M. "Undue Process of Law—Here and There," in Francis B. Rissari, ed., *Brand Book of the Denver Westerners.* Boulder: Johnson, 1965: 257–279.

Rockafellow, B. F. "History of Fremont County," in Anon., *History of the Arkansas Valley, Colorado.* Evansville, Ind.: Unigraphic, 1971, originally published 1881: 541–687.

Rohrbough, Malcolm J. "The Continuing Search for the American West: Historians Past, Present, and Future," in Gene M. Gressley, ed., *Old West/New West: Quo Vadis?* Worland, Wyo.: High Plains, 1994: 123–146.

Sheldon, A. Z. "History of El Paso County," in Anon., *History of the Arkansas Valley, Colorado.* Evansville, Ind.: Unigraphic, 1971, originally published 1881: 415–476.

Waldrep, Christopher. "Word and Deed: The Language of Lynching, 1820–1953," in Michael Bellesiles, ed., *Lethal Imagination: Violence and Brutality in American History.* New York: New York University Press, 1999: 229–256.

GOVERNMENT DOCUMENTS

Colorado State General Assembly. *Laws Passed at the Fifth Session of the General Assembly of the State of Colorado, Convened at Denver on the Seventh Day of January, A.D. 1885.* Denver: Collier and Cleaveland, 1885.

———. *Laws Passed at the Tenth Session of the General Assembly of Colorado.* Denver: Smith and Brooks, 1895.

Colorado Territory, Legislative Assembly, Council. *Council Journal of the Legislative Assembly of the Territory of Colorado Eighth Session, Convened at Denver, January 3d, 1870.* Central City, Colo.: David C. Collier, 1870.

U.S. Congress. *Congressional Record.* 74th Congress, 1st Session, April 24, 1935, 79:6, 6291. Washington, D.C.: Government Printing Office, 1935.

U.S. Department of Commerce, Bureau of the Census. *Statistical Abstract of the United States 1942.* Washington, D.C.: Government Printing Office, 1943.

———. *Thirteenth Census of the United States Taken in the Year 1910, Volume II, Population 1910, Alabama–Montana.* Washington, D.C.: Government Printing Office, 1913.

U.S. Department of State. *Papers Relating to the Foreign Relations of the United States With the Annual Message of the President Transmitted to Congress Dec. 5, 1881.* Washington, D.C.: Government Printing Office, 1882.

———. *Papers Relating to the Foreign Relations of the United States With the Annual Message of the President Transmitted to Congress Dec. 2, 1895, Part II.* Washington, D.C.: Government Printing Office, 1896.

———. *Papers Relating to the Foreign Relations of the United States With the Annual Message of the President Transmitted to Congress Dec. 7, 1896, and the Annual Message of the Secretary of State.* Washington, D.C.: Government Printing Office, 1897.

Wright, Carroll D. *A Report on Labor Disturbances in the State of Colorado From 1880 to 1904.* Senate Executive Document No. 122, 58th Congress, 3d Session, 152–159. Washington, D.C.: Government Printing Office, 1905.

ARTICLES

Allen, Alonzo. "Pioneer Life in Old Burlington, Forerunner of Longmont." *Colorado Magazine* 14 (July 1937): 145–157.

Beasley, Joan Ostrom. "Unrealized Dreams: General William Larimer Jr." *Colorado Heritage* (summer 1996): 2–20.

Benson, Maxine. "Port Stockton." *Colorado Magazine* 43 (winter 1966): 22–29.

Berwanger, Eugene H. "Hardin and Langston: Western Black Spokesmen of the Reconstruction Era." *Journal of Negro History* 64 (spring 1979): 101–115.

Block, Augusta H. "Old Burlington." *Colorado Magazine* 19 (January 1942): 15–17.

Bohme, Frederick G., ed. and trans. of Giovanni Vigna Dal Ferro, *Un Viaggio Nel Far West Americano. Colorado Magazine* 35 (October 1958): 290–302.

Burg, B. Richard. "Administration of Justice in the Denver People's Courts, 1859–1861." *Journal of the West* 7 (October 1968): 510–521.

Cassidy, Belle. "Recollections of Early Denver." *Colorado Magazine* 29 (January 1952): 52–56.

Clark, George T. "Across the Plains and in Denver, 1860: A Portion of the Diary of George T. Clark." *Colorado Magazine* 6 (July 1929): 131–140.

Cornwall, Henry C. "My First Years in the Gunnison Country," ed. Duane Vandenbusche. *Colorado Magazine* 46 (summer 1964): 220–244.

Dorsett, Lyle W. "The Ordeal of Colorado's Germans During World War I." *Colorado Magazine* 51 (fall 1974): 277–293.

Dykstra, Robert R. "Field Notes: Overdosing on Dodge City." *Western Historical Quarterly* 27 (winter 1996): 505–514.

Ferguson, Olivia Spalding. "A Sketch of Delta County History." *Colorado Magazine* 5 (October 1928): 161–164.

Giddens, Paul H. "Letters of S. Newton Pettis, Associate Justice of the Colorado Supreme Court, Written in 1861." *Colorado Magazine* 15 (January 1938): 3–14.

Glasrud, Bruce. "Enforcing White Supremacy in Texas, 1900–1910." *Red River Valley Historical Review* 4 (fall 1979): 65–74.

Gower, Calvin W. "Kansas Territory and the Pike's Peak Gold Rush: Governing the Gold Region." *Kansas Historical Quarterly* 33 (autumn 1966): 289–313.

———. "Vigilantes." *Colorado Magazine* 41 (spring 1964): 93–104.

Hafen, LeRoy. "Claims and Jurisdictions Over the Territory of Colorado Prior to 1861." *Colorado Magazine* 9 (May 1932): 95–102.

Hanchett, William. "'His Turbulent Excellency,' Alexander Cummings, Governor of Colorado Territory, 1865–1867." *Colorado Magazine* 34 (April 1957): 81–104.

Harner, Ariana. "No Time for a Trial: The Abrupt Fate of the Reynolds Gang." *Colorado Heritage* (autumn 2000): 37–45.

Harvey, James Rose. "'Pioneer Experiences in Colorado': Interview With Elizabeth J. Tallman." *Colorado Magazine* 13 (July 1936): 141–149.

Inouye, Ronald K. "Alamosa, Colorado: Some Highlights of Its Early History." *San Luis Valley Historian* 19(1) (1987): 5–31.

Irion, John W. "Lynching of Hull's Slayers." *The Trail* 2 (April 1910): 23–24.

Johnson, David A. "Vigilance and the Law: The Moral Authority of Popular Justice in the Far West." *American Quarterly* 33 (winter 1981): 558–586.

Johnson, Jerome W. "Murder on the Uncompahgre." *Colorado Magazine* 43 (summer 1966): 209–224.

Leary, Hal. "A Rope for Mary Rose." *Frontier Times* 48 (January 1974): 32–34, 53–54.

Leonard, Stephen J. "Swimming Against the Current: A Biography of Charles S. Thomas, Senator and Governor." *Colorado Heritage* (fall 1994): 29–34.

Linton, Charles T. "An Early Western Experience." *Sons of Colorado* 1 (May 1907): 37–38.

———. "An Experience With Horse Thieves." *The Trail* 1 (September 1908): 27–28.

Maiden, R. R. "Records Show 87 Colorado Lynchings." *Colorado Sheriff and Peace Officer* (May-June 1965): 13.

———. "Sheriffs of Colorado Counties, 1871–1965." *Colorado Sheriff and Peace Officer* (February-March 1965): 61–66.

Manson-White, Laura. "Reminiscences of Uncle John B. Heilman Retold by Laura Manson-White." *San Luis Valley Historian* 16(2) (1984): 1–31.

Marshall, Thomas Maitland. "The Miners' Laws of Colorado." *American Historical Review* 25 (April 1920): 426–439.

Mathews, Carl F. "Rico, Colorado—Once a Roaring Camp." *Colorado Magazine* 28 (January 1951): 37–49.

McKimens, William. "Letters From Auraria, 1858–1859." *Colorado Magazine* 13 (September 1936): 167–170.

Moore, Jesse T., Jr. "Seeking a New Life: Blacks in Post–Civil War Colorado." *Journal of Negro History* 78 (summer 1993): 166–187.

Oggel, L. Terry. "Speaking Out About Race: 'The United States of Lyncherdom' Clemens Really Wrote." *Prospects: An Annual of American Cultural Studies* 25. New York: Cambridge University Press, 2000: 115–138.

Ophus, John. "The Lake County War, 1874–1875." *Colorado Magazine* 47 (spring 1970): 119–135.

Owen, James. "Reminiscences of Early Pueblo." *Colorado Magazine* 22 (May 1945): 98–107.

Perrigo, Lynn I. "Law and Order in Early Colorado Mining Camps." *Mississippi Valley Historical Review* 38 (June 1941): 41–62.

Pierce, James H. "With the Green Russell Party." *The Trail* 13 (May 1921): 5–14.

Root, George A. "Gunnison in the Early Eighties." *Colorado Magazine* 9 (November 1932): 201–213.

Sanford, Albert B. "John L. Routt, First State Governor of Colorado." *Colorado Magazine* 3 (August 1926): 81–86.

Schulz, Vauna S. "Pioneer Justice in Douglas County." *Colorado Magazine* 24 (May 1947): 123–126.

Secrest, Clark, abstracter. "The 'Bloody Espinosas' Avenging Angels of the Conejos." *Colorado Heritage* (autumn 2000): 10–17.

Sharp, Verna. "Montezuma and Her Neighbors." *Colorado Magazine* 33 (January 1956): 17–40.

Spencer, Frank. "Early Days in Alamosa." *Colorado Magazine* 8 (March 1931): 41–46.

Taylor, Morris F. "The Coe Gang: Rustlers of 'Robbers Roost.' " *Colorado Magazine* 51 (summer 1974): 199–215.

———. "Confederate Guerrillas in Southern Colorado." *Colorado Magazine* 46 (fall 1969): 304–323.

Thom, William B. "Early Day Marshals of Tin Cup." *Colorado Magazine* 10 (July 1933): 143–144.

Thomas, Charles. "The Pioneer Bar of Colorado." *Colorado Magazine* 1 (July 1924): 193–204.

Thomas, J. J. "In the Days of the Overland Trail." *The Trail* 2 (May 1910): 5–9.

Thompson, D. Claudia. "Driven From Point to Point: Fact and Legend in the Bear River Riot." *Montana* 46 (1996): 24–37.

Waldrep, Christopher. "War of Words: The Controversy Over the Definition of Lynching, 1899–1940." *Journal of Southern History* 66 (February 2000): 75–100.

Warford, Sherrill, and Nancy Manly. "The View From Both Sides of the Badge: Edward Frodsham Patrick A. Kelly." *Mountain Diggings* 18 (1988): 21–35.

Westermeier, Therese S. "Colorado Festivals." *Colorado Magazine* 28 (July 1951): 172–183.

Williamson, Joel. "Wounds Not Scars: Lynching, the National Conscience, and the American Historian." *Journal of American History* 83 (March 1997): 1221–1253.

Willing, George M. "Letters of George M. Willing, 'Delegate of Jefferson Territory.' " *Colorado Magazine* 17 (September 1940): 184–188.

Wortman, Roy T. "Denver's Anti-Chinese Riot, 1880." *Colorado Magazine* 42 (fall 1965): 269–291.

THESES AND DISSERTATIONS

Hasse, Carl L. "Gothic, Colorado: City of the Silver Wires." M.A. thesis, Western State College, Gunnison, 1971.

Knapp, Anne Curtis. "Making an Orderly Society: Criminal Justice in Denver, Colorado 1858–1900." Ph.D. diss., University of California–San Diego, 1983.

Leonard, Stephen J. "Denver's Foreign Born Immigrants, 1859–1900." Ph.D. diss., Claremont Graduate School, 1971.

Rudolph, Gerald. "The Chinese in Colorado, 1869–1911." M.A. thesis, University of Denver, 1964.

Woodall, Conrad L. "The Italian Massacre of Walsenburg, Colorado, March 1895." M.A. thesis, Colorado State University, Fort Collins, 1989.

MANUSCRIPTS

Blecha, Arvid D. "Colorado Place Names." 2 vols. Typescript in Western History and Genealogy Department, Denver Public Library.

Cairns, Elizabeth. "Interview With J. H. Maxey, December 12, 1933." Civil Works Administration Interviews, Pueblo County, CWA 344/3. Typescript in Colorado Historical Society.

Calvert, Charles. "United States Marshals, Territory and State, District of Colorado, 1861–1958." Typescript in Western History and Genealogy Department, Denver Public Library.

Colorado State Census, 1885, Ouray County. Microfilm in Western History and Genealogy Department, Denver Public Library.

Colorado State Penitentiary. "List of Inmates at the Colorado State Penitentiary." Colorado State Archives, Denver.

Cuddigan, Michael, Estate Records. "Administrator's Bond January 22, 1884." Ouray County Probate Court records, Box 3341, Colorado State Archives, Denver.

Draper, Benjamin P. "Manuscripts in the Bancroft Library Relating to Colorado." Entry on George P. Costigan in Volume 1. In Western History and Genealogy Department, Denver Public Library.

Johnson, Edward L., to Charles Devens, November 11, 1880. Letters Received by the Attorney General, 1871–1884 [microform], Western Law and Order, Colorado Reel II. Bethesda, Md.: University Publications of America, 1996. In Western History and Genealogy Department, Denver Public Library.

Londoner, Wolfe. "Vigilance Committees in Colorado." MSS XA Bancroft 401–426. Typescript in Colorado Historical Society.

Miller, W. J., to James B. Grant, February 28, 1884. James B. Grant Papers, Box 26689, Colorado State Archives, Denver.

Monroe, A. W. "Interview With Robert M. Ormsby, December 11, 1933." Civil Works Administration Interviews, CWA 357/64. Typescript in Colorado Historical Society.

Ouray County, Probate Court Records, Box 3341. Colorado State Archives, Denver.

Owen, Elizabeth. "Crimes in Denver, 1859–1864." Typescript in Colorado Historical Society.

Rathmell, William. "A Brief History of Ouray Co., Colorado." Typescript in Western History and Genealogy Department, Denver Public Library.

Servant, Robert, to James Grant, February 9, 1884. James B. Grant Papers, Box 26689, Colorado State Archives, Denver.

Soens, A. L. "Interview With John Davis [undated, ca. February 1934]." Civil Works Administration Interviews, CWA 362/2. Typescript in Colorado Historical Society.

———. "Interview With Dr. W. C. Folsom, March 20, 1934." Civil Works Administration Interviews, CWA 362/40. Typescript in Colorado Historical Society.

Sopris, Richard. "Settlement of Denver." Typescript in Collection 1897, Bancroft Manuscripts, Colorado Historical Society.

U.S. Census Bureau, 1880 Census, Colorado, Arapahoe County, Denver. Microfilm in Western History and Genealogy Department, Denver Public Library.

———, 1880, La Salle County, Illinois, Township of Manlius, Village of Crotty [Seneca]. Microfilm in Western History and Genealogy Department, Denver Public Library.

SCRAPBOOKS

George A.H. Baxter Scrapbook, Colorado Historical Society
Thomas Dawson Scrapbooks, Colorado Historical Society
Sam Howe Scrapbooks, Colorado Historical Society

NEWSPAPERS

Alamosa Journal
Animas Forks Pioneer
Boulder County News
Boulder Daily Camera

Boulder Tribune

Buena Vista Democrat

Cañon City Record

Cañon City Times

Carbonate Chronicle [Leadville]

Central City Register

Chicago Tribune

Colorado Catholic [Denver]

Colorado Chieftain [Pueblo]

Colorado Livestock Record [Denver]

Colorado Miner [Georgetown]

Colorado Republican [Denver]

Colorado Springs Gazette

Colorado Springs Weekly Register

Colorado Topics [Hyde, Washington County]

Colorado Transcript [Golden]

Colorado Tribune [Golden]

Creede Candle

Daily Mining Journal [Black Hawk]

Daily Register-Call [Central City]

Daily Sentinel [Grand Junction]

Daily Times [Leavenworth, Kansas]

Delta Chief

Denver Post

Denver Republican

Denver Times

Denver Tribune

Denver Tribune Republican

Denver Weekly Tribune

Dolores News [Rico]

Durango-Cortez Herald

Durango Daily Idea

Durango Herald

Evening Chronicle [Leadville]

Fairplay Flume

Fort Collins Courier

Grand Junction News

Greeley Tribune

Guardian [London]

Gunnison Daily News-Democrat

Gunnison Daily Review

Gunnison Review-Press

Huerfano Herald [La Veta]

La Plata Miner [Silverton]

SOURCES

Las Animas Leader
Leadville Daily Herald
Leadville Democrat
Leadville Herald-Democrat
Miner's Register [Central City]
Mining Register [Lake City]
Montrose Enterprise
Montrose Messenger
Montrose Press
Mountain Mail [Salida]
New York Times
Ottawa [Illinois] *Republican*
Pueblo Chieftain
Pueblo Indicator
Pueblo Sunday Opinion
Queen Bee [Denver]
Rico Record
Rocky Mountain Herald [Denver]
Rocky Mountain News [Denver]
Salida Mail
San Juan [Silverton]
San Juan Prospector [Del Norte]
Silver World [Lake City]
Silverton Democrat
Silverton Democrat-Herald
Solid Muldoon [Ouray]
Summit County Journal [Breckenridge]
Summit County News [Breckenridge]
Transcript [Golden]
Trinidad Chronicle News
Tri-Weekly Miners Register [Central City]
Weekly Commonwealth and Republican [Denver]
Weekly Transcript [Golden]
Western Mountaineer [Golden]
White Pine Cone [White Pine, Gunnison County]

INDEX